Lebanese in Australia:
A Changing Mosaic

Trevor Batrouney
and
Andrew Batrouney

Published in 2019 by Connor Court Publishing Pty Ltd

Connor Court Publishing Pty Ltd
PO Box 7257
Redland Bay QLD 4165
sales@connorcourt.com
www.connorcourtpublishing.com.au
Phone 0497 900 685

ISBN: 978-1-925826-66-1

Front Cover Design: Ian James

Printed in Australia

Photos used with permission

FOREWORD

As this book goes to press, the streets of Beirut are once more filled with protestors demanding serious reform from their Government.

The politics of Lebanon are complex and deeply rooted in its history. No wonder that many Australians struggle to understand what their Lebanese neighbours, friends and workmates have endured in their country's recent past.

As with their other writings on Lebanon and the Lebanese, Trevor and Andrew Batrouney perform a valuable service in explaining, passionately but objectively, the many-sided reality of being Lebanese.

When they wrote their first major history on the Lebanese in Australia, back in 1985, Trevor and Andrew Batrouney were describing a community that was mostly Christian. Today, thanks to the civil war, Australia's Lebanese include a significant Muslim element. It is to their credit that Trevor and Andrew write about the experiences of more recent Lebanese settlers with as much scholarly care and insight as they did with their writings on the earlier Lebanese community.

This is what a genuinely multicultural intelligentsia can achieve. It is important that our schools, technical colleges and universities continue to celebrate cultural diversity, not in a tokenistic way, but as part of a genuine dialogue between and among groups of Australians from distinctly different backgrounds.

Certainly, my university, Victoria University in Melbourne, strives to meet this objective. Our staff and students represent every imaginable social, religious and ethnic group in Australia. Every day in our classrooms and in our meetings my colleagues learn from each other new ways of thinking about the issues and challenges we face as a society in a turbulent era.

This book should inspire Australians from all backgrounds to listen to each other's stories, and perhaps to produce new books and other media that give voice to the multiplicity of narratives that is the great Australian conversation.

Having read this book, the evening news, with its version of events in contemporary Beirut, should suddenly make much more sense and we should feel joined to the people whose faces appear on our TV and laptop screens.

Robert Pascoe

Dean Laureate and Professor of History

Victoria University, Melbourne

ACKNOWLEDGEMENTS

The authors gratefully acknowledge the many people, both in Australia and internationally, who have contributed to the development of this book in many ways.

We are indebted to our academic colleagues for the information and insights we have gained from their research and writing. This applies particularly to those who have conducted research and written about the migration and settlement of Lebanese in Australia.

Our special thanks go to those Lebanese who have shared with us their accounts of life in Lebanon and their experiences of migration and settlement in Australia. Their individual and family stories have enabled us to document their experiences and identify patterns in the larger story of the Lebanese in Australia.

In writing this book we also chose to reflect on our own experiences of the Lebanese Community in Melbourne and as descendants of an Australian-Lebanese family which extends over seven generations in Australia

At the same time, in recognition of the size and significance of the Lebanese Community in Sydney and the settlement of Lebanese throughout Australia, we interviewed key personnel to gain some understanding of the current dynamics in those communities.

This work represents an abiding interest and passion for us. It has sustained us for many years and through many community projects and tasks on which we have worked. These have helped us develop and refine our understanding of the nature of the Lebanese community, which is hopefully reflected in the following pages.

We acknowledge with gratitude the critical assistance provided by Dean Laureate Professor Robert Pascoe and Dr Dunia El-Badaoui from Victoria University. Professor Desmond Cahill, formerly of RMIT University Melbourne, was a valued early adviser. In the later stages of the book, Professor Ken Cruickshank of Sydney University and Judy Saba, cross cultural psychologist with NSW Police, provided valuable insights into the Lebanese communities of Sydney. Our thanks go to Tom Batrouney for his diligent copy editing and enthusiastic support for the project.

Two people have supported us throughout this entire project: our wives, Shamla and Mae. Our special thanks go to them for their love and unfailing support as we wrestled with ideas and explanations, deadlines and re-writes.

Finally, we present this book as a tribute to the courage of our great-grandparents, George and Annie Batrouney, and grandparents, Nicholas and Amy Antees. They left Lebanon from El Mina, Tripoli in the 1880s to seek a better life for themselves and their children and make their homes in far-flung Australia. For this we are eternally grateful.

Trevor Batrouney and Andrew Batrouney
Melbourne
October 2019

CONTENTS

INTRODUCTION

I find him in the garden. Staked tomato plants are what
he walks among, the apples of paradise. He is eighty
and stoops, white-haired in baggy serge and braces. His moustache
once warrior-fierce for quarrels in the small town of Zahle,
where honour divides houses, empties squares, droops and is thin
from stroking, he has come too far from his century to care...
This is his garden,
a valley in Lebanon; you can smell the cedars on his breath
and the blood of massacres, the crescent flashing from ravines
to slice through half a family. He rolls furred sage between
thumb and stained forefinger, sniffs the snowy hills; bees shifting
gold as they forage sunlight among stones, church-bells wading
in through pools of silence. He has never quite migrated.

This extract from a poem by David Malouf (1974), in which he remembers his grandfather, reveals that the past never quite leaves migrants but always remains a part of their lives. In some cases, they recall their past lives with warmth and nostalgia; in others they suffer from on-going trauma caused by the deaths and destruction during the many conflicts in Lebanon; and in a few cases, they turn their backs on their former homeland forever.

Major Changes in Lebanon and Australia since 1985

In 1985 the authors produced the first edition of *The Lebanese in Australia*. It is still widely read today – there are 61 copies sitting on library shelves throughout Australia alone. But over the past three decades much has happened in Lebanon and in Australia which has had a major impact on the migration of Lebanese throughout the world, including Australia. These demand a second updated edition of this work.

Lebanon

When we wrote *The Lebanese in Australia* (1985), Lebanon was in the throes of a turbulent and destructive civil war which caused major loss of life and disrupted the lives of the Lebanese in both Lebanon and Australia.

The Lebanese Civil War (1975–1990) ushered in a period of uneasy peace, punctuated by violent episodes, between the various political and religious groups in the country. Following the civil war, the relative weakness of Lebanon among the nations in the Middle East was illustrated by three conflicts which had their origins in the divided Lebanese nation, and in the regional states surrounding Lebanon, during the civil war. These were: the Syrian occupation of Lebanon (1976–2005); the Israeli invasion of Lebanon in 2004, which led to the Summer War of 2006 between Israel and Lebanon; and the ongoing Syrian Civil War (2011–present).

This period has also been marked by the continual emigration from Lebanon to elsewhere in the Middle East, as well as to Europe, the Americas, Australia and Africa. The impact of this emigration further altered the demographic balance between the Muslims and Christians in Lebanon. This would become the basis for the 1943 Lebanese Constitution, which was adopted upon Lebanon's declaration of independence. This demographic shift upset the precarious power-sharing arrangements that had been active since the National Pact of 1943, which established that: the President must be a Christian; the Prime Minister must be a Sunni Muslim; and the Speaker of the Parliament must be a Shi'ite Muslim.

The National Reconciliation Act (1990) – henceforth known as the Ta'if Accord – recognized, at least to some extent, that the Muslims formed a majority in Lebanon and therefore could claim a greater say in the affairs of the nation. Following the implementation of the Ta'if Accord, the Prime Minister was to be nominated by the Parliament, rather than the President, and the number of deputies was increased to give the Muslims an equal number of seats, resulting in the Christians no longer having the upper-hand in Lebanese politics.

A related development has been the rise of Muslim fundamentalism in Lebanon, as shown in the increasing prominence of Hezbollah in the nation's military and political systems. In 1985, Hezbollah was introduced into Lebanon. Originally a secret organisation originating from Iraq in the 1960s, Hezbollah became an Iran-backed militia with considerable authority in the Lebanese community, based on its capacity to provide local social services and its resistance to the Israeli occupation of southern Lebanon.

The 2011 uprising against the Assad regime in Syria, led to an influx of over 2 million refugees seeking a haven in Lebanon. Thereby contributing to Lebanon once again suffering from social and political instability.

Australia

The changes in Australia since 1985, while less dramatic, have been no less significant. During this period, the population of Australia grew from 15,791,042 to 23,401,892 in 2016 with 97 per cent of the population living in the major urban centres in each of the states and territories. Post-Second World War immigration increased the size and diversity of Australia's population to the extent that by 2012 as many as 22 per cent of Australians were born overseas and 43 per cent had one or more parents born overseas. Australia's parliamentary democracy has remained firmly in place with alternate periods of governance by a Liberal/National Coalition and the Labor Party.

These governments presided over an economy which has enjoyed a stronger economic performance than any other nation of the Organisation for Economic Cooperation and Development, transforming itself from a manufacturing and primary producing economy to one that is post-industrial, relying on a strong financial services industry, a healthy flow of foreign university students, and a moderate communications sector. Its mining industry ebbs and flows.

These economic and demographic changes held major implications for the size, composition and employment prospects of Australia's intake of immigrants and refugees.

Equally profound changes have been taking place in the Lebanese-Australian community. Australia's Lebanese-born population has grown in size from about 5,000 in 1971 to 78,650 by 2016. The 1971 cohort was mostly Christian, self-employed, with some living the across the length and breadth of Australia. Today three-quarters of Australia's Lebanese-born live in Sydney, mostly in the West with high Muslim numbers. Sydney's Muslim Lebanese have become the target of right-wing criticism in politics and the media, putting Australia's much-vaunted multicultural policy at risk.

Five Periods in Lebanon's Modern History

This book is organised around key periods in recent Lebanese history. These have formed the backdrop to the migrations that have created the Lebanese Diaspora across the world, including Australia.

Late Ottoman Lebanon

The Ottoman Period, which dates back to 1516, lasted until 1918 with the defeat of the Ottomans by the Entente during the First World War, followed by the Treaty of Versailles in 1920. In the devolved system of rule that characterised the Ottoman Empire, it was possible to bid for the task of tax collection. The Maronites successfully bid for tax collection in what had been traditional Druze lands further south in Mount Lebanon, leading to the arrival of new Christian farmers on what had historically been Muslim territory. This disruption lay behind the 1860 massacres of Maronites in the region, and the beginnings of large-scale international migration of Maronites and other Christian Lebanese to elsewhere in the Middle East, to France and to the countries of the new world, including Australia.

The French Mandate

Following the end of the Ottoman Empire and during the transformation of Anatolia into the new republic of Turkey, in 1920 Lebanon and Syria were entrusted by the new League of Nations to France as a mandate. The size of Lebanon was increased by the addition of the Anti-Lebanon mountain range to Mount Lebanon, thus creating the State of Greater Lebanon in 1926.

Lebanon was declared a republic on 1 September 1926, and the Lebanese Constitution became the law of the land. Unlike their Muslim neighbours, the Lebanese Christians had the existing networks worldwide that enabled them to leave French Lebanon; increasing numbers took this opportunity to do so. Foreign governments often classified them as Syrian or as Turku, in South American countries.

Independent Lebanon

In 1941 Vichy France proclaimed the independence of Lebanon, and on 8 November 1943 general elections were held and the new Lebanese Government unilaterally abolished the mandate. In March 1945 independent Lebanon became a founding member of the new League of Arab States (usually called the Arab League) and, shortly after, in October 1945, was one of the 51 founding members of the new United Nations. The National Pact of 1943 institutionalised the form of confessional politics that had prevailed in Lebanon for almost a century. Following World War Two there were major migrations of Lebanese around the world. This period saw substantial migration to Australia of emigrants, who were now recognised as Lebanese.

The Lebanese Civil War

Mismanagement of the new nation's economic development during the post-Second World War years, and the increasing strains on Lebanon's capacity to resolve these economic problems via political processes ignited the vicious civil war in 1975 that lasted until 1990.

Now Muslim Lebanese were as likely to attempt emigration as their Christian compatriots. An important feature of this civil war was the occupation of Lebanon by Syrian forces. The occupation by Syria, which lasted from 1976 to 2005, led to a flow of Syrian workers and military forces into Lebanon, based on Syria's belief that Lebanon was historically part of the Syrian nation.

Contemporary Lebanon

With the cessation of hostilities in 1990 and return to independent government after 2005, the flow of migration out of Lebanon has been counterbalanced by some back into Lebanon from parts of the Diaspora, including Australia. Following the Civil War there was a major increase in return visits to Lebanon. The period from 2005 to 2016 was marked by the on-going modernization of Lebanon and an increase in political and economic contacts between Australia and Lebanon.

Two significant events in contemporary Lebanon were the rise of Hezbollah and the Israeli invasion of Lebanon in 2006. Following the uprising against President Assad in 2011 over two million refugees and immigrants from Syria flooded into Lebanon.

SOCIAL CHANGES IN AUSTRALIA

Australia underwent a series of social changes and cultural transformations from the post- Second World War period to the early 21st century. The following policies were attempts to respond to these changes brought about by the different waves of migration. Although there have been obvious continuities across the periods (economic opportunity, adaptations to the host society, ongoing cultural or religious identities), the migrants in each period were the product of unique circumstances, both in Lebanon and in Australia. Australian migration policy has undergone dramatic shifts, which roughly coincide with the five phases of Lebanese history.

Colonial Australia

As a settler nation in the making, the Australian colonies were open to immigration from both British and non-British sources. Although colonial governments drew the line on Chinese immigration, European, American and some Middle Eastern groups settled in all parts of the continent. The camel trade was operated by Afghans; Americans were influential in the transport business; haberdashery was the province of early Lebanese arrivals.

White Australia

The newly federated nation of 1901 agreed upon the Australian settlement, with protective tariffs to grow industry, centralised arbitration to protect employees, and restricted immigration (the White Australia Policy). A system of nomination enabled some new Lebanese immigrants to build on the older network of Lebanese already in parts of Australia, especially in New South Wales and Victoria.

Assimilation

The involvement of Japan during the Second World War brought the conflict much closer to Australia than during the Great War. This, in turn, prompted a large-scale immigration program after 1945. Between 1947 and 1964 the policy underpinning this program and making it more acceptable to Australians who had grown up in the White Australia period, was one of assimilation. During this period the adoption of assimilation policies by governments was strongly supported by the public. These policies expected immigrants, especially those of non-British backgrounds, to abandon their languages and cultures and to adopt the language, culture and institutions of the host society. The response of Lebanese migrants was to publicly embrace the prevailing mainstream attitudes and values but retain valued elements of their Lebanese culture within the private sphere of their lives.

Integration

There was resistance to the policy of assimilation from some immigrant groups. As a result, government policy, from about 1964 to 1972, began to favour a policy of integration. Governments now began to respond to the needs of immigrants and their children, partly as a result of the activities of ethnic community organizations. This was followed by the emphasis on ethnic pluralism from 1972 to 1975 with further attempts to respond to diversity as well as the beginnings of multicultural policies. The period of integration from 1967 to 1972 saw substantial numbers of Lebanese and other immigrants continue to arrive from Middle Eastern countries.

Multiculturalism

The next distinct stage was the policy of multiculturalism from 1975 to 1988, based on two cardinal principles. One was equality, to ensure immigrant participation in all societal institutions. The second was the principle that migrants have the right to pursue their own religion and languages and to establish communities.[1] These principles supported the notion that membership of ethnic communities and their organisations are legitimate and consistent with Australian citizenship as long as certain principles (such as respect for basic Australian institutions and democratic values) are adhered to. This policy was given concrete expression in the Government's adoption of the Galbally Report in 1978 and then the National Agenda for a Multicultural Australia (1983) which advocated Government recognition of, and support for, ethnic community organizations as a means of providing settlement assistance for newly arrived migrants.

The policy of multiculturalism adopted in Australia coincided with a substantial increase in emigration from Lebanon following the Lebanese Civil War. During the 1980s, the Lebanese in Sydney and Melbourne responded to the official policy by establishing a range of welfare and cultural bodies to serve their large and diverse communities. In these capital cities the Lebanese established communities and a range of organisations, including churches and mosques, welfare bodies, political and cultural organizations, village and town associations, and media outlets. Together, these reflected the diversity and complexity of the Lebanese community.

Post-multiculturalism

The post-multiculturalism period from 1988 contains a mix of policies and communal attitudes. On the one hand, there has been the increasing diversity of the Australian population which ensured the retention of multicultural policies, including the National Agenda for a Multicultural Australia. However, the policy of multiculturalism came under sustained attack from right-wing groups, conservative politicians and commentators during the 1990s. A number of international events also led to widespread reappraisal of multiculturalism: the Tampa Incident in 2001, the destruction of the Twin Towers in New York on 11 September 2001 and the Bali bombing of 2002 when attacks by the Islamist Group Jemaah Islamiyah killed 202 people, of whom 102 were Australians.[2]

The criticisms of multiculturalism extended beyond political attacks. The notion of multiculturalism, based on clear-cut dichotomies of origin and destination, has been challenged on a number of levels. Recent research reveals that migrants may have commitments that flow in a number of directions. Some may have a sense of commitment to their locality but not necessarily to their national identity. Others may have simultaneous commitments to two or more societies, rather than exclusive loyalty to either their society of origin or destination.[3]

These Australian concerns reflect a change in worldwide conditions. Now there are 100 million refugees throughout the world, symbolised by the victims of the long-running Syrian Civil War, which began in March 2011. Governments, even those like Australia which had emphasised settlers ahead of guest workers, have been adopting new policies that favour the circulation of workers ahead of their permanent settlement in host societies.

Migration as a Link between Lebanon and Australia

Australia and Lebanon have been linked by migration since the latter third of the 19th century. While the motivations of Lebanese migrants varied over time and across groups, essentially the Lebanese were searching for a viable life (economic, political or cultural) denied to them in their homeland. Each of these five periods, which provide the structure of this book, can be understood in the terms of the interplay between the factors (economic, political or cultural) making for emigration from Lebanon and the corresponding opportunities (also economic, political or cultural) for Lebanese in the Australian part of the larger global Diaspora.

Although there have been obvious continuities across the periods (economic opportunity, adaptations to the host society, ongoing cultural or religious identities), the migrants in each period were the product of unique circumstances, both in Lebanon and in Australia.

The Lebanese migrated to Australia in five major waves spanning some 140 years:

- The First Wave extended from around 1880 to the beginning of the First World War in 1914.
- The Second Wave commenced in the years immediately following the Second World War, lasting from 1946 to 1966.
- The Third Wave began in 1967, with the Arab-Israeli War, and lasted until the beginning of the Lebanese Civil War in 1975.
- The Fourth Wave, which saw the largest number of migrants from Lebanon to date, took place between 1975 and 1990.
- The Fifth Wave, being the most current migration wave to date, occurred following the cessation of hostilities in 1990 and covers a series of smaller movements between Australia and Lebanon.

The arrival of immigrants, together with their descendants, plus subsequent smaller migrations, led to as many as 230,869 Australians claiming Lebanese ethnicity in 2016. These included the Lebanese-born in Australia who numbered 78,653, an increase from the 56,118 in 1985. The size and composition of each of the major waves were different, producing a diverse Lebanese community in religion, political affiliation, social background and adaptation to Australia. The earliest Lebanese immigrants were often to be found in country areas in the occupations of hawking, or peddling, and shop-keeping. By the early 20th century the Lebanese-born began to be concentrated in the more populous states of Victoria and New South Wales. This has continued with around 20 per cent living in Victoria and 75 per cent in New South Wales by 2012. The Lebanese reside mainly in the capital cities of Australia, particularly in Melbourne and Sydney, where they initially formed enclaves but later spread throughout the metropolitan areas in search of businesses and better housing.

Writing about the Lebanese in Australia

It was not until the multicultural phase that Australian intellectuals began to research and write about the Lebanese experience in Australia. This of course reflects the dominant assumption of earlier periods that the newcomers should be looking forward as new citizens of their adopted land rather than dwelling on their past or on their group experiences in the process of migration and settlement.

It took almost 100 years of living in Australia before there was any systematic writing and research on the Lebanese in this country. It was not until the early 1980s that the first works appeared. These were studies of settlement needs of the newly arrived Lebanese who fled to Australia during the Civil War in Lebanon.

A second category includes histories of Lebanese families in Australia, usually families who came to Australia during the First Wave migration. In uncovering family stories these works often express a sense of family identity and pride in achievement.

Studies of Lebanese occupations and businesses ushered in a new phase in documenting the success of the Lebanese-Australians, and their gratitude and contribution to the country that embraced and supported them. These include works on hawkers and shopkeepers and their families' transitions to a range of other, more varied, businesses.

A related group of studies are the biographies of prominent and successful Lebanese-Australians which emphasize their contributions in various businesses. The authors of these biographies explored the trials and triumphs of these people and highlighted the contribution of the close-knit Lebanese family to their business success. These studies focused on the biographies of the most successful and inspiring Lebanese-Australians, who mastered the fields of fashion, retail, hospitality, real estate, and other businesses.

Academic research and writing represents the largest body of work on the Lebanese in Australia. Academic studies present empirical, conceptual and theoretical perspectives on the Lebanese in Australia and enable them to be seen in the wider contexts of research and writing on migration, ethnicity, nationalism, race, comparative religion, and globalisation. Much of this work finds its way into books of readings.

A separate but important body of writing covers studies of Lebanese community organisations. These works reveal collective action by Lebanese to establish organisations to provide religious, welfare, social and recreational services for their communities.

Of the few attempts to write a general history of the Lebanese in Australia; such as *The Lebanese* (1978) by Drury, and *The Lebanese in Australia* (1985) by Batrouney and Batrouney; none have covered the last 33 years of Lebanese experience in Australia nor benefited from research and writing during that period. Therefore, they cannot be said to present a comprehensive and contemporary picture. It is this gap which we hope to fill with the publication of this book.

Theoretical Perspectives

This work approaches the study of the Lebanese in Australia from two theoretical perspectives. The first is an historical narrative which will examine the concepts of change and continuity in the migration and settlement of Lebanese over time. This enables analysis of issues such as:

- Changes and developments in the economy, society and power relations in Lebanon and Australia over the migration period.

- The different waves of Lebanese immigrants to Australia, with an emphasis on their diversity, including their different motivations for migration, their varied socio-economic backgrounds and social capital.

- The significant role of Lebanese families in migration and settlement.

- The changing roles of women in migration and settlement, including in families, employment, business and communal activities.

- The occupations and businesses of Lebanese migrants and their children.

- The education of Lebanese immigrants and their children.

- The communal activities of Lebanese migrants and their children and relations with groups in the wider Australian society.

This approach includes an emphasis on the diversity and complexity of the Lebanese immigrants, both within, and between, the migration waves. It will also enable us to identify changes and continuities in the total story.

The second approach is based on the concept of group or collective identity applied to the history of the Lebanese migrants. This raises the significance of family, religion and locality as key signifiers of identity, each of which will be examined in this work. Both in their homeland and in Australia the questions of national identity and nomenclature of the Lebanese have been subjected to many different interpretations and emphases. In their homeland in the 19th and early 20th centuries the common term applied to the Lebanese was Syrian, with the term Lebanese not coming into general use until after the State of Greater Lebanon was proclaimed in 1943.[4]

Australia, along with the United States of America, made the transition from Syrian to Lebanese by the middle of the 20th century. However, this was by no means universal: for example, in a number of South American countries, the common term for immigrants from Lebanon during the 19th and early 20th centuries was Turku, reflecting Ottoman control over the region. Throughout this work we will examine the different identities and nomenclatures attached to the Lebanese in Australia. While some were claimed by the Lebanese themselves, others were imposed by those in authority and yet others were used to denigrate Lebanese.

Two major theoretical paradigms have emerged to explain different forms of collective identity. These have been termed the primordialist and constructivist perspectives.

Primordialist perspectives emphasise that individual attachments to collective identities are based on sentiments, ties and obligations which are embedded in the individual from an early age and remain as a fixed point of reference. This often takes the form of strong emotional attachments and ties to family, kin and local community as evidenced by immigrants' feelings of loyalty and obligation to parents, other relatives, and village or town of their birth.

On the other hand, social constructivist approaches support the view that many of the characteristics that were previously perceived as being ascribed at birth or primordial…are now conceived as being subject to individual construction and personal choice; that is, individuals are largely responsible for shaping their own identity.[5]

The above represent two ideal types of immigrant identities. While these approaches have conceptual value, they need to consider the findings of a recent study: that the identity of many immigrants is changeable and influenced by the situations in which they find themselves and the activities they engage in.[6] This situational identity suggests that immigrant identities depend on contextual issues including class, ethnicity, gender, nationality and religion. In some cases, immigrant identities may transcend particular national identities and may be termed transnational or cosmopolitan identities.[7]

These considerations will be employed in our analysis of group identities of Lebanese migrants in Australia.

Lebanese in Australia: A Changing Mosaic

This book presents an overview of 140 years of Lebanese migration and settlement in Australia from the late 19th to the early 21st century, which outlines the history of the Lebanese from their first arrival in Australia to the present. The story is set against the background of the Lebanon the immigrants left and the Australia to which they came. It will involve tracing key developments and changes in both Lebanon and Australia, with a particular focus on the economic and political conditions in both countries. However, as the title of the book suggests, the major emphasis will be on the story of the Lebanese in Australia and their contacts with the wider Australian society.

The story of the migration and settlement of the Lebanese in Australia can be divided into five periods:

- The First Wave (1880–1914) ~ Late Ottoman Lebanon
- The World Wars (1914–1945) ~ The French Mandate
- The Second & Third Waves (1946–1975) ~ Independent Lebanon
- The Fourth Wave (1976–1990) ~ The Lebanese Civil War
- The Fifth Wave (1990–present) ~ Contemporary Lebanon

We will examine who the immigrants were, where they came from in Lebanon, why they emigrated and where and how they settled in Australia. We will focus on Lebanese families and two major processes which were vital for their settlement: occupations and education. For each period we will also discuss Lebanese communities and how they organised themselves to meet the settlement needs and interests of their members. This will include a discussion of religious bodies, welfare services, village organisations and political parties. A particular focus will be on how Lebanese in Australia maintained contacts with their former homeland. Parts One to Five will provide a picture of the unique characteristics of each of these waves.

In the final part, we seek to identify some contributions of Lebanese-Australians to Australian society. The narrative approach also enables us to identify patterns in the story of the Lebanese in Australia over the total period, including changes and developments in both Lebanon and Australia. Finally, we will examine changes in the identity and nomenclature of Lebanese in Australia over time.

The approach taken is to present the story based largely on existing research and literature, most of which is historical and sociological. While acknowledging the work of others, we have relied heavily on our own research and writing, both published and unpublished. Our aim is to present a readable story based on an understanding of work that has already been undertaken. We hope to give life to the story through the presentation of case studies, vignettes and photographs. This work meets the often-expressed need for a study of Lebanese migration and settlement in Australia over time; this is picked up in the title of the book.

Major Terms Used in the Book

A word about nomenclature. When the First Wave immigrants came to Australia from the 1880s Lebanon was a semi-autonomous district in the Ottoman province of Syria until the French Mandate of 1920. Therefore, when people from this district migrated to Australia they were commonly known as Syrians. After semi-autonomous statehood was achieved in 1926 individuals began migrating with Lebanese passports. However, it was not until 1954 that Australian census officials classified Lebanese and Syrian immigrants in separate categories. In this book we will use the term Syrian/Lebanese for the First Wave period (1880–1920), and the term Lebanese for the later periods.

In terms of religious affiliation, the great majority of Lebanese identify with one of the branches of Christianity or Islam. Some of the terms used to describe the major Christian Churches in Lebanon such as Maronite, Melkite and Orthodox, will be unfamiliar to some readers. The same applies to the major branches of Islam: Sunni, Shi'a, and Alawi as well as the Druze. Given the significance of religious affiliation for the great majority of Lebanese, brief descriptions are provided below for the largest religious communities in Lebanon.

The Maronites, or followers of Saint John Maroun, had their origin in Antioch in the 4th century, later spreading to the mountainous regions of northern Lebanon. There they remained until their contact with the Catholic Crusaders from the 11th century, which led the Maronites to look to the west for support and assistance. The contacts with the Papacy were consolidated during the 16th century with the opening of a Maronite College in Rome in 1584. Today the Maronite Church is one of the patriarchates of the Catholic Church and is guided by its patriarchs and bishops in unity with the Pope. The Maronite Church has its own unique liturgy, theology, spirituality and law, and is characterised by its own history and cultural identity. Although it is an Eastern Catholic Church, some devotional practices and traditions used by Maronites today, for example the Rosary and devotion to the Sacred Heart, have been introduced by western missionaries who were sent to the east at various times. However, the Maronite Church still follows its own Antiochene, or west Syrian Rite, and its liturgy is conducted in Aramaic and Arabic.

The Antiochian Orthodox Church is part of the Eastern Orthodox Church, the second largest Christian denomination in the world. The Eastern Orthodox Church consists of a large number of national churches in Eastern Europe and the Middle East, such as Russian Orthodox, Greek Orthodox, Serbian Orthodox, Antiochian Orthodox and many others. Although each church is independent, they are united by their common faith and religious practice. The divine liturgy is normally celebrated in the language of the country. The pioneer Syrian/Lebanese in Australia identified their Church as the Syrian Orthodox Church. Following Lebanese independence, the Church became known as the Antiochian Orthodox Church as it comes under the Orthodox Patriarch of Antioch. The Antiochian Orthodox Church provides spiritual leadership for the majority of Arabic-speaking Orthodox and converts to the Orthodox faith in Australia.

The Melkites trace their origins to the Council of Chalcedon in 451, after which the term was adopted. However, it was not until 1724 that the Melkite Catholic Church began its separate existence when some members of the Eastern Orthodox Church changed their allegiance from the Patriarch of Constantinople to the Pope. The Church today is another patriarchate of the Catholic Church. It differs from Roman Catholicism in that its mass is a Byzantine Liturgy which is conducted in Greek and Arabic. The term Melkite refers to those who followed Emperor Constantine's interpretation of Christianity, as 'malick' means king in Arabic.

The faith of Islam is based on five pillars:

- The declaration that there is no God but God, and Muhammed is God's messenger.

- Ritual prayers five times a day.

- Giving alms to the poor and needy.

- Fasting and self-control during the holy month of Ramadan.

- Pilgrimage to Mecca.

The Quran is the central religious text of Islam which Muslims believe to be a revelation from God. It is accepted by all sectors of Islam. Another religious text, the Hadith, is based on the oral traditions of the early history of Islam.

The main divisions of Islam are Sunni Islam and Shi'a Islam. Sunni Islam, which is followed by 87 to 90 per cent of the world's Muslim population, is the largest denomination. The term Sunni refers to usual practice, custom, or tradition. Shi'a Islam refers to the followers, faction or party of Muhammed's son-in-law and cousin, Ali, whom Shi'a believe to be the divinely appointed successor to Muhammed in the caliphate. Shi'a Islam is followed by 10 to 13 per cent of the world's Muslim population. The Alawis are also Shi'a Muslims who have retained some older beliefs that predate Islam. They are centred in Syria where they constitute 12 per cent of the population.

The Druze are a Middle Eastern religious sect characterised by an eclectic system of doctrines and by cohesion and secrecy among its members. The Druze religion is an outgrowth of Islam which incorporates elements of Judaism and Christianity. The Druze are to be found in the isolated mountains of Lebanon, Syria and Israel where they number about 250,000 followers.

A more extensive glossary of terms is provided in an appendix covering additional unfamiliar terms.

We turn now to the pioneer Syrian/Lebanese migrants who came to Australia between the 1880s and 1920s.

NOTES

1   Castles S et al. 2012 *The Internal Dynamics of Migration Processes and their Consequences for Australian Government Migration Policies*, University of Sydney.
2   *Ibid.* p.18
3   *Ibid.* p.18
4   Salibi, P. 1988, *A House of Many Mansions: The History of Lebanon Reconsidered.* University of California Press
5   Batrouney, T & Goldlust, J. 2005, *Unravelling Identity: Immigrants, Identity and Citizenship in Australia.* Common Ground p. 19 - 21
6   *Ibid.* p.112
7   Castles, S et al. 2012, *Op. Cit.* p.18

PART 1

LATE OTTOMAN LEBANON

When it was part of the declining Ottoman Empire, during the latter decades of the 19th century and into the early 20th, the land that is now the modern state of Lebanon underwent a number of major changes. These economic, social and political changes led to a major emigration to countries of the 'new world'. From the late 1870s Australia became a recognised destination for emigrants from Lebanon. Their motives for emigration and their patterns of settlement were diverse and varied with different groups of migrants.

From the 1870s to 1900 Australia comprised a series of colonies which came together as a nation through a British parliamentary Federation in 1901. Challenges for the new nation involved ensuring sole control over its enormous land mass and over its increasingly diverse population, as well as maintenance of its ties with Great Britain. The early years of the young nation were marked by the passing of legislation designed to maintain social cohesion by ensuring that immigrants, other than those of 'white' British or European stock, were excluded from entry, let alone citizenship. This policy was intended to reduce competition for Australian-born workers and, importantly, to maintain the numerical and cultural dominance of the British in the new nation. It was against this background of exclusionary legislation and often negative social attitudes that the early 'Syrian' or 'Lebanese' immigrants, and indeed all 'ethnic' immigrants, came to Australia.

Four Christian Militiamen with their full set of weapons at the time of the Maronite/Druse conflict in Lebanon in 1860 as shown on a French post card. (Source: mideastimage.com/result.aspx)

Christian refugees, during the 1860 strife between Druze and Maronites in Lebanon. (Source: http://mideastimage.com/ photo)

1

LEBANON: ECONOMIC AND POLITICAL CONDITIONS, 1880-1918

The consulates of almost every nation are found here. The city has commercial firms, hotels, shops full of goods, a European pharmacy and even a casino, a luxury establishment which only first-class sea ports in the Levant can afford.

French Consul 1847 in Mt Lebanon district of Syria.[1]

On 22 May 1860, at the entrance to Beirut, a small group of Maronites fired on a group of Druze, killing one and wounding two. This sparked a torrent of violence which spread through Lebanon from 29 to 31 May 1860. Scores of villages were destroyed in the vicinity of Beirut, while 33 Christians and 48 Druze were killed. By June, the disturbances had spread throughout Lebanon. The Druze peasants laid siege to Catholic monasteries and missions, burnt them to the ground and killed the monks. After these horrific massacres, in which over 10,000 Christians were killed, France intervened on behalf of the Christian population, and Britain on behalf of the Druze.[2]

After 1861 and the creation in June of *Règlement Organique*, the autonomy of the so-called Mount Lebanon District of the Ottoman Empire was guaranteed by interested European powers of the time, including England, France, Russia, Austria, Prussia and, later, Italy. These nations all had vested interests in the relationships of Mount Lebanon with both the Arab and European worlds. Of the interventions of western powers based on economic, strategic and religious interests, this was the first of many.

'Confessional politics', the ongoing bane of Lebanese political life, can be detected even at this early stage. In 1861 the European powers established a ruling body in Mount Lebanon known as the *Mutasarrifate*. This body provided for the control of Mount Lebanon by an Administrative Council that comprised two elected representatives of the six main religious sects: Maronite, Melkite, Orthodox, Sunni, Shi'ia and Druze. In 1864 the composition of the Administrative Council was reformed and simplified to include seven Christian representatives and five Muslim representatives, a proportion which reflected the numerical superiority of Christians in Mount Lebanon at the time.[3] To administer the separate nation of Lebanon, this *Mutasarrifate* ushered in a period of stability which lasted until the end of the Great War and the creation of a French Mandate. Arguably, this period of stability derived from the political structure which included representation of the major religious groupings. 'Confessional politics' seemed to work in practice, albeit within an imperial framework.

This imperial framework owed its origins to the significant European presence in Mount Lebanon in the second half of the 19th century. This included British and French companies which created business opportunities for the inhabitants of Mount Lebanon. Beirut was the centre of trade that was dominated by the cultivation, spinning and export of silk. The proliferation of the silk industry across Mount Lebanon saw it engage about half the population and, as a result, generate one-third of its income. At the time, silk production in Mount Lebanon employed 14,500 people (8,500 Maronite, 2,500 Melkite, 2,500 Orthodox, 1,000 Druze), of whom 12,000 were women. The numbers of women employed may have been the cause of poor working conditions and low wages. Male wages in the silk industry were three times those of women while free child labour was being provided by orphanages run by French missionaries and convents.

Of the 67 silk reeling factories in Lebanon in 1867, the seven largest were French-owned. By 1885, there were 105 factories in Mount

Lebanon with five of the largest being French. Silk production occupied 45 per cent of the arable land in Mount Lebanon, often at the expense of more diversified subsistence crops such as grains and cereals, which consequently had to be transported from Syria and the Beka'a. Such was the French dominance of this industry that the Lyon Chamber of Commerce viewed Mount Lebanon as a 'colony' because of its trading importance.[4]

Young boy using primitive silk reeling equipment
(Lebanon) 1914
(Source: Underwood and Underwood Stereograph Collection.
Library of Congress)

The importance and extent of the silk trade within Lebanon, and between Lebanon and Europe, was apparent in the creation of a new and significant group in society in the last quarter of the 19th century. The landed middle class and administrators, as well as members of the liberal professions, merchants and those directly involved in the silk trade were known as the *mudabbir* families. These families grew to have significant power in Lebanese society during this period and were recognised as educated and resourceful people. Their number was swelled by successful and wealthy returning emigrants. The significance of the *mudabbir* families lay in their intermediary role between the commoners and the sheikhs. They also were familiar with European ways and, as such, set the stage for a nation that would look towards Europe for trade and culture more than towards the Arab world.

When the *Mutasarrifate* was set up in 1861 not only had the demographic structure of Mount Lebanon changed dramatically in favour of a Christian and, specifically, a Maronite majority, but also Druze leaders who, prior to 1861, held significant power were now losing the social and political control they had under the *Mutasarrifate*. This was reflected in the change of ownership of land: three-quarters of those who sold land after 1860 were Druze and two-thirds who bought land were Christians. This was made possible through remittances and purchases of returning immigrants, most of whom were Christians. Maronites were anchored in the privileged sectors of society, particularly in the trade, services and agriculture sectors.[5] The Druze were marginalised to artisanal and agricultural production.

A number of factors created the conditions and impetus for emigration from Mount Lebanon in the last quarter of the nineteenth century. These included economic changes that altered the structures and means of making a living in villages and towns. Population growth, due to peace and prosperity after the 1860 uprising, saw numbers of young adults looking for work in a changing economy. Where peasants and rural workers had been able to make a living in villages, the reduction in cultivable land due to the growth in mulberry leaf production for the silk industry had limited their ability to find meaningful work. In the last twenty years of the nineteenth century, the resulting surplus of peasant workers saw many begin to travel overseas looking for greater opportunities.[6] Peasant workers were also dislocated and expelled from church lands because of the extension of the church *wa'qf* (property rights). Accompanying these economic changes was the growth of a social and political climate that included the emergence of a pan-Arab identity that overrode religious and regional differences and began to gain traction in the latter half of the 19th century.

The impulse to leave Mount Lebanon was strengthened by the failure of the peasant revolts and the impact of these on the lowest stratum of society.[7] Between 1860 and 1914 approximately one-third of the population of Mount Lebanon left for overseas. They were aided in this movement by shipping agents who travelled throughout the towns and villages of Syria/Lebanon selling tickets on ships bound for the countries of the 'new world'. During this period these emigrants sent back remittances valued at 45 per cent of the total revenue of Mt Lebanon. When they returned with money made overseas, they often sought to purchase property and gain respectability. However, few of the Lebanese who remained were prepared to sell their land that had been so hard come by. Many potential emigrants were forced to live overseas permanently with the expectation that one day they would return to purchase a stake in their village that had been impossible for them when they were growing up.

The attraction of returning to Lebanon was severely disrupted by the events of the Great War. As many as 100,000–200,000 Lebanese died due to war, pestilence and a dire famine in 1916. The major cause of this loss of life was the Ottoman blockade of Lebanon as a means of preventing any support for the British defending the Suez Canal. The hardships of life in Lebanon and the precarious nature of its relationship to Istanbul and to the European powers provided an incentive to commit to a more stable, safe and fruitful life in the United States, South America, Canada or Australia.[8]

The modern state of Lebanon commenced with the defeat of the Ottoman Empire by the British in 1918 and the occupation of the coastal areas and Mount Lebanon by the French. At the Conference of Versailles, Lebanon was granted to the French as a mandate, a status it held from 1920 to 1943. Lebanon now included the coastal region as far south as the border of Palestine and the entire Beka'a plain. On 23 May 1926, Lebanon was formally established as a semi-autonomous state, with Beirut as its capital. Complete independence from France was not gained until 1943, during the Second World War. The newly independent nation recognised as many as 17 distinct religious communities and allocated positions in government based on their size and significance. The six major religious communities in Lebanon were the Maronite Catholics, the Sunni Muslims, the Shi'ite Muslims, the Greek Orthodox, the Melkite Catholics and the Druze.

2

SYRIAN/LEBANESE IMMIGRANTS TO AUSTRALIA 1880 TO 1918

When your prospects narrow in your town and you're afraid of not being able to earn your living anymore then leave, for God's earth is wide.

Amin Maalouf

Syrian/Lebanese emigration may be seen in the wider context of an increased global movement of peoples to the 'new world.' Emigration from the Middle East to the United States, South America, Australia, Africa and New Zealand was part of a larger movement of migrants around the world between 1880 and 1914.[8] Therefore, the migration and settlement experiences of Syrian/Lebanese were part of, and yet different from, the migration experiences of other national groups. This applied to their motivations for migration, the importance of return visits to Lebanon and 'double' migration where migrants moved from one destination country to another, as illustrated in the story of Julia Antees, née Menayer (chapter 3).

In the first great migration wave an estimated 120,000 had left Syria/ Lebanon by 1900 seeking economic opportunities in countries of mass migration. While the goal for most was the United States, many ended up in Brazil, Argentina and other Latin American countries. By 1896 emigration from Syria/Lebanon was running at 5,500 a year. During the period 1900-1914 some 225,000 'Syrians' or 'Turks' (the designations for Lebanese in the United States and Latin America respectively) had emigrated. It is estimated that during this first wave period some 350,000 had left: two thirds to the United States and most of the rest to Latin America.[9] Much smaller numbers were to be found in Canada, Australia and New Zealand.

The numbers of Lebanese-born who came to Australia during these years were consistently small. In 1901 there were 1,498 Lebanese-born in the whole of Australia. This number had grown to only 1,803 by 1921. This was, no doubt, caused by the application of the White Australia Policy and the impact of the Great War. The addition of the second generation in Australia meant that the Lebanese community may have reached an estimated total of around 5,000 people by the first quarter of the century at a time when the total Australian population was 5.41 million.

In the 1880–1918 period, emigrants from Syria/Lebanon could be characterised in different ways: by family, by religion, by region or by village. Those who came to Australia from Mount Lebanon shared similar characteristics to those who arrived in America after the 1880s. According to an estimate by the Lebanese-American professor Philip K. Hitti in 1924, the vast majority (95 per cent) were Christian. Estimates indicated that Lebanese immigrants to the United States were made up of 45 per cent Maronite, 43 per cent Orthodox, 5 per cent Catholic, 2.5 per cent Protestant and 4.5 per cent Muslim and Druze.[10]

The early emigrants were, on the whole, fairly young, unattached, and unmarried males, with relatively low levels of skills or formal schooling. In Australia the early Lebanese immigrants soon brought out their wives and families so that the ratio of males to females was higher than that of other Mediterranean immigrants. Many of these first immigrants were drawn from rural villages and, as such, depleted the villages of large numbers of young people. There were low levels of literacy among many of those who migrated to the United States with only 45 per cent being able to read and write Arabic.

On the other hand, there was also a small group of educated immigrants who had gained some schooling and an even smaller group who had attended university. The more educated and professional groups cited their reasons for emigration as a quest for liberation from an oppressive political atmosphere.

Two debated areas in the study of Syrian/Lebanese emigration in this early period are their motivations for leaving their homeland and their reasons for returning home. Did emigrants leave for economic reasons to make a better life in their chosen destination, or did they leave for issues to do with political and social liberty in Lebanon? The reality is likely to vary for different groups, as will become evident, but we can identify seven main factors at play in this early emigration from Syria/Lebanon.

Firstly, the bulk of immigrants were members of lower socio-economic groups who left Lebanon mainly because of economic and demographic pressures. Changes in trade routes by sea and over land and the decline of the silk industry contributed to 'push factors' of 'economic insecurity, ruinous taxation and, above all, the awareness of a better life elsewhere'. Thus, farmers and the poorer levels of society justified their departure on economic grounds. Recent research has shown that these Syrian/Lebanese immigrants were not peasants who worked for landowners but came from a range of occupational backgrounds to be found in villages and towns.[11] An analysis of their Applications for Naturalisation documentation confirms that many had held village or urban jobs as well as farmed small plots of land.[12]

On the other hand, intellectuals and more educated groups claimed the attraction of a freer political culture overseas. The growth of foreign schools and universities in Mount Lebanon contributed to an intellectual, cultural and literary awakening at a time of persecution, censure and oppression under Ottoman rule. This may be seen in the town of Zahle which, by the 1880s, had a population of about 15,000. Its foreign schools included two Jesuit boys schools, a Roman Catholic girls school, a Russian Orthodox school, a British Anglican school and one American Protestant school. It also had a Jesuit College and one Catholic and one American Library.[13] Newspapers and journals aroused greater awareness on issues of social equality, freedom, liberty and social and civic consciousness, the so-called *naqdah* (Arab Renaissance). The Lebanese-American writer, Ameen Rihani, claimed that he and his friends 'left our mother country with nothing but curses for her government on our lips'.[14]

Thirdly, the role of foreign missionaries also points to a factor that may have influenced emigration for some: the creation of missionary-run public schools and religious schools at primary and secondary levels. In addition to education, the missionaries from the United States and Europe and their supporting religious organisations began publishing texts, both religious and secular, that increased literacy and the spread of new social and political ideas. The intention of the Presbyterian missionaries was not to prepare young people to emigrate but to teach them English so they could be better educated and help their country benefit from what they had learned, not so they would go and open grocery stores in Detroit or Baltimore. The hope of these preachers was to create a little America right there in Levant—virtuous, educated, industrious, and Protestant.[15] The commencement of tertiary education in 1866, with the establishment of the American University in Beirut, helped to create an educated professional and intellectual class. The impact of education, even for a few years at primary level, qualified a young person beyond what he was expected to do in a village which was, perhaps, limited to tending crops or animals. For educated young people, the promise of a more exciting and fulfilling life outside the village became an irresistible lure.[16]

There was a fourth factor for some, the motivation to escape military conscription. The Young Turks 1908 Constitution created equality between Christians and Muslims in terms of military conscription, from which Christians had been exempt for centuries. The impact of conscription weighed heavily on small rural farms requiring family labour. Avoidance of conscription, for Muslims and Christians, saw many Lebanese flee Syria/Lebanon or take other drastic measures, including self-mutilation to avoid service, in the Ottoman army.

Religious persecution was a fifth factor given by some as the major reason for emigration, especially after the massacres of 1860. Different writers and commentators view the importance of religion differently. The fact that that large numbers of emigrants did not leave Syria/Lebanon until the 1890s, some thirty years after the 1860 massacres, raises questions about the significance of religion as a major push factor.

Steamship agents and money lenders played an important role in presenting visions of a better life to be gained by emigrating to countries where one can 'pick gold from the trees.' These well-dressed raconteurs, by tapping into the story-telling, oral traditions of the communities, told tales of the adventures of emigration and of the fortunes to be made. Some agents helped smuggle passengers out of Syria/Lebanon when exits from Ottoman ports were forbidden. Unscrupulous agents were more committed to getting fares than to the welfare of their passengers. Some Lebanese travellers were barred from entry to the United States on health grounds. For a few emigrants, the promise of arriving in America actually led to their arriving in France, Italy, South America or even Australia.

Finally, the tales of success and evidence of wealth enjoyed by returning migrants provided another impetus to emigration. Some returning migrants displayed their wealth by building houses with red tiled roofs in their village in a copy of the villas being built in the cities by the wealthy. The capital they brought with them also had an impact on their family by sharing some of their riches to raise the status of the family, including the education of the younger members. In this context, emigration was not seen as a liability or a burden on the family. In fact, it was seen as a 'felicitous or positive phenomenon'.[17]

Whatever the reasons for their emigration, Lebanese emigrants often entered into onerous financial arrangements that included mortgaging property, borrowing from family and friends and later repaying creditors with money earned. In one instance George and Joseph Hamra borrowed only sufficient money to fund their passage to Singapore. They had to borrow the rest of the fare from a fellow passenger to enable them to reach Fremantle in 1920. They then made their way by boat to Adelaide where they joined their aunt Maryanna.[18]

All too often studies of Lebanese emigration focus on those who left with scant attention paid to those who remained in Lebanon. A family memoir of the time speaks of the pain of separation for the families left behind:

> Here families have sons buried in Beirut, Egypt, Argentina, Brazil, Mexico, Australia and the United States. Our fate is to be as scattered in death as we were in life.[19]

Australia: Economic and Political Conditions

In many respects the Syrian/Lebanese who came to Australia in the 1880s and early 1890s could not have chosen a more difficult time to start a new life in Australia. Their earliest years in Australia were marked by a combination of economic depression, popular feelings of nationalism and racism, and a pervasive imperialist ideology.

By the mid-1880s, the eastern Australian economy was in the final stages of a boom. This was soon to descend into depression in the mid-1890s. In addition to its economic decline, the eastern colonies were suffering from a cruel drought that slashed the wheat yields by a third and culled the sheep population by a half. As economic conditions worsened, unemployment spread and demand dried up. Although Victoria was hardest hit, other major centres were also feeling the effects of the economic downturn. During the depth of the depression, unemployment claimed 30 per cent of the skilled workers and even more of the unskilled. In the cities many small factories closed their doors and many city dwellers ventured into the country in search of work. For example, by the early 1890s the population of Melbourne had fallen by 50,000 people, particularly with migration to Western Australia. By 1901 the situation had improved somewhat but many Australians remained out of work and desperate.

The economic depression of the 1890s meant that the early experiences of Syrian/Lebanese immigrants were ones of constant struggle. In the late 19th century hawking was not always profitable and some Lebanese families were living in poverty for a number of years. This is suggested by the fact that some were buried in unmarked graves. For example, the Dobley family in Ballarat buried two of their children in the 1890s in the grave of a member of another Lebanese family, which itself was unmarked.

Hawking also involved separation from family, often for long periods of time, and even on those occasions when wives accompanied their husbands, other family members were left behind. In order to minimise competition, Lebanese hawkers would strike out in different directions, establishing depots in settlements along their routes. These depots sometimes became drapery and fancy goods stores. Thus most of the early Lebanese, who were living in country areas, were deprived of the sense of security and belonging that membership of their own community could bring. Lebanese community life had to wait until enough families congregated in certain localities within the larger towns and cities.

Then there were the physical dangers confronting hawkers and merchants in the harsh outback of Australia. Floods and bush fires took their toll of early hawkers. In July 1898 two Lebanese hawkers, Michael Aidouh and George Naideff, lost their lives when the Criterion Hotel at Gormanston on the west coast of Tasmania was burnt to the ground. Two years earlier the fancy goods store owned by Michael's brother, Bandali, was destroyed in the fire that engulfed

Penghana, the shantytown near the Mt Lyell mine, that was later rebuilt as Queenstown. Having lost a brother and a business it is no wonder that the single Bandali returned to Lebanon.

The disastrous impact of the flood of 28 December 1916 on the population of Clermont, Queensland, is vividly described in Roger Nasser's family history. It was in that flood that Nicholas Nasser was drowned and most of the family's hard-won possessions were lost.[20]

Travelling alone or in pairs in the outback also attracted the unwelcome attention of bushrangers, one of whom 'killed a Syrian hawker just for fun' (Anonymous). This led to some violence against them as was the case in the murder of Salim Matta, a single Lebanese hawker travelling alone in country New South Wales:

> A Syrian hawker named Salim Matter [sic] was murdered at Bumbaldry, Grenfell District, last night. He was camped near an hotel when a man came to his wagon under pretence of making a purchase, and as Matter was going into his van, the stranger struck him on the head. His cries brought assistance, and he was carried into the hotel, where he died today.[21]

The police caught his killer.

Cowra Wednesday. In connection with the murder of Salim Matter [sic], at Bumbaldry goldfield, Sub-inspector Kenny Forbes, with Senior-sergeant Butler, of Cowra, have arrested a youth on suspicion. The hawker's body has been brought to Cowra to be entrained to Cootamundra for internment. Deceased's widow and family are residing there.[22]

Grenfell Wednesday. An inquest was held at Bumbaldry on Salim Matter [sic], an Assyrian [sic] hawker and has been adjourned. The remains have been sent on to Cootamundra, for burial at Young.[23]

The reporting of this episode reveals a number of common elements in the lives of the early hawkers: the dangers of the life, especially when travelling alone; the common confusion of the nationality of 'Syrian' with 'Assyrian'; and the common misspelling of their names.

'White Australia Policy'

The agitation for White Australia was fully developed by the mid-1880s and had moved from labour protection (Australia as a 'working man's paradise') to openly racist arguments. The trend was sustained by growing popular journalism, particularly in the *Bulletin* (founded in 1880) and the *Boomerang* (founded in 1888). Their propagation of a racist ideology through articles and cartoons exerted a powerful effect on the population. This racist ideology was given tangible expression in 1888 when the Chinese passengers on two ships, the *Afghan* and the *Burrumbeet,* were refused landing rights in Melbourne. This decision reflected popular outrage and political panic which was to extend beyond the Chinese to become a crusade against all non-European immigrants.[24] The argument employed was that the living and dignity of the working man was being undermined by cheap labour and, as such, immigrants were perceived to be a threat to their way of life based on Anglo-Celtic values.

Writers such as Henry Lawson and Banjo Patterson contributed to this dominant ideology by idealising shearers, farmhands and other itinerants in the Australian bush as model Australians. Lebanese hawkers were not only excluded from this idealised group but were also the subject of some popular agitation and parliamentary criticism.

The push for Australian nationalism, which gained strength in the latter part of the nineteenth century, included the notion of 'Australia for the Australians' meaning, of course, Australia for the Anglo-Celtic majority. This led to the establishment of the White Australia Policy as a means of maintaining racial and cultural homogeneity. Thus the first attempt to ensure social cohesion in Australia was by exclusion of those who were not British. The notion of 'Australia as British' provided the basis for Australia's social cohesion until the onset of mass migration after the Second World War.

Immigration Restriction Act 1901 and Commonwealth Naturalisation Act 1903

The years from 1880–1920 may be termed the period of the 'White Australia Policy.' When the six independent colonies came together in a federation in 1901, one of the first acts of the Commonwealth Parliament was the Immigration Restriction Act of 1901 designed to preserve 'racial purity' and to protect labour conditions. This was achieved through the introduction of a dictation test in any European language for the inhabitants of all countries classified as 'Asiatic', including the Syrian/Lebanese.

This was soon followed by the Commonwealth Naturalisation Act of 1903 which denied Asians and other non-Europeans the right to apply for naturalisation. Similarly, they were prohibited from receiving the pension and enrolling as electors. Through these measures the new Federal Government assumed control of immigration. The government vigorously pursued policies which debarred entry of immigrants to Australia on criteria based explicitly or implicitly on racial characteristics and which involved preferential treatment for particular nationalities.[25]

The Immigration Restriction Act of 1901, the first major Commonwealth piece of legislation, was only part of the legislative armoury of White Australia. Colonial and state laws relating to immigration, occupation, citizenship and Aborigines were all part of a consistent campaign to prevent anyone from contributing to Australian nation-building who was not of European descent and appearance.[26]

The genesis of these acts goes back to the gold rushes of the 1850s in the colonies of New South Wales and Victoria. The gold rushes led to a great influx of immigrants from all parts of the world in which hundreds of thousands were drawn to the goldfields of eastern Australia. During the 1850s alone, Australia's population grew from just 405,400 non-Indigenous settlers to 1,145,000. After the gold rushes of the 1850s, the populations of the colonies of

New South Wales and Victoria changed dramatically in both size and composition. A major effect of the increase in population was a boom in demand for housing, clothing, food and amusements. Equally important were the significant concentrations of ethnic groups, such as American, French, Italian, German, Indian, Japanese, Chinese and Canadians who had been attracted to Australia by the lure of gold. The Anglo-Celtic immigrants came to a nation that was already sympathetic to their values and ways. On the other hand, the influx of a heterogeneous group of immigrants led to popular feelings of racism within the Anglo-Celtic majority, particularly against the Chinese and other Asians. As a result, Asian and other non-British immigrants experienced exclusion as well as discrimination based on their culture, colour and inability to speak English.

Prejudice against these groups was justified by the native Australians and other Caucasian settlers concocting stories of Chinese abducting white women or smoking opium or stealing from whites. Above all, the factor that rankled most with the Australians was the single-mindedness with which the Asians worked and sent money home to improve the living standards and raise the status of their families. It was against this background that 'White Australia' feelings were generated with the stated aim of retaining racial homogeneity.

The Great War, like the Boer War before it, gave rise to a powerful expression of nationalist and imperialist ideology among Anglo-Australians. Not only was Australia 'white' and British, but it would fight alongside the mother country in protection of the Empire of which it was a proud member. At the time of Federation, the greater part of Australia's sense of identity came from its connection with the British Empire.

Syrian/Lebanese immigrants arriving in Australia between 1880 and 1920 were eager to settle and begin earning a living as best they could. They had heard little about Australia other than, like America, it was a land of great opportunity. However, the Australia which these pioneer immigrants encountered was vastly different from the Lebanon that they had left.

Officially the Syrian/Lebanese were grouped together with other Asiatic immigrants largely because their birthplace was listed as east of the Bosporus in Turkey, which was regarded as the demarcation line between Asia and Europe. They were at times incorrectly called 'Assyrians' and confused with other national groups such as Afghans, Indians, Greeks, and Italians.[27] Just one example of incorrect nomenclature was the description of the two Syrian/Lebanese hawkers as 'Assyrians' in the reports of the hotel fire in Gormanston, Tasmania in 1898 in which they were burned to death.

The Syrian/Lebanese were the subject of a racist commentary in which their negative attributes were spread throughout the colonies in both metropolitan and provincial newspapers. Certain accusations, mainly unfounded, were taken up and amplified in these newspapers as a warning to colonial society: that Syrian hawkers terrorised and threatened unprotected women to force them to purchase their goods; that the Syrian made his womenfolk work while he lazily enjoyed the proceeds of their toil; that Syrian hawkers were 'of the lowest type of humanity' and were 'a curse to the country;' and that they should be prevented from holding hawkers' licences.[28]

Not only were they considered a threat to migrant workers but were regarded as an inferior race in every respect:

> These aliens undersell both their goods and their labour. Besides breeding disease and hybrid children—neither black nor white nor brindle they live on a lower scale, and can consequently outbid us in every departure [sic] of trade...In short, they are an inferior race ---inferior in morals, inferior in enlightenment, and inferior in standards of living....[29]

Being denied citizenship, Syrian/Lebanese were prohibited from receiving the pension and enrolling as electors. In this limbo, no one was quite sure how they should be treated administratively. They were arbitrarily classified with the Asians, not by race but by region. Therefore, any restrictive legislation worked against them. As a result, they presented a dilemma to the immigration authorities. This may be seen in this extract from a letter to the Minister, written just at the commencement of the Great War, from his chief bureaucrat, pointing out the intermediary status:

> [T]hey are of swarthy appearance with dark hair and of sallow complexion, but approximate far more closely European types than those of India or parts of Asia further East. So far as their general appearance goes, they cannot be distinguished from the people of Southern Italy, Spain or Greece.[30]

These comments reveal the importance attached to skin colour and general appearance in determining their eligibility for naturalisation and gaining the full rights of citizenship.

The Secretary for the Department of External Affairs, Attlee Hunt, indicated that Syrian/Lebanese were suitable as immigrants and settlers on several grounds. Firstly, the relatively high number of female immigrants, with only 62 per cent of the total in 1901 being male, meant that they could not be considered a threat to the safety of Australian women or racial purity. Secondly, their physical appearance was regarded as more similar to Europeans than to Asians. Thirdly, some of them were considered to have a relatively high educational standard compared with other immigrant groups. Hunt gave examples of this in the bilingual ability of some of the early Lebanese settlers. They were familiar with French, Italian and other European languages and customs, owing to the presence of European educational and religious institutions in Lebanon. Finally, the great majority of the Syrian/Lebanese immigrants were Christians. This contributed to the official view that the Syrian/Lebanese were a unique group.

While this view appears to sit uneasily with earlier claims of illiteracy among pioneer Syrian/Lebanese settlers, it is likely that Mr Hunt and other government officials came into contact with the more skilled and educated Lebanese who were acting as representatives of their community. In any event, Syrian/Lebanese settlers in Australia felt they should be classified differently. To this end, a letter was written by W. Abourizk of Melbourne on 27 January 1910, to the Prime

Minister, Alfred Deakin, pointing out, rather provocatively, the many good qualities of Lebanese settlers:

> Syrians are Caucasian and they are a white race as much as the English. Their looks, habits, customs, religions, blood etc. are those of Europeans but they are more intelligent.[31]

In this debate it was conceded that the Syrian/Lebanese settlers exhibited a number of characteristics that distinguished them from Asian immigrants with whom they were classified. As a result, the Lebanese strongly rejected their classification as Asians. Many Lebanese applied unsuccessfully for citizenship until the passing of the Nationality Act in 1920 which allowed people who had been resident in Australia for five years or more to become naturalised. Single 'Asiatic' males were barred from gaining citizenship. However, even after gaining naturalisation, Lebanese, being classified as Asians, were still not permitted to enrol and vote in elections.

Some Syrian/Lebanese immigrants made strenuous efforts to overcome these Asian immigration restrictions. Some listed their place of birth as European Turkey while others claimed to be Greek, or another European nationality, by birth. Some were also quick to learn through word of mouth which centres and which officials were likely to be more sympathetic to their desire to be naturalised. Accordingly, if one application for naturalisation was unsuccessful, another would be made at another centre, even if it involved travelling some distance. Some also used solicitors to help argue their case as well as obtaining the support of government officials. These efforts led to some success in gaining citizenship. This is apart from those who had already been granted citizenship by colonial administrations before 1901. For example, in a group of Syrian/Lebanese immigrants in Queensland as many as 34 per cent had been naturalised before 1904.[32]

There were also collective efforts to protest against the application of the Immigration Restriction Act to Syrian/Lebanese, as indicated by a gathering held at the Melkite Church Hall in Waterloo NSW in 1908.

At a meeting of the Syrian Progressive Association, held last night
at St Michael's Hall, Waterloo, it was resolved that a petition be
signed by the Syrians resident in Australia, and presented to the
Commonwealth Parliament asking it to amend the Alien Immigration
Restriction Act with regard to the Syrian Community in Australia.[33]

During this period the Syrian/Lebanese did not challenge prevailing
public norms about race or discriminatory immigration and
citizenship legislation on grounds of moral principle but only as it
applied specifically to them. In other words, their desire was simply
to become accepted and respected as members of British Australia.

A sample of correspondence at this time reveals the depth of
feeling with which the Lebanese responded to their alien status.
It also exhibits a growing sense of confidence and assertion with
which Lebanese community leaders approached authorities directly
or requested others to intercede on their behalf in their attempts to
gain full citizenship status. They based their claims on a number of
factors: their racial similarity to Europeans and their distinctiveness
from Asian 'races'; their integration into Australian society; their
commercial endeavours including, in many cases, the important roles
they played in their local communities.

As a result of their suitability for settlement, authorities began to
treat the Lebanese as a special case even before the Immigration Act
was amended in 1920. The passing of this act was a milestone in
the acceptance of Lebanese immigrants as reliable and enterprising
citizens.

The outbreak of the Great War in August 1914 proved to be
detrimental to relations between the Australian Government and
Syrian/Lebanese immigrants. Although the majority of settlers
came from the district of Mount Lebanon and were described as
Syrians, they were classified as Turkish subjects by the Australian
Government. Consequently, they were required to register as enemy
aliens at their local police station at regular intervals during the war. At
least they were spared the ignominy of being interned as a danger to

society. For the Syrian/Lebanese settlers who perceived themselves, and were seen by others, as law-abiding and diligent members of the Australian community, the obligation for them to register as enemy aliens rankled. Nonetheless, they fulfilled what they saw as their duty as citizens, registered as enemy aliens at their local police station and reported there each month.

List of Turkish subjects ... 19-8-18

(Surname) first	Race	Age	Address	
...yon, Morris	Jewish	28	18 Pitt Str. Carlton	Vic
Abbott, Michael	Syrian	39	Tallangatta	
Abosaid, Abraham	"	40	311 Exhibition Str. Melb.	
Aboomey, Alex. Amin	"	41	Carlyon's Hotel, Spencer St. Melb.	
Abourizk, Elias	"	35	36 Lonsdale Str. Melb.	
Abourizk, Michael	"	32	36 Lonsdale Str. Melb.	
Abrey, Joseph, Mich.	"	38	190 Queensberry St. Nth Melb.	
Addoon, Joseph	"	41	Koroit	Vic
Atta, Faris	"	58	29 Latrobe Str. Melb.	
Attleir, Abraham	"	65	9 York Str. Nth Fitzroy	
Attleir, Leslie	"	23	9 York Str. Nth Fitzroy	
Batrouney, Farah	"	37	59 Little Lonsdale St. Melb.	
Batrouney, James	"	40	298 Drummond Str. Carlton	
Batrouney, John	"	30	496 Drummond St. Carlton	
Batrouney, Spiridon	"	39	291 Exhibition St. Melb	
Berinson, Morris	Jewish	26	55 Pitt Str. Carlton	
Beshara, Asuf	Syrian	60	28 Douglas Parade W'town	
Beshara, Michael	"	30	30 Douglas Parade. W'town	
Bossad, George	"	55	Back Creek Ballarat	Vic
Buzeid, Khaleel	"	48	Koroit	Vic
David, Badwee, George	"	59	13 Cumberland Place, Melb.	
David, George	"	57	3 McCormack Place, Melb	
Davis, Joseph	"	35	207 Moulton Str. Ballarat	
Davis, Walter	"	30	610 Doveton Crescent, Ballarat	
Dabley, George	"	65	High Str. Avoca	Vic
Elias, George	"	41	9 Mercer St. Geelong	Vic
Ellis, Michael	"	60	1 McCormack Place, Melb.	
Fakhrey, Joseph. Ch.	"	22	150 Bridge St. Bendigo	
Fakhrey, Michael. M	"	35	150 Bridge St. Bendigo	
Fakhry, Rasheed. Dr.	"	37	16 Carlton Str. Carlton	

List of Turkish subjects (males), including many Syrian-Lebanese, 19 August 1918. During the First World War, Turkish subjects were classified as Enemy Aliens and were required to report weekly to police stations for registration.
(Source: National Archives MP series 707. General Correspondence, Attorney General's Department, Commonwealth Investigation Branch, General Correspondence 1914 – 1918).

3

SYRIAN/LEBANESE SETTLEMENT IN AUSTRALIA 1880-1918

Everything in the world is much greater when heard about than when seen
Arabic proverb

Lebanese immigrants arrived by ship to the capital city that they, or their shipping agent, had arranged. Often, they would arrive in the company of an experienced immigrant or a returning immigrant. As such, some were anonymous. Shipping records in the 1880s and 1890s showed migrants travelling 'with friends', usually in steerage (third) class. In this way, some immigrants arrived without official identification. However, they were required to identify themselves when they sought to rent or purchase properties or to apply for a hawker's licence or for citizenship or to make some other official application. At this point, identification may have been obscured by anglicising names or falsifying information based on their particular needs at the time.

Upon arrival the Syrian/Lebanese immigrants soon set about making a living, often by hawking. However, those who arrived with some capital or were more educated and resourceful, opened warehouses and shops. These early immigrants established homes and raised families in capital cities and country towns. They developed a pattern of work and settlement which was followed by their relatives and fellow-villagers. At the same time, they created small communities in the capital cities and founded their first places of worship.

A guide to the Syrian/Lebanese populations of Victoria, New South Wales and Queensland at the outbreak of the Great War, may be found in the lists of Turkish subjects compiled by the Australian Attorney-General's Department, Commonwealth Investigation Branch.[34] These lists provide an indication of both the Syrian/Lebanese populations in each state and their places of residence. In Victoria, of 109 Turkish subjects, 87 were Syrian/Lebanese. In New South Wales, of 277 Turkish subjects, 257 were Syrian/Lebanese. In Queensland, of 42 Turkish subjects, 34 were Syrian/Lebanese.[35]

Once they landed in Australia, Syrian/Lebanese immigrants had to adapt to a society very different from the one they had left. Differences included the physical environment in which they lived and worked, either the inner urban districts, or country areas and towns. Their immediate tasks were to learn the currency, obtain a place to live, and acquire enough ability with the English language to enable them to earn a living and manage their daily lives. Syrian/Lebanese immigrants also had to adjust to living among the 'Inglees' in a period of strident Australian nationalism which was reflected in both political and public rejection of 'Asiatics'.

Picture of Queenstown and Mt Owen, Tasmania. Queenstown was a centre for mining copper, lead and zinc in the 1890s. Here Nicholas and Amy Antees and their family worked as hawkers and shopkeepers serving the miners and their families.

(Source: National Library of Australia. Photographer: Stephen Spurling III)

In these tasks the newly arrived immigrants were guided and assisted by their compatriots who had preceded them to Australia, especially by those who had some ability with the English language. This often involved introducing the newcomers to the work of hawking by escorting them to warehouses which supplied suitable goods, extending credit, applying for hawker's licences at police stations and courts, and accompanying them on their initial hawking rounds. Gold crosses, shirt studs, coins and religious medals were just some of the items which hawkers left with suppliers as a surety against the items of clothing and other lightweight goods they purchased for hawking. (Some of these items remain in the possession of the descendants of the Callil family, who were a major supplier of hawkers' goods from their clothing factory and warehouse in Melbourne).

Help and advice extended to renting and, later, purchasing, shops and houses. Support took the form of loans of money from family members or relatives and friends to help them start a business. This support was expected to be reciprocated in later ventures in which the earlier immigrant might participate. This indicates that the traditional village ties of Syria/Lebanon were extended to small networks of Syrian/Lebanese immigrants in Australia. Of course, interactions were not all devoted to learning about life in Australia. There was an opportunity to converse about the lives they left behind as well as to participate in cultural and religious rituals. The gatherings of Syrian/ Lebanese settlers, often just the men, who met at the Exhibition Gardens in Melbourne or Redfern Park in Sydney in the early 20th century provided the occasions where they would meet and speak Arabic and learn about their new life from each other. Often this took the form of a *mishwaar*, the traditional afternoon promenade. These gatherings constituted the very beginnings of Syrian/Lebanese communities in both cities.

Syrian/Lebanese families in Australia

At every stage in the migration and settlement of Syrian/Lebanese in Australia the role of the family was paramount. In most cases the initial decision to emigrate was a family decision and undertaken with the family's blessing. This applied to individuals, groups of family members, or the family as a whole. In the first instance, travelling with a family member, perhaps a father, brother or cousin, was the most common arrangement. In some cases, husbands, wives and children travelled and worked together as hawkers and shopkeepers. Earnings were generally pooled and remittances were sent home to meet family expenses and commitments. Not only was the family essential in the earning of money but it provided for the emotional and sociability needs of newly arrived immigrants. While this may be true of all recently arrived migrants, it particularly applied where there was no expatriate community, as in most country towns. This made the role of women all the more important in the first wave families, as illustrated by the story of Elizabeth Davis who took up hawking in and around Ballarat with her two young sons after the death of her husband.

Elizabeth Davis

In 1891 Tannous Dabes (later known as Davis) made the long journey to Ballarat, Victoria, from his home village of Bkfaya, in Mount Lebanon. He left behind his young wife, Elizabeth, and three young children – Joseph, Walter and Victoria. Elizabeth came from a well-educated family in Lebanon. She had been a schoolteacher before she married and she left behind one brother who was a doctor of medicine and another who was an Orthodox priest and, later, a bishop. Nevertheless, she was prepared to join her husband as he tried his luck in a remote country.

Tannous joined the tiny colony of Lebanese in Ballarat and began hawking in and around the Ballarat area. Other families in Ballarat at the time included the Batrouney and Dobley families and others whose names have not been recorded. Just six years later Elizabeth and her three children came to Australia on the German steamer, *Frederick der Grosse*, arriving on 6 January 1897.

Elizabeth Davis (nee Shammah) 1865-1935, hawked in and around Ballarat, Victoria, circa 1900-1908.
(Source: Ron Davis)

Tannous continued hawking in and around Ballarat and two years after the family's arrival a fourth child, Minnie, was born in September 1899. The stage was set for the steady progress of this young Lebanese family in the colony of Victoria. However, tragedy struck the family when Tannous, the father and breadwinner of the family, died of pneumonia on 26 October 1899. Elizabeth was left a young widow with four young children, the youngest of whom was a newly born babe. Tannous died a pauper and was buried in an unmarked grave in the new Ballarat cemetery. It was not until some years later that his sons were able to afford a tombstone for their father. The early Lebanese families in Ballarat experienced the hardships of hawking, separation from family, and considerable poverty. The unmarked graves provide sad testimony to the hardships and poverty experienced by this small group of pioneers.

How were Elizabeth and her family to survive? Government assistance was non-existent and the small Lebanese community had precious few resources to help each other. So Elizabeth had to fend for herself and her family by continuing the hawking business her husband had started. She pulled her two boys, Joseph (12) and Walter (10), out of their Catholic primary school and, with her four children in a horse-drawn cart, commenced hawking in and around the Ballarat area. Fortunately, Joseph had completed primary school and Walter was well educated for a boy of his age. This was to serve the family well in the future.

Elizabeth's determination and resourcefulness and the assistance of her two sons enabled the family to pull itself out of poverty. Over the next few years their hawking business prospered and the range of their activities widened. By 1906-1908 they were able to hire a railway carriage in a train en route to Mildura stopping at country towns, sometimes for a week, to sell their goods before moving on to the next town. An elderly lady in Mildura recalled the great excitement of the hawkers' visits and the lovely goods they would sell. Despite the success of these ventures and the use of modern technology, (namely the train) from which to sell goods, by the first decade of the 20th century their hawking days were rapidly drawing to a close.

Then came the second stage in the business activities of the Davis family: the establishment of drapery businesses. The first venture was a white goods factory in Prahran, Victoria, which Joseph ran for a short while with his mother, Elizabeth, in 1908, while Walter continued hawking. Walter then opened a shop in 1917 at Bakery Hill, Ballarat. He was there only three years before he bought a larger shop at 86 Bridge Mall in the centre of the Ballarat retail area. Although this shop was originally quite small, it offered ladies, men's and children's wear as well as Manchester, carpets and other household furnishings. Over the years it began to specialise by becoming a ladies and girls fashion store which it remained until its closure in the 1990s.[36]

The Davis family is noteworthy in that two of Elizabeth's grand-children achieved notable success in their fields: Steve Bracks as Premier of Victoria and Joe Saba, as originator of the Saba brand of clothing.

These first wave Syrian/Lebanese immigrants relied for communication with family in Lebanon and elsewhere on exchanges of letters containing photographs sent by post and, less frequently, delivered by hand by those returning to Lebanon or coming to Australia. Remittances were sent from Australia to Lebanon to help support the extended family. These remittances were intended to fund further migration of family members, to build or refurbish homes in case of future return, and to support aged parents and relatives. The significance of remittances for the Lebanese economy can be seen in the fact that by 1917 they accounted for some 40 per cent of the estimated national income of Lebanon.[37] They were also an indicator of the success of family members in the migration enterprise and helped prompt others to consider emigration.

It was through these letters, photographs and remittances that a limited form of contact was maintained with family members, not only in Lebanon but also in the United States, Canada, Argentina, Brazil and other diasporic communities. However, the expense and rarity of travel meant that these family members dispersed throughout the world would typically never meet again. These international contacts were essential in the formation of Lebanese communities in major cities of the diaspora. People emigrating from Syria/Lebanon were informed about those who had preceded them to a particular city or region and subsequently made contact with them.

It is important to note that, despite some common features, each Syrian/Lebanese family was unique, as illustrated by the story of Julia Elias Menayer. Her story reveals a number of less common themes found in the pioneer Syrian/Lebanese immigrants. These included double migration as her family moved from one location to another to join other family members; shopkeeping, which provided an early economic base for the family to prosper and provide their daughters with a superior education fit for ladies; and contacts with the Syrian/Lebanese communities in Melbourne, Queenstown Tasmania, and Dunedin, New Zealand.

Julia Elias Menayer

Julia Elias Menayer was born in Alexandria, Egypt, during her family's emigration from Beirut, Lebanon to Havana, Cuba, in 1897. The family established a haberdashery shop in Havana and Julia and her three sisters were sent to a private school for young ladies. Julia was raised in Bejucal, a small town 40 kilometres from Havana renowned for its street festivals called 'Las Charangas'. During that time, 1904-1907, she created an album of Spanish poetry and postcards. Julia and her sisters were fluent in three languages – Arabic, English and Spanish – and were brought up as ladies of leisure knowing fancywork, poetry, languages and music.

On 27 September 1911 Julia's family left Cuba to join her mother's family who had already settled in Dunedin, New Zealand. On arrival in Melbourne, en route to Dunedin on 7 March 1911, Julia started a diary with 20 entries covering a period of four months, including her stay in Melbourne and travel to Dunedin. Julia's diary was like a friend to her and in it she reveals all her inner thoughts, observations and dreams. Her diary is the voice of a young girl trying to cope with her sense of displacement at the loss of her carefree life in Cuba and her long-lost love, Claudio, for the more forbidding climate of New Zealand.

After rejecting two suitors when she was in Melbourne, Julia accepted the hand of Joe Antees in February 1912. Joe came from a pioneer Lebanese family from the mining town of Queenstown, Tasmania. However, this was not a particularly happy marriage and, after about eight years, Julia and Joe went to Sydney where Julia had a sister. So once again Julia had to adjust to a new life in Australia where she brought up her six children alone after the marriage broke down.[38]

Occupations and Business

The Syrian/Lebanese immigrants dispersed throughout the country areas of New South Wales, Queensland and Victoria. Their frequently chosen occupation as hawkers led to their moving to different regional areas in these colonies in search of markets for their merchandise and to avoid competition with each other. Hawking was a deliberately chosen initial step for many immigrants. It required little capital to pack a bag, a wagon or a cart with goods for sale; it relied on the energy and endeavour of the Syrian/Lebanese immigrants to travel to mostly country areas to sell their goods door to door and earn an income. In Queensland there was an official requirement for Syrian/Lebanese males to work in country areas, or with family members, rather than compete for jobs in the main cities. This had the effect of preventing competition for jobs where, it was feared, that immigrants would undercut the price of labour at a time of strengthening union activity.

The life of Raymond Betros, a hawker after 1926, touches on many of the common themes in the story of Lebanese hawkers in the early years of the 20th century. These included the early struggles to make a living by selling door to door, before using a horse and cart and later a truck for transport. The later stage for Raymond Betros, and others like him, was shop-keeping in country towns or perhaps warehouses in larger cities. A second theme was the beginnings of a Syrian/Lebanese community as those who had arrived earlier would offer later arrivals various forms of assistance such as helpful advice, goods on credit, loans of money and, above all, companionship. The *koora* or meeting place, included Syrian/Lebanese with the common experience of leaving their homeland, travelling to a strange and distant land, speaking in a foreign tongue, and engaging in a common occupation.[39]

Women played an important role in the settlement of their families during the first wave period. The Syrian/Lebanese had a higher percentage of females in their number during this period than Asian or other Mediterranean immigrants. For example, in 1911 and 1921 there were 71 and 76 females per 100 males compared with the much lower numbers for Greece (6 and 16) and Italy (21 and 29) for the same period. This was a clear indication that the Syrian/Lebanese were not sojourners but settlers who intended to raise families and make Australia their home. It was also a factor in the relatively high fertility rate of the Syrian/Lebanese families.

Not only were these women homemakers, who brought up their families in a largely alien environment, but a significant number also played major economic roles as hawkers or shopkeepers, either alongside their husbands or independently. This is confirmed by an analysis of the granting of hawkers licences in New South Wales and Queensland which indicated that approximately one third of all licences were granted to Syrian/Lebanese women.[40] In some cases there appeared to be a family tradition of women working in business. For example, Adele Moriarty reports that her grandmother and mother were both hawkers in the 1950s and into the 1960s. In 1953 Adele Moriarty became a bread deliverer with a horse and cart, reputed to be the first female bread carter in New South Wales.[41]

Many Syrian/Lebanese women were self-employed as shopkeepers, dressmakers and retailers of other goods. Sometimes their work was complementary to that of other members of their family as they made goods that were in demand and suitable for hawking. For example, Amy Antees, who was both a shopkeeper and dressmaker, made warm woollen singlets which were hawked by her husband, Nicholas Antees, to the miners who worked in the Mt Lyell Mines in Queenstown, Tasmania.

The work of these first wave women as hawkers set a pattern for the involvement of later generations of Lebanese women in family enterprises such as shop-keeping, warehouses and factories, milk bars and coffee lounges, among others.

Not all immigrants took the first step of hawking to accumulate capital in order to open a business. Some of the more educated immigrants or those arriving with sufficient money opened businesses on arrival. There were several examples of immigrants who were fluent in English as well as other languages. These included the Arida brothers who opened a store in Charters Towers in 1886 and, subsequently, elsewhere in rural Queensland and Daher Aboud who, according to a police report, 'was well educated and had brought a lot of money into the Colony'. Abraham Lutvey and his sister Regina were both fluent in English. The well-educated immigrants provided support and help for others in the local Syrian/ Lebanese community. Their bilingual ability made them unofficial intermediaries between their local community and wider colonial society. They also provided a means, either formal or informal, to take care of their fellow countrymen and women who might have met with misfortune.[42]

Immigrants from Syria/Lebanon responded differently to the situations in which they found themselves. Some moved swiftly from hawking to shopkeeping, while others, who perhaps enjoyed the life of travelling around, or were working to save more money, continued hawking for some years before settling in a particular area. In some cases, those who continued to hawk were employed by other family members or other members of the Syrian/Lebanese community. This transition to shopkeeping was noted by the Minister, Atlee Hunt, in a memorandum in 1914:

> ... by occupation they are mostly hawkers, and subsequently, as they manage to save some money, small storekeepers.[43]

Whatever the occupations of the first wave settlers, they were invariably self-employed. The reasons for this were complex. Sometimes the Syrian-Lebanese chose to become self-employed because of exclusion from the workforce based on political and popular discrimination. In other cases, hawking was seen as more profitable than employment on farms or in factories.

An important explanation for the predominance of hawking

and shop-keeping among early Syrian immigrants lay in the establishment of warehouses and factories in Redfern by Syrians who had preceded them in Sydney. These included George Malouf from Zahle (1888), George Dan (1890), Anthony Coorey (1891), and Stanton Melick's firm (1888). These warehouses supplied hawkers in New South Wales, Queensland and elsewhere in rural Australia. The relationship between warehouses and hawkers was a mutually beneficial one. Hawkers were given goods on credit by the warehouses and taught the fundamentals of trading and shop-keeping. The warehouses benefited by recruiting a ready supply of traders to market their goods far and wide throughout the country areas of Australia.[44]

It was not uncommon for members of the one family to live in different country towns which they used as bases for their hawking activities. In this way, the area covered by their hawking activities was extended and the family income increased. Some of the larger country towns had sufficient numbers of Syrian/Lebanese to provide social interaction and mutual assistance in their commercial activities. These included towns like Albury in New South Wales, Taree in Queensland, Zahle in Queensland (renamed Kilburnie in 1925) and Ballarat in Victoria, where they would meet informally in homes or public places like parks or picnic grounds. However, in most cases, the Syrian/Lebanese in country towns were too small in number and their occupations too transitory for a Lebanese community to develop fully.

The story of Peter Callil Fakhry and the successful businesses he created clearly demonstrate the characteristics displayed by some early Lebanese immigrants: entrepreneurial business activities; an early commitment to settle and establish families in Australia; extensive family involvement in business; public spiritedness and loyalty, especially in times of war, and eventual integration into wider Australian society.

Peter Callil Fakhry

When Peter Callil Fakhry sailed from Lebanon to Australia in 1881 he thought he was going to al Nayurk (New York). His arrival was the earliest recorded of the first wave of Lebanese/Syrian migration, which started in the 1880s.

Born in Bcharre, Lebanon in 1863, Peter worked in a Melbourne hotel for a few years before deciding to find a place to settle. He travelled and traded in Australia and New Zealand until finally settling in Melbourne, Victoria, where his brother, Latoof, joined him.

In 1884 Peter opened 'Latoof and Callil', a small warehouse in Exhibition Street. Latoof returned to Lebanon but Peter continued the business. He supplied goods to the Chinese, Indian, Afghan and Syrian hawkers who arrived at the warehouse in their horse-drawn covered wagons. They bought supplies to service the remote country areas of the colonies of Victoria, South Australia and southern New South Wales.

Peter Callil Fakhry, founder of Latoof and Callil Pty Ltd in1884. Peter Callil was naturalised in the late 1890s as a citizen of the Colony of Victoria. After 1903 Lebanese were generally denied the right to apply for Australian citizenship until 1920.

(Source: Peter Callil)

Four years later Peter visited Lebanon and returned with his bride, Anna Yazbek. Over the years their six sons, two daughters and their extended families became involved in the prospering family business. He built a large five story building on the adjacent site in Exhibition Street and, by 1916, the company's best customer was the Coles family who had a shop in Smith Street, Collingwood. Over the years, the expansion of Coles and Latoof and Callil went hand in hand. By the late 1930s Latoof and Callil had expanded both warehousing and manufacturing operations and built a modern manufacturing plant on a large site in Brunswick.

During the Second World War, Latoof and Callil manufactured military uniforms and other items for the Australian war effort. The family decided to donate all the profits generated during the war to wartime charities and projects, including the provision of field ambulances and amenities to military hospitals. Employees were encouraged to support Food for Britain parcels and knitting of balaclavas for the Red Cross.

After the war the company workforce had grown to 1500 employees, and had established factories at Benalla, Euroa, Mooroopna, Greensborough, Werribee, Watsonia, Ballan and Highett. But when Australia's tariff barriers and import quotas were lifted in the 1970s, many clothing manufacturers were severely affected, including Latoof and Callil. Slow to embrace modern production techniques and financial management methods, the company suffered. In 1981, after successfully trading for 99 years and becoming the largest clothing manufacturer and fabric importer in the southern hemisphere, Latoof and Callil was voluntarily placed in the hands of receivers. All creditors were paid in full by 1982.[45]

Education of Syrian-Lebanese children

Once settled in an area, Syrian/Lebanese children would be enrolled in a local school, either a Catholic school or a state run one. For children, many of whom only spoke Arabic at home, the demands of an English-speaking school at a time of assertive Australian nationalism challenged their sense of self and identity. Their initial lack of facility in speaking English and in understanding the behavioural nuances of the school and peer groups saw them either isolated or in fights in the playground. In the classroom there was a sense that teachers were looking down on them.[46]

Something of the problems facing some Lebanese children at school is captured in the following poem:

> And I think of my days at primary school in Sydney
> A school with 'wogs' from neighbouring Thornleigh--"Little Lebanon" it was called
> Oily, dark-skinned kids who were teased and shunned because of how they
> Looked and spoke and smelt
> I know now why I felt sorry for them
> Why my little heart reached out to them
> Why I got angry and felt the injustice
> Why I tried to be friends with them
> Why I tried to take the Outsiders In
>
> My Jiddee*
> was one of them
> And so was my dad
> And deep down, so too am I
>
> (Richard Mellick, 2016.[47]) *grandfather

As their language proficiency improved, and depending on the family's valuing of education and the child's ability, some Syrian/Lebanese children became proficient at learning at school and formed friendships with their fellow students. Those children, whose English language proficiency quickly outstripped that of their parents, were embarrassed when they had to speak Arabic to their parent at school or around school friends. For many, attendance at school was secondary to the needs of the family business. Girls would help serve in shops or work in factories. Boys travelled with their fathers and other family members hawking goods and later worked in the family businesses.

The type and level of education of the children of immigrants varied according to the resources and values of their parents. Three case studies will reveal different experiences of schooling. While the majority of Syrian/Lebanese families gained only a modest income through hawking, a few children came from families which had become wealthy through establishing warehouses and factories in the clothing industry. One such was the Peter Kahlil Fakhry (later Peter Callil) family in Melbourne. As we saw, Peter was one of the first arrivals from Syria/Lebanon and the first in Melbourne to open a warehouse and factory. His venture quickly prospered and the Callil family was able to provide a superior education for their children. This is illustrated in the education and academic career of one of their sons:

Frederick Alfred Louis Callil

Frederick Alfred Louis Callil was born in Melbourne on 17 April 17 1899, the sixth son and eighth child of the nine children of Butros Kahlil Fakhry (Peter Callil) and Henineh Yazbeck (Anna Callil). When he was only six he was sent back to Lebanon for his education, as was the custom of the time. There he attended St Joseph's School and University in Beirut. He returned to Melbourne in 1911, went to the Christian Brothers School in East Melbourne, and won a scholarship to Trinity College at the University of Melbourne in 1917. He completed his University years at Newman College and graduated in Arts with honours in 1918. He won the Mollison Scholarship three times – in French, English and Arabic. After his Arts degree he studied law, also at Melbourne University, and became a practising barrister at the Melbourne Bar in the 1930s.

Because of his many languages (he also spoke Italian) as a barrister he was much in demand by the immigrant communities of Melbourne. He continued his work at Melbourne University, being awarded his MA in 1930 and LLB in 1940. From 1930 to 1946 he was associated with the French department at the University of Melbourne, working with Professor A.R. Chisholm and V.N.T. Karagheusian. The latter was senior lecturer in the French department, and Fred Callil tutored in French from 1930 to 1946. Both Karagheusian and Callil were notorious amongst the generations of French students to whom they introduced French language and culture, for various and considerable eccentricities which included, in the case of Fred Callil, occasionally lecturing in his pyjamas.[48]

Our second case study deals with the education of Adele Antees, who, as we saw, came from a family which had pursued the traditional pathway of hawking and shopkeeping in Queenstown, Tasmania with some success. This led Adele's mother to encourage her daughters to acquire dressmaking or some other skills. In Adele's case this was typing, shorthand and bookkeeping.

Adele Antees

Adele Antees was born in Queenstown, Tasmania on 6 February 1911, the youngest daughter of Nicholas and Amy Antees. Adele's parents migrated from Tripoli, Lebanon in the 1890s to join two of Amy's brothers, Bundali and Michael, who had already made their way to the west coast of Tasmania. During her early childhood Adele's father and uncles were hawkers in the Mt Lyell region of Tasmania. Her mother was a busy and successful businesswoman so Lily, the oldest sister at home, took much responsibility for Adele's upbringing.

Adele attended the local primary school and Sunday school at St Martin's Church of England in Queenstown, where she was dux of the Sunday School one year, which pleased her devout parents. At the age of ten years, Adele, her parents and unmarried sisters, Julia and Mary, left Queenstown in 1921 to join their married daughters and the small Lebanese community in Melbourne.

In September 1921 Adele commenced at Lee Street State School in Carlton, Melbourne. Adele enjoyed her schooling and was a capable student. Her mother did not know what to do once she completed Grade Eight and received her Merit Certificate, as she wanted her to receive training at a business college. However, Adele was too young to be enrolled in college and options such as completing secondary schooling or higher education were not even considered by her parents. The solution was for her to repeat Grade Eight until she was old enough to enrol in Stott's Business College in Melbourne, where in twelve months she learned typing, shorthand and bookkeeping. Her training was testimony to her mother's drive to educate her daughters. Adele inherited her mother's love of education and passed it on to her family in good measure.

Adele Antees, was born in Queenstown Tasmania 1911. Her parents opened a general goods store in Queenstown tended by her mother and sisters. Her father hawked goods around the local area. Her family came to Melbourne in the early 1920s to live close to their daughters who had moved there once they married. As her parents knew little of the education system, she had to repeat her merit certificate (Year 8) to be old enough to enter a business studies college.

(Source: Andrew Batrouney)

After Adele married she devoted herself to her family and Church. Her love of children and education saw her start Sunday school classes in two Orthodox churches in Melbourne where she was much loved by the hundreds of children she taught over the years.[49]

The final case study describes the more common experience whereby young peoples' schooling had to give way to working in the family business.

Muriel 'Bubs' Saleeba

Muriel ('Bubs') Saleeba was the third daughter of George and Elsie Saleeba. George Saleeba was born in Rashaya, Lebanon in 1882, and came to Australia with his father Essa at the age of 10 in 1892. George did not attend school in Melbourne but was thrust into earning a living at an early age to enable the rest of his family in Lebanon to join them. Essa and George became hawkers of clothing and soft goods in country areas outside of Melbourne. The Saleeba family next established a business at 324 Smith Street, Collingwood, consisting of a small factory, a shop front where the goods were sold, and rooms upstairs where the family lived. In 1916 George described his occupation as a draper.

Bubs describes her experiences at school in unsentimental terms: 'I never passed an exam. At home we were never taught to do homework. Who could we talk to about our books? Mum was always having babies or working at the factory, we had no encouragement. In the sixth grade we had our qualification exam, I never passed that. In the eighth grade when you were about fourteen we had the merit. I never passed that.' Failing did not bother her 'because I knew I had to go to the factory and work'.

What Bubs lacked in formal qualifications she more than made up for in her drive and determination to succeed. In 1938 at the age of twenty Bubs took over the running of her father's clothing factory: Saleeba Manufacturing. Soon after, she started her own business, later joined by her husband, Victor Batrouney, and one brother, Ron. In 1944 the company's name was changed to Merlvic Modes, specialising in children's and women's night wear. Merlvic became a highly successful, nation-wide company before Bubs retired in 1984 aged 68 after 60 years in business.[50]

4

EARLY SYRIAN/LEBANESE COMMUNITIES

Follow in the footsteps of the fortunate and you will come to fortune.

Arabic Proverb

The limited and delayed communication between Australia and Lebanon and rare return visits resulted in the isolation of these Syrian/Lebanese communities in a sea of Anglo-Celtic Australians. Together with other factors, this was a recipe for their rapid and extensive assimilation.[51] The difficult times and discrimination endured by many of the first wave settlers produced a number of defensive responses by the immigrants themselves and even among their descendants. These sometimes involved obscuring, and at other times an outright denial of, their ethnic and religious backgrounds. This led some second-generation Lebanese to claim a presumably higher status 'French' or 'Mediterranean' background in preference to their Lebanese one.

The practice of Anglicising surnames and first names to Anglo ones, which more or less approximated their Lebanese names was partly a defensive response to their circumstances. Yet another example can be seen in the attempt to change the first names of a newly arrived second wave family to Australian names. Thus, Milhem became Bill,

Fatine became Victor, Mounah was to be called Jack and the names of two of the girls in the family were changed: Najla to Lily and Shamla to Mary. In some cases, these adopted names were readily accepted while in other cases the family reverted to their original names. Another common occurrence was changing religious affiliation from one of the Lebanese Christian churches such as Greek (later Antiochian) Orthodox, Maronite and Melkite Catholic Rites to affiliation with Anglican and Latin Catholic churches. In these ways first wave Syrian/Lebanese sought to assimilate into Australian society and thereby justify their suitability as permanent settlers and their rights to equal status within Australian society.

During this period, there were small Syrian/Lebanese communities in Sydney, Melbourne, Brisbane and Adelaide as well in some provincial towns. These communities initially congregated in inner metropolitan areas such as Redfern in Sydney, the north-east quarter of the city of Melbourne and spreading into Carlton, and around South Brisbane and the northern parts of Adelaide. The Syrian/Lebanese families living in these areas had much in common. They had all migrated from Syria/Lebanon during the 1880s and 1900s, so their first language was Arabic, their culture was Syrian/Lebanese and the great majority were Christians – Maronites, Orthodox or Melkites.

The Syrian/Lebanese in Melbourne and Sydney, Australia, provide examples of early community formation. By the early years of the 20th century, a small colony of Syrian/Lebanese had settled in Melbourne. This was noted in the mainstream Press:

> These districts are centred in the very heart of the city, and form in themselves small colonies of many undesirable aliens. In one district especially---that bounded by Spring, Lonsdale, Exhibition and La Trobe streets – there are massed together many nationalities...But the Syrians may particularly claim to represent the greater proportion of this heterogeneous population...[52]

Khyatt family group in front of their drapery shop 221 Exhibition Street,
Melbourne, circa 1904.
(Source: Khyatt Family; State Library of Victoria)

These Syrian/Lebanese families made initial contact with each other
through word of mouth and maintained this contact over the years.
They often worked together as hawkers, shopkeepers or wholesalers
and shared social activities such as visiting each other and meeting on
Sundays in the Exhibition Gardens on the edge of the city. The larger
Syrian/Lebanese community in Sydney was centred in Redfern and
would meet informally in Redfern Park to enjoy each other's company
and share information about life and work in their new home as well as
provide help to each other. In this way, these early Lebanese migrants
sought to recreate the communal life of the villages they had left
behind. One newspaper report of the Syrian colony in Redfern was
positive:

The colony covers the greater portion of the eastern side of Redfern Park, the Syrian houses lying between the numbers 37 and 141. Within these limits the Syrians are located in 23 shops.... [T]he list of pursuits will at once suggest that the Syrian is not an undesirable colonist.

Some Syrian/Lebanese were successful proprietors of retail businesses and warehouses, others found that 'times were very tough for Redfern and especially for most of the Lebanese who by and large eked out livings as workers in the clothing trade, proprietors of tiny businesses or as hawkers'.[53]

**Joseph and Susan Malouf and family outside their shop and dwelling at 58 Lonsdale St., Melbourne, 1918.
(Source: Eileen Malouf)**

Given the small size of these communities in Australia and the infrequency of return visits to Lebanon, maintaining contact by mail with Lebanese families in other cities or countries in the diaspora was an important means of obtaining suitable marriage partners, at least in terms of ethnicity and religion. For example, one Melbourne family of four sons obtained marriage partners in the early years of the 20th century from Dunedin, New Zealand; Adelaide, South Australia; Albury, New South Wales; and from Ballarat, Victoria.

Against the background of being denied citizenship after 1903, and registration as Enemy Aliens after 1914, the small communities of Sydney and Melbourne were keen to demonstrate their public spiritedness and loyalty, which they did through community collections for hospitals and charities as well as professions of loyalty to those in authority. As early as 1914 the small Syrian/Lebanese community in Sydney subscribed over £400 to the Lord Mayor's Patriotic Fund and £600 to the building of the South Sydney hospital. At the end of the War the Syrian/Lebanese community of New South Wales sent the following message of congratulations to the Australian Governor-General:

> Please accept for your Excellency and convey to His Gracious Majesty the King our humble congratulations of the Syrian community of New South Wales at the great victory achieved by the British Empire and its Allies, and our unswerving loyalty to His Majesty's person and throne.[54]

These collective examples of loyalty and community spirit were more than matched by the charitable works of community–minded Syrian/Lebanese shopkeepers, especially in country towns. Many examples have been provided of their active participation in local welfare, religious and sporting activities as well as their generous donations to these bodies and other local charities. Another dimension of their charitable works were the individual acts of generosity to the needy, particularly during the Depression years of the 1930s, that have been fondly remembered by the descendants of both the helpers and those who were helped.

> James Batrouney was essentially a kindly and benevolent man who worked in his grocery businesses from 1907 to 1949. His son, Leo, recalls how James would extend credit to poor families during the Depression and when his sons would remonstrate with him, he would reply 'But she's got three children'. On another occasion Leo was puzzled that they never seemed to get the right number of pounds of sugar out of a large bag. The problem was solved when James admitted that he always gave customers an extra ounce! Many years

later another son, Phillip, recalled meeting a man who claimed that, 'during the Depression, Mr Batrouney kept my family from starvation'. Another example of James' benevolence![55]

It is understandable that these acts of collective and individual generosity by the pioneer settlers were remembered by their families and others in the Lebanese communities while other, perhaps less praiseworthy, actions were not recalled or made public. It is possible also that the difficulties of migration and settlement, which were encountered by the pioneer families, provided the impetus for them to seek to prove beyond doubt their worth as community members and citizens of Australia.

Syrian-Lebanese community in Albury, NSW

After their time as hawkers, many Syrian-Lebanese later opened businesses in country towns throughout Australia. While most eventually moved to the capital cities, others settled in the country towns and became part of the local community. This occurred with the town of Albury, on the border of New South Wales and Victoria.

Albury proved attractive to hawkers because of its situation on the Murray River and its plentiful supply of water, a vital resource for hawkers and their horses during the drought years of the 1890s. Some of the families who lived and worked in the Albury area over the years included the Sarroff, Malouf, Bounader, Azzi, Wessen, Jabara, Elias, Salamy, Galletti, David, Nadar, Nash, Nasser, Nesire, Keamy, Mellick, Farrah, Dihood, Sedawie, Corban, Buckley, Doumanie, Dobley, McConnell, Assada, Beca, Batrouney and Metry families.

Following the hawking period Syrian-Lebanese and their descendants opened clothing shops, warehouses and clothing factories. After the Great Depression they could be found in a wide range of activities, including ice works (Elias Family); service station and motor mechanics garage (Jim and Daniel Abikhair); pie shop and later reception centre (Jim and Vicky Bacash); fruit and vegetables, real estate, auction rooms, and furniture store (Batrouney family); bookmaking (Assad and Sarroff families); dry cleaning and insurance (Sarroff family); jewellery (Jabara Family); shoe repairs, poultry farming and auctioneering (Metry family); Moteliers and horse racing (Farrahs).

Wal Abikhair at work in his drapery shop in Albury, circa 1958.
(Source: Abikhair Family)

The Lebanese also made a lasting contribution to building in Albury. Over the years Butros Abicare built the 'Big Store' on one corner of Dean Street and the Regent Theatre on the opposite corner, as well as a service station on the third corner. George Malouf built the T and G building. A number of shops and dwellings were built or acquired by the Dihoods, Corbans, Farrahs, Buckleys and Nesires. Sometimes they lived above or behind their shops. In all, Lebanese families made a lasting contribution to the built environment of the town.

Given their prominence in the community life of Albury a number of Lebanese-Australians have been duly recognised for their many contributions. These included Norman Batrouney (British Empire Medal); Eddie Batrouney (Order of Australia Medal and Paul Harris Fellow); Gwen Abikhair (Paul Harris Fellow), among others. Lebanese families have been involved in local government (Eddie Batrouney as Mayor of Albury), Rotary, Apex, Hospital and School Committees, Riding for the Disabled, YMCA, RSL, Scouts and Guides.

The first churches

In the earliest period of settlement, contacts among Syrian/ Lebanese were informal and based on relationships derived from their former homeland. The most important of these were family and kin, who provided the new arrivals with guides and companions in their hawking and shopkeeping activities. Other key relationships were formed with former fellow villagers and those who shared the same religion. Even when they gathered together for a specific purpose such as making a declaration of loyalty or supporting a charity, these were essentially informal gatherings.

The first formal community organizations established by first wave Lebanese immigrants were churches. For most of the Lebanese immigrants to Australia during this period, religion was an integral part of their upbringing and a strong means of ordering their lives. Likewise, the religious affiliations of these immigrants played an important part in explaining their relationship with the host society and the degree to which they were integrated into it. As we have seen, the great majority who settled in Australia between 1880 and 1920 were Christians, divided into Maronite Catholics, Syrian (later termed Antiochian) Orthodox, and Melkite Catholics.

Although these churches established places of worship in Sydney around the turn of the century, the many Syrian/Lebanese working and living in country towns and in the other major cities of Australia had no access to worship in their own churches and in their own native tongue. This was especially so during the early stages when they were earning their living as itinerant hawkers or as shop-keepers in country towns. The few priests from Sydney travelled throughout New South Wales, Queensland, Victoria and even as far as New Zealand, visiting their flock and performing sacraments, especially baptisms and marriages.

The first Antiochian Orthodox priest to arrive in Australia was Father Nicholas Shehadie in 1913. He not only served the Syrian Orthodox community of Sydney but travelled throughout eastern Australia where he performed sacraments and conducted Divine Liturgies for the local populations.[56] One such visit to the Mission House in Spring Street, Melbourne was recorded in the Day Book of the Anglican Community of the Holy Name:

> In November 1922 we had another visit from the Syrian priest of the Orthodox Church who comes occasionally from Sydney to minister to the Syrians in Melbourne. The Liturgy was celebrated in the Mission Hall and the Syrians turned up in great force. Arabic was the language used which most of the older people could follow, but those born in Australia rarely learn their parents' language and refuse to attend services after they grow old enough to assert themselves.[57]

The Anglican Mission Hall in Spring Street Melbourne was used for worship by the first Pan-Orthodox group, including the Syrian Orthodox, in the 1890s. It was also used by Syrian Orthodox before their church of St Nicholas was established in 1932.
(Source: History of St Nicholas Orthodox Church)

The desire to practise their own religion developed more strongly with the increasing economic stability and permanence of the expatriate Syrian/Lebanese communities. Before establishing their own churches, the Christian Lebanese attended churches of other denominations on festival days to participate in religious rituals such as weddings and baptisms. This practice was more acceptable to the Maronites and Melkites, who attended Australian Catholic Churches, than to the Syrian Orthodox. However, with the establishment of Greek Orthodox Churches in Sydney (1898) and in Melbourne (1900), with the financial help of key members of the Lebanese community, Syrian/Lebanese Orthodox now had a place of worship to attend. In Melbourne hawkers would journey from outlying areas to share, with the rest of the community, special religious festivals like Easter and Christmas as well as marriages, baptisms and funerals. Whether these were conducted in Anglican, Catholic or Greek Orthodox churches, most Lebanese were still not worshipping in their own churches or in their own language. During this initial period of Lebanese settlement, religion took second place to their economic survival and family welfare.

The only formal Syrian/Lebanese community organisations during this period in Sydney were three churches and a handful of priests. The small communities in Brisbane and Adelaide were not serviced by their own clergy. However, during this time, the Sydney priests travelled throughout Australia to serve their scattered adherents.

With its larger population of Lebanese than Melbourne, Sydney saw the establishment of Lebanese churches for the Syrian/Lebanese in the last decade of the 19th century. Despite the small numbers of Maronites, as early as 1889 the Maronite Patriarch decided to establish a Maronite Mission in Australia. Two priests, Father Abdallah Yazbeck and Father Joseph Dahdah, arrived in Sydney on 8 May 1893 and, not long after their arrival, a Maronite chapel was set up in Waterloo in 1894. This served as the first Maronite place of worship in Sydney until 10 January 1897 when the new church of St Maroun was consecrated by Cardinal Moran. From this period there has been a constant and expanding Maronite presence throughout Australia with significantly larger numbers in New South Wales than in Victoria and elsewhere in Australia.[58]

The first Syrian/Lebanese church established in Australia was that of St Michael's Melkite Church in Waterloo, Sydney, in 1895. This church was established by Archimandrite Silwanos Mansour, the first Lebanese priest to settle in Australia in 1891. This was quickly followed by the establishment of St Maroun in Redfern in 1897. Shortly after, in 1901, the Orthodox community of St George was also established in Redfern to service the needs of the Orthodox in Sydney.

Archimandrite Silwanos Mansour, the first Lebanese priest to settle in Australia in 1891. He helped establish St Michael's Melkite Church in Waterloo, Sydney in 1895. Until churches for the other Christian denominations were established, Archimandrite Mansour ministered to all Lebanese (then Syrian) Christians in Sydney (Source: St Clements Catholic Church, Brisbane Queensland)

Very Reverend Father Nicholas Shehadie arrived in Sydney in 1910 and served the Syrian Orthodox community throughout eastern Australia. He established St Georges in Sydney in 1920, the first Antiochian Orthodox church in Australia. He passed away on 15 May 1974. (Source: Dan E & Mansour N, St Georges Cathedral: Past, Present and Future, 2004).

The establishment of these churches indicates that the initial phase of hawking had largely come to an end and that each of the religious communities was organised to the point where they could gather congregations, purchase churches and bring out priests to serve their needs. The earlier establishment of the Sydney churches indicates that the Sydney Lebanese community was larger, more organised and settled earlier than its Melbourne counterpart.

The first communal activities of the Syrian/Lebanese in Melbourne were aided by an Anglican nun, Sister Esther Silcock, who took it upon herself to assist the Orthodox in conducting services in their own tongue and according to their own rite. This she did by offering the Anglican Mission Room in Spring Street, Melbourne, as a place of worship for the Syrian/Lebanese. For example, in 1889 at the first Orthodox service, the Anglican Bishop of Melbourne was present and pronounced the blessing in Arabic after delivering an address which was translated by the leading Orthodox layman, Katarr Keamy. Even though they were without a priest, the Orthodox celebrated their own Easter at the appropriate time. The following account of one of the first Orthodox Easters in Melbourne conveys something of the joyousness with which it was celebrated by both Orthodox and Anglicans:

> The Greek Easter, of course, was at a different date from the Western, but the Mission room was arranged with equal care for the Orthodox festival and the Sisters enjoyed the fun of the crackers and candles distributed at the close of the service, treasuring Katarr's reply to a passer-by who asked the reason of all this noise of a Sunday morning: 'If the King of England came to Melbourne you would let off crackers. We do this because the King of Kings has come back to us from the grave'.[59]

The Syrian Orthodox also worked closely with the Greek Orthodox and helped establish a Greek Orthodox Church in East Melbourne in 1902. However, attendance at the Greek Church did not fully meet the spiritual and social needs of the small group of Lebanese Orthodox families in Melbourne. Despite the fact that these families had been living in Melbourne without their own place of worship for up to forty years, the desire to establish their own church did not fade over time. By the late 1920s, most families had become established in business and their children were either attending school or had commenced work. Now seemed the right time to found their own church. Thus St Nicholas Antiochian (then called 'Syrian') Orthodox Church was established in 1931. This church was to provide the sole communal centre for Lebanese in Melbourne until the 1950s.

The Lebanese Christians in Brisbane also sought a church of their own. Partly because of their small numbers, they decided to build a church for all of the Lebanese Christians – Melkites, Maronites and Orthodox – together. Each of these groups provided funds and support for the establishment of St Clement's as a single church to serve the three major faiths. The foundation stone was blessed on 29 March 1929 and the church was opened for public worship by 1936. The church was served by priests of the Basilian Melkite Order and it soon came under the jurisdiction of the Melkite Rite. St Clements provided the community centre for all Lebanese from its inception in 1936 until the Orthodox and Maronites of Brisbane established their own churches in the 1980s.

Contacts with Syria/Lebanon

Following immigration, most first wave settlers had limited contact with their home country. Their contacts were mostly confined to sending and receiving letters and photographs from their family in Lebanon and in other immigration countries. In many cases family members made their homes in different countries and were never or rarely able to see their relatives again. For example, the first wave Facoory family from El Mina, Lebanon, found themselves spread across the world in the United States, New Zealand, Brazil and Australia as well as in their home country. It was only when the original Facoory family members were older that they were able to visit each other and meet their sisters, brothers, nephews and nieces. Sadly, the eldest sister, Katy, died when she visited Melbourne from her home in the United States.

As we have seen, a major form of contact was sending remittances to family in Lebanon to assist them in difficult economic times and to help with the education of young family members. Those immigrants who had amassed riches were able to build homes in Lebanon for their future use and to make donations to churches and village charities.

Some few families, who had the resources, were able to send their children to Syria/Lebanon to become educated in Church schools, as we saw in the case of Frederick Callil. While this provided some early family contact with the home country there is little evidence that this was a significant influence in their lives.

5

LEBANESE IDENTITY IN AUSTRALIA
1880 – 1918

The geography and history of the region now known as Lebanon contributed to the identity of its immigrants. The location of Lebanon meant that Syrian/Lebanese immigrants were influenced by traders and missionaries from other Mediterranean nations and the Arab hinterland, as well as from the United States. Added to this were the success stories of returning immigrants from Africa, the Americas and Australia. These influences, together with their own oral traditions, helped forge a Syrian/Lebanese identity as a nation of traders willing to travel far and wide to earn a living.

From their first arrival Australian-Lebanese immigrants had to confront questions of their identity and nomenclature. The main signifiers of their identity in their homeland and on arrival in Australia were family, religion and locality. Given their place of birth east of the Bosporus, Syrian/Lebanese were classified by the Australian authorities as 'Asiatic' and, after Federation, excluded from entry and citizenship. This was a particularly hurtful misnomer as it identified Lebanese together with the so-called 'undesirable' Chinese and other Asian immigrants. At this time some Syrian/Lebanese were mistakenly identified as 'Assyrians,' a term familiar to those in the West through Biblical stories.

Questions of identity were also raised during Syrian/Lebanese applications for citizenship and hawkers' licences after 1903. In addition to offering testimonies as to the applicant's good character it became important for applicants to claim citizenship of a European nation, such as Greece or 'European' Turkey. So, we find many Syrian/ Lebanese seeking to identify magistrates who might be sympathetic to their claims to be eligible for Australian citizenship on these or other grounds.

Even when volunteering to serve their new country in the AIF during the Great War, questions of identity and nomenclature came to the fore. In view of Ottoman control over their former homeland, Syrian/ Lebanese immigrants were classified as Turkish subjects. During the War they were required to report to local police, as we saw, on the grounds that they were subjects of a nation with which Britain and its Empire, including Australia, were at war. This cast a long shadow over Syrian/Lebanese families and their loyalty to Australia, which they were always keen to dispel.

We also noted that local magazines such as the *Bulletin* and *Boomerang* idealised workers and miners as true Australians and those who did not fit this idealised picture were subject to satirical and critical commentary. In this way Syrian/Lebanese immigrants were depicted as culturally and racially inferior and not being worthy Australians. So the media of the time played its part in disseminating critical comments and caricatures of Syrian/Lebanese and other so-called 'non-desirables'.

What impact did this negative treatment and commentary have on the small Lebanese communities in the early decades of the 19th century? The treatment they received from Australian colonial and national authorities challenged the sense of their own worth. There was a gulf between how they viewed themselves and how they were viewed officially. This may help explain the strong desire of Syrian/Lebanese immigrants to identify themselves as loyal Australians and worthy of Australian citizenship. They rejected any treatment as 'second-class citizens' and sought to be regarded as equal to other 'favoured' races in Australia. This may be seen in their expressions of loyalty to the British monarchy and their collections for local charities and in their high take-up of Australian citizenship in the 1920s. Despite this official discrimination, Syrian/Lebanese shopkeepers gained positive reputations in local communities.

Another possible impact relates to the terms in which some first wave immigrants, and especially their children, described, or sought to obscure, their origins in order to gain public respect. For example, some chose to identify themselves or their families as of French or European background.

During this period Syrian/Lebanese identity may be seen as split along two lines: a private identity within their family, church and ethnic community, and a public one in which they related to the wider Australian society through work, schooling and mainstream social activities. This suggests a combination of primordial and constructivist forms of identity.

In this manner, the identity of Syrian/Lebanese was both primordialist and constructivist. Certainly, first wave immigrants and, to a lesser extent, their children, tended to retain attachments to family, religion and aspects of Lebanese culture, not least of which was their traditional food. This could be seen in their feelings of loyalty and obligation to their family (both in Lebanon and Australia), their establishment of churches and later mosques, and their retention of elements of Lebanese culture.

Over time, these immigrants, and especially their children, tended to construct their own identities influenced by the work and schooling they engaged in and the social situations they experienced. In a sense, the second generation may be seen as living in both worlds: the Syrian/Lebanese ethnic community and the wider Australian society.

Despite this limited contact with their homeland, the identity of these early immigrants was Syrian/Lebanese, marked by their primordial attachments to their Arabic language, religion and culture. Although their direct contacts with their home country were limited, they still retained their traditional culture and identity as Syrian/Lebanese. However, this did not apply to their children who, during the course of their lives, constructed Australian identities or, at least, hybrid identities: part Australian, part Lebanese.[60]

NOTES

1 Jidejian, N 1992, *The Story of Lebanon in Pictures*. Librairie Orientale. p. 260

2 Traboulsi, F 2012, *A History of Modern Lebanon*. Pluto Press. 2nd Edition. p. 33

3 *Ibid.* p. 43

4 *Ibid.* p. 48

5 *Ibid.* p. 46

6 *Ibid.* p. 44

7 Burke, E 1988, 'Rural Collective Action and the emergence of modern Lebanon: A comparative historical perspective.' In Shehadi, N & Haffar Mills, D (eds) 1988, *Lebanon: A history of conflict and consensus* Centre for Lebanese Studies, London. p. 28

8 *Ibid.* p. 72

9 Owen, R *1992*, 'Lebanese in the world: a century of emigration', in Hourani AH & Shehadi N 1992 *The Lebanese in the World: A century of emigration*. Centre for Lebanese Studies, University of Oxford. p. 34

10 Issawi, C 1992, 'The Historical background of Lebanese Emigration' in Hourani, AH & Shehadi, N *The Lebanese in the World: A century of emigration*. Centre for Lebanese Studies, University of Oxford. pp 13 -32

11 Hitti, PK cited in Khalaf, S 1987, *Lebanon's Predicament*. Columbia University Press, New York p. 21

12 Tannous, A I 1949, 'The Village in the National Life of Lebanon', *Middle East Journal*, vol. 3, no. 4, Middle East Institute. p. 151 - 163

13 Monsour, A 2010. *Not quite white: Lebanese and the White Australia Policy 1880 to 1947*, Post Pressed. p.96

14 Naff, A 1992. 'Lebanese Immigration to the United States: 1880 to the Present', *The Lebanese in the World*, Centre for Lebanese Studies in association with IB Tauris& Co.

15 Khalaf, S *Op. Cit.* p 27

16 Monsour, A *Op. Cit.* p. 52

17 Khalaf, S *Op. Cit.* p.30

18 *Ibid.* p.32

19 Interview Dianne Anderson née Hamra, November 2016

20 Maalouf, A 2008, *Origins: A memoir*. Farrar, Strauss & Giroux, New York. p. 24

21 Nasser, R 2001, *From Kousba to Clemount: The Nasser and Solomon Australian Story*, J.R. Durington & Sons. p.38

22 *The Argus* 5 April 1905

23 *Sydney Morning Herald*, 6 April 1905

24 NSW Government, *Archives in Brief*, 62: Lebanese migration and settlement in New South Wales

25 Jupp, J 1991, *Immigration: Australian retrospectives*, Sydney University Press p. 47

26 Foster, L & Stockley, D 1984, *Multiculturalism: The changing Australian paradigm.* Clevedon: Multilingual Matters. p. 22

27 Jupp, J 1991, *Op. Cit.* p. 46

28 Monsour, A 2010, *Op. Cit.* p. 116

29 *Goulburn Evening Penny Post*, Saturday 4 January 1896 p. 4

30 *Quiz and Lantern* (Adelaide), 12 October 1899, cited by Monsour, A. 2014, 'But what are ya? Identity, Belonging and In-Between-ness in early Lebanese Australian communities' in Batrouney, T, Boos, T, Escher, A & Tabar, P 2014, *Palestinian, Lebanese and Syrian Communities in the World: Theoretical Frameworks and Empirical Studies.* Heidelberg: Universitätsverlag Winter   p. 8

31 Memorandum to Minister from Secretary, 27 October 1914

32 Batrouney, A & Batrouney, T 1985, *Lebanese in Australia* AE Press p. 26

33 Monsour, A 2010, *Op. Cit* p. 47

34 *Sydney Morning Herald*, Friday 6 November 1908. p. 6

35 MP707 1914 -1918

36 Monsour, A *Op. Cit.* 2010. p. 127.

37 Interview Ronald Davis, July 2008.

38 Issawi, C *Op. Cit.* p. 27

39 Copeland, S 1995, *Julia's Diary* (unpublished) p. 12

40 Pascoe, R 1990, 'Raymond Betros: Hawker', *Open for business: immigrant and Aboriginal entrepreneurs tell their story*, Office for Multicultural Affairs

41 Monsour, A *Op. Cit.* pp. 8-9.

42 *ALHS Newsletter.* 2015

43 Monsour, A 2009, *Raw Kibbeh: Generations of Lebanese Australian Enterprise*, Lebanese Australian Historical Society p. 239

44 Monsour, A 2014, *Op, Cit.* p. 7

45 Monsour, A 2004, *Syrian/Lebanese Traders and the Customs Prosecutions of 1897*, Professional Historian's Association (Queensland) Conference

46 Batrouney, T 1991.

47 Monsour, A 2010, *Op. Cit.* p. 132

48 Mellick, R 2016, 'Tears for My Jiddee'

49 Callil, J 2001, *Frederick Alfred Louis Callil*, Unpublished Monograph

50 Batrouney, T 2013, *Adele Batrouney – A Memoir*, Unpublished monograph.

51 Ansell, K 2001, *The Business of Life*, Merlvic Schrank Pty Ltd. p. 35

52 McKay, J 1989 *Phonecian Farewell: Three Generations of Lebanese Christians in Australia*, Ashwood House.

53 *The Herald*, Saturday 27 September, 1904.

54 *The Illustrated Sydney News*, November 1908.

55 Australian Lebanese Historical Society, 2015 'Growing Up in Redfern' from Notes of a discussion with Adele Moriarty, ALHS

56 Interview Phillip, February 2013.

57 Dan, E & Mansour, N (eds) 2004, *St George Cathedral and its people, past present and future*. Longueville Media, p. 26

58 Community of the Holy Name, Day Book, 1922 p.105

59 Batrouney, T 2008, *Living our Heritage: The Maronite Catholic Church in Victoria*, The Victorian Maronite Community.

60 Community of the Holy Name, Day Book, 1949, p. 105

PART 2

THE FRENCH MANDATE 1920 – 1943

The period 1920-1943 was marked by the economic, political and cultural dominance of France over Lebanon. For Lebanese settlers and their children, the time between the two World Wars and to the end of the Second World War was a quiescent period. It was marked by reduced immigration from Lebanon and a consolidation of the small and somewhat isolated communities in Sydney, Melbourne, Brisbane and Adelaide and in some regional towns.

Australian society in this period continued to suffer from the impact of the Great War. Many families were left to cope with the casualties of war, including the loss of life or life-long disability of husbands, fathers and sons. During the war Australian society was divided by sectarian disputes between Catholics and Protestants over conscription. This, together with the continuation of the White Australia Policy and assertive Australian nationalism, overflowed into an attitude whereby Lebanese immigrants experienced a degree of defensiveness about their Lebanese background.

Lebanese emigration between the two World Wars was affected more by restrictive conditions in the receiving countries than 'push' factors from Lebanon. The total number of Lebanese-born settlers in Australia grew only slowly from 1,527 in 1911 to 2,020 in 1933. The decline in numbers of Lebanese emigrating in the late 1920s and early 1930s reflected economic and social conditions caused by worldwide depression. This was followed by the outbreak of the Second World War in 1939 which again halted Lebanese emigration until the late 1940s.

6

LEBANON AND AUSTRALIA: ECONOMIC AND POLITICAL CONDITIONS, 1920 – 1943

Better to be in the city collecting garbage than be a Sultan in the village.
Arabic proverb

The years during and after the Great War were disastrous for Lebanon, its society and economy. Many Lebanese suffered extreme poverty and famine, caused partly by the commandeering by the Ottoman army of food and other necessities of life and the forced recruitment of young Lebanese men into the Ottoman military. The devastating impact of natural disasters, including a locust plague, stripped crops and worsened the famine. Furthermore, the decline of the silk industry destroyed an important source of income for Lebanese in rural areas and led many to seek a living in the coastal cities and towns.

The defeat of the Ottomans in 1918 and the Versailles Peace Treaty the following year realigned the states in the Middle East. Lebanon as a political entity was brought about by competition between France and England which led to the partition of the Middle East. The status of Lebanon changed from being part of the province of Syria within the Ottoman Empire to that of a French Mandate which gained semi-autonomy in 1920. This small nation came to life in 1920 as a separate structure, albeit against the will of the majority of its people.[1]

Within Lebanon, the period covering the 1920s and 1930s was a time of move and counter-move by Muslim and Christian religious and political groups and Lebanon's French administrators. The French initiative to grant Lebanon a constitution in 1926 was a means of forestalling disruptions brought about by a revolt in Syria in 1925–1927. Greater Lebanon was renamed the Lebanese Republic in 1926. This change did little to appease political tensions between the factions. In the Constitution, the state gave religious communities the rights to rule on matters to do with individuals such as marriage, baptisms, inheritance and custody.

The overarching issue causing great schisms in Lebanese society was the perceived political and social attachments of its Muslim population to Syria, a Muslim Arab nation. The French believed that they had created 'too great a Lebanon.' With 405,000 Muslims and 425,000 Christians, Emil Iddi (former head of the Administrative Council) complained to the French Government that there were insufficient numbers to make an effective Christian majority that could 'defend the country'.[2]

France saw Lebanon as another French satellite. This was evident in the urban re-design of Beirut, the growth of middle-class farmers, the development of an economic sector of middle-class workers, supported by an education system that produced middle class bureaucrats and educated intellectuals. The French economic vision for the country was that Lebanon should act as a banker for the region and as a tourist destination. For these reasons, the dominant Christian view of Lebanon was as the 'Switzerland of the East.' However, it soon became apparent that incorporating the needs and views of Muslims, who amounted to nearly fifty per cent of the population, could not be addressed under French control.

By 1936, tensions between Muslim and Christian groups over their treatment in an independent Lebanon had reached breaking point. France formally recognised Lebanon as an independent state in September 1936 and, in return, Lebanon guaranteed French capital and interests and the continuation of monetary parity. France pledged to support Lebanon if attacked by a third party and Lebanon would be allied to France if there were a war.[3] The result of these arrangements was to fragment and polarise disaffected groups in Lebanese society. Between 1932 and 1936, a number of organisations emerged, ranging from pro-Syrian groups to right wing Lebanese nationalist groups, some Christian and some Muslim. The growth of many diverse groups in Lebanon was a response to a delicate and complex political situation. Although the existence of each group was acknowledged, they were not incorporated in the Government's decision making.

Australia

The nation's development was hindered during the 1920s and beyond by the great loss of life among the young Australians who fought for the British Empire during the Great War and the impact of the war on the returning servicemen and women and their families. This was followed by the Great Depression which hit the nation in the late 1920s and extended throughout most of the 1930s. The impact on Australia's economy and society was profound, leading to the closure of factories, shops and widespread unemployment. This pushed some families into poverty as they were forced to rely on food handouts dispensed by local councils and churches and to live in inadequate and makeshift housing. Unable to find work in the cities, some Australian men became itinerants as they tried their luck in country areas, seeking casual employment on farms and living off the land.

These economic and social developments provided fertile ground for the rise of extremist groups in Australia, both of the Right and Left. These included right-wing groups such as the Old Guard, which was formed in 1930, and the New Guard a year later. As a counterbalance to these right-wing movements, the Communist Party of Australia, founded in 1920, reached its greatest strength in 1940 when it achieved influence in some trade unions and the Labor Party.

By the late 1930s Germany's industrial development and its resentment at the reparations imposed on it by the Treaty of Versailles culminated in its aggression towards neighbouring European nations. The network of alliances among European nations led inevitably to Britain and its Empire declaring war on Germany. As a loyal member of the British Empire, Australia willingly joined the war against Germany and its allies in 1939. In many respects, Australia was unprepared for war with its underdeveloped secondary industries and neglected armed services.

At the request of Britain, young Australians served in many theatres of war across both Europe and Asia. However, by the early 1940s, the Australian Government realised that the most imminent threat to Australia came from Germany's ally, Japan, with its aggressive push into south-east Asia and across the Pacific.

The Labor Government under John Curtin began wholesale mobilisation of the nation to defend the country against imminent invasion by the Japanese. Able-bodied men were conscripted into the armed services, manpower regulations were invoked as factories were required to manufacture weapons, armoured vehicles, ammunition, uniforms, parachutes, tents and a host of other necessities for defending the nation. While some women joined the Armed Services in a range of jobs, particularly nursing, others looked after their families alone or took over jobs that had previously been undertaken by men. Women worked in factories, on farms and in a host of other occupations as required. Some goods and foodstuffs were in short supply and their distribution was controlled by ration coupons for the major items such as meat, butter and petrol.

Since its formal adoption in 1901 the White Australia Policy had remained securely in place in legislation and in practice, supported both by governments and the people. However, one thing had changed. During and immediately after the war, the Japanese had supplanted the Chinese as the major target of popular racism and xenophobia. The fear of invasion and the continued relative isolation of Australia left the White Australia Policy unchallenged. Returned servicemen and women, especially those affected by their wartime experiences, supported the conservative political and social values of the Australian governments and people. Australia was still predominantly British, not only in terms of its population, but in all aspects of life, including its political, legal and educational institutions.

> As an eight-year-old I recall being in a class at primary school towards the end of the war when it was apparent that the Allies, including Australia, were about to be victorious. The teacher proudly informed the pupils: 'all you children have British blood in your veins… except you, Trevor, but you are very close.' I went home, looked at the Ampol map of the world with the British colonies all coloured red and how I longed to be part of the winning team—the British Empire.[4]

Australia's reliance on the United States during the Second World War led to closer military and political ties and increasing American influence on Australia and its way of life. However, it was Australia's large-scale immigration program after the war which led to an increase in the numbers and diversity of Australia's population. It was this that changed the face of the nation.

7

IMMIGRATION FROM LEBANON TO AUSTRALIA, 1920 – 1943

Love of one's country is but a weakness of character, have the courage to leave and you will find another family to replace yours.

Amin Maalouf

The religious and political machinations of this period, while highly significant for the national development of Lebanon, seemed not to have had a major impact on emigration. Rather, Lebanese emigration was affected more by restrictive conditions in the receiving countries than 'push' factors from Lebanon. This was in contrast to the initial phase of emigration from 1880 to 1918 which saw Lebanese emigrants attracted by extensive opportunities in America, South America, Canada, and Australia because of booming national development and growth in those countries. Another explanation is that after the privations of war and famine, families wanted to re-unite and enjoy each other until the diaspora of economic necessity pulled them apart again.

During the period 1920 to 1939, significant barriers were erected in the receiving nations to restrict immigration. In Australia, the Immigration Restriction Act of 1901 and the Commonwealth Naturalisation Act of 1903 provided a national approach to restrict Asian Immigrants, including Ottoman subjects, and to deny them citizenship rights. In the United States the Emergency Quota Law of 1921 and the Johnson-Reed Act of 1924 similarly restricted Lebanese immigration.[5] Canada also set up barriers through the Canadian Order-in-Council PC 926 in 1910.[6] Exclusion from Australia was largely based on racial and labour grounds and implemented by Australian governments through the classification of Lebanon as part of the Ottoman Empire. After the war, the White Australia Policy continued to be supported by the public and formed the basis for national restrictive legislation.

The decline in numbers emigrating from Lebanon in the late 1920s and early 1930s reflected economic and social conditions in destination countries due to the worldwide depression affecting Britain, Australia, the United States and Europe. The population censuses of 1921 and 1932, the last two censuses conducted in Lebanon, give some indication of the numbers, religions and former localities of Lebanese emigrants during the period. The total number of Lebanese-born settlers in Australia grew only slowly from 1,527 in 1911 to 2,020 in 1933 (Table 1).

The 1932 Lebanese Census data allow us to make some general observations about the movement of Lebanese to Australia. In 1932 return migration to Lebanon was greater than emigration with 1,640 Lebanese emigrants outnumbered by 2,744 return migrants during that year (see Table 4). Throughout this period New South Wales received more than half of the Lebanese settlers (57 per cent), while Victoria (14 per cent), South Australia (15 per cent) and Queensland (12 per cent) accounted for most of the other settlers. The numerical dominance of New South Wales during this first period of settlement set a pattern that was to continue in future years with around 75 per cent of all Lebanese immigrants settling in that state.

The migration of Lebanese males (57 per cent) outnumbered that of females (43 per cent) during this period (Table 5.2). However, the Lebanese-born population in Australia had a higher proportion of women than did Asian and other Mediterranean immigrants.[7] These figures indicate the importance of family to these Lebanese immigrants, as well as their early and ready commitment to settle in Australia. Even if they did not always emigrate as family groups, Lebanese emigrants soon took steps to bring out their families and settle in their new country. This pattern of early family reunion was also a factor in the relatively high fertility rate of Lebanese women. The economic contribution of Lebanese women was to be found not only in their nurturing and support of their families but also in their own hawking, shop-keeping and other business activities.

The 1921 Lebanese Census lists the numbers of emigrants from various municipalities in Mount Lebanon by religion. This confirms the generally held view that the early emigrants were predominantly Christian and came from municipalities in central and northern Lebanon. By 1921, Christian emigrants of various sects numbered 42,195, Muslim emigrants accounted for 4,703 and Druze 3,792 emigrants (see Table 3).

We turn now to the settlement of Lebanese migrants in Australia during this period.

8

LEBANESE SETTLEMENT BETWEEN THE WORLD WARS

Toil and you shall procure.

Arabic proverb

Settling into their new home created a number of issues for Lebanese immigrants as they went about building their lives in Australia. The learning of English – the pathway to transacting business – was a challenge that many faced with varying degrees of success. The relationship of Lebanese settlers with elements of their own culture such as their extended family, their ties to their village in Lebanon, and their religious adherence all changed over time. Likewise, their relationship with the wider Australian society also changed significantly as did their links to aspects of their original culture which ebbed and flowed but, inevitably, were diminished.

This period was marked by the assimilation of the Syrian/Lebanese families to the dominant British-Australian culture. This was aided by the Australian-born families whose children and young people attended Australian schools and workplaces. At the same time, the Lebanese sought to retain valued elements of their culture, within their families, community gatherings and churches. In this way total assimilation was resisted, but quietly and privately. This supports the contention that Lebanese identity in Australia was a mix of traditional Lebanese and emergent Australian cultures, with the latter achieving dominance over time.

Settlement in Australia

During the Great War, as we noted, anti-alien sentiment saw Ottoman subjects, including Lebanese settlers, treated with suspicion. Not only were there legal requirements to which these so-called 'enemy aliens' had to comply, but Lebanese settlers felt they needed to prove their allegiance to Australia at a time when they were denied citizenship. As Lebanese settlers became more established, they sought ways to express their patriotism to Australia, especially during the two world wars. This involved donations to wartime charities, public professions of loyalty to the nation and the Crown and enlisting in the armed services.

A group portrait of attendees at Lebanon Ladies Maronite Ball at the Wentworth Hotel, Sydney, Australia, 17 August 1938. At the 1938 ball (during the sesquicentenary of European settlement in Australia) the President of the Republic of Lebanon, M. Émile Eddé, presented the Commonwealth of Australia with six six-foot cedar saplings from the historic cedar grove, Arz-el-rub (Cedars of God). Also, the Consul-General for France, M. Jean Tremoulet, presented to Mrs Therese Alam the purple ribbon of the Officier de l'Académie. (Source: National Arborium, Photographer Tom Lennon)

Between the wars, the Australian-born children of the first-wave arrivals from Lebanon made their own adaptations to life in Australia. They were the pivotal generation who changed from being predominantly Lebanese early in their lives to becoming more Australian in their later years. By the Second World War, many of the Australian-born children had adopted a blend of Lebanese and Australian values and activities. This they achieved through their schooling, work and social activities in the wider community. During this period some Lebanese immigrants and their children lived active public lives in business and local community affairs. At the same time, they remained members of Lebanese families and participated in Lebanese community activities and institutions.

Archimandrite Antonios Mobayed, first priest of St Nicholas Orthodox Church, with the Church cricket team comprising Australian-born Lebanese: Melbourne 1934.

(Source: Trevor Batrouney)

On the other hand, there were always some immigrants who chose not to mix with other Lebanese but to strike out on their own. Some chose to study at tertiary level in an attempt to complete qualifications started in Lebanon; some tried their hand at new occupations; and some chose to live in areas where there were few Lebanese immigrants.

In these instances, they came into contact with a wide section of Australians with whom they struck up friendly relations which lasted many years.

Men's egg and spoon race St Nicholas Antiochian Orthodox Church picnic 1938.
(Source: St Nicholas Antiochian Orthodox Church Archive Photos)

The few Lebanese community organisations in Sydney and Melbourne also adopted a blend of Lebanese and wider Australian activities. This was true of the churches, which met the needs of the first-wave settlers by maintaining their traditional forms of worship and language. On the other hand, their children introduced into church and other Australian-Lebanese organisations, values and activities derived from their experiences in the wider society.

Occupations and Business

Not all Lebanese made the transition in the early years of the twentieth century from itinerant hawkers to more sedentary businesses. Some few continued hawking during the inter-war years and even beyond the Second World War. One such was Hassan Ali

(Harry) Monsoor who continued to work as a hawker through the outback of South Australia until 1954.

Mary Moses (nee Nasser) in front of the Nasser shop West Wyalong New South Wales circa 1930. A feature of pioneer Lebanese settlement was the establishment of rural small businesses, especially drapery and clothing shops (Source & Permission: ALHS Collection – sourced from Judy Atallah Family papers)

Hassan Ali (Harry) Monsoor

Hassan Ali (Harry) Monsoor was born 1 March 1884 at Beit Meri, Lebanon and came to Australia in 1900 at the age of seventeen. He commenced work as a hawker in 1902 in the far north region of South Australia, visiting places such as the Nepabunna Aboriginal Mission in the Flinders Ranges and travelling as far west as Lake Eyre... Harry carried goods such as blankets, towels, rugs, hats, soap, patent medicines, watches, mouth organs, boots, gabardine trousers, shirts, razor blades, tobacco, sweets (Minties, Almond Rock and Jubilee Mix), linen, haberdashery, bolts of cloth and underwear... At Christmas time he would make a special trip to the Nepabunna Mission with talcum powder, hair oil, ribbons and brooches.

Hassan (Harry) Ali Monsoor came to Australia in 1900 and commenced work as a hawker in 1902 in the outback of South Australia. He travelled first by donkey and cart and, after 1926, by truck. Harry later opened a shop before retiring in 1954 at the age of 71. (Source: ALHS Collection [Paul Convy photographer])

In 1925 Harry travelled to Lebanon to marry Mahiba Ali Solomon, returning to Australia soon after and setting up house in Copley, near Leigh Creek. His first transport as a hawker was with a cart and a team of donkeys. But in 1926 he purchased his first and only truck... He returned to Copley for two-week periods to re-stock and service the vehicle. His route took him over difficult terrain, rocky roads, flooded creeks and dangerously steep tracks.

In 1939 the family moved to the small town of Beltana where Harry opened a shop, continuing the hawker's run from there until retiring in 1954 at the age of 71.[8]

Lebanese business ventures were characterised by the involvement of family. During the period when hawking was the dominant activity it was common to see fathers, sons and brothers engaged in hawking, often in the same district but in separate locations. This meant that they would not be competing with each other but could meet together after a few days' hawking. Wives would either accompany their husbands on their hawking expeditions or strike out on their own, while others, as we observed, would sew garments and other goods to be sold by the hawkers in the family.

Toofey Nesire, Albury in his hawking van, circa 1926.
(Source: Michael Bacash)

The involvement of family members was even more marked when Lebanese opened shops, factories or warehouses. Families included not only husbands, wives and children but other members of the extended family. The Australian-born children of Lebanese migrants often worked in the family businesses, at first part-time while they were still at school, and later full-time. On the other hand, when school-aged children were required to work in family businesses it led, in some instances, to truancy and leaving school early.

Ashkar family members outside their well-known pie shop in the provincial city of Ballarat, Victoria, in the late 1930s. This shop became the economic and social centre for the family during the 1930s and 1940s.
(Source: Yvonne Ashkar, 2016)

By 1931 there was a concentration of Lebanese families and family businesses in the upper end of Exhibition Street in Melbourne, known to the Lebanese as the *Koora*. The variety of businesses owned by Lebanese in this locality included:

Exhibition Street:

east side

242	Khyat, Jas., confectioner
262-266	Latoof and Calil, importers fancy goods
308-310	Haddad C.F., Clothing Manufacturer
308-310	The Palestine Club

west side

287	Batrouney Bros, grocers
291	Batrouney, Spiridon, hairdresser & tobacconist
293	Haddad,A., fruiterer
295-297	Haddad, Jos., white work manufacturers
299-301	Jaboor, Simn. N., importer
311	Bosaid Mrs F., confectioner
311	Bosaid Abraham
313	Khittar, R. tobacconist & soft drinks.[9]

On the other hand it seems that Lebanese across rural Victoria were more likely to own haberdashery businesses. Some of the Lebanese families who established these businesses continued to engage in hawking at the same time. The following examples from the 1928 and 1931 *Sands and MacDougall's Directories* included:

Abikhair, Abraham, Rushworth

Aboumady, Jas, Alexandra

Antoon, J., West Geelong

Bashara, N., 24 Bridge Street, Ballarat

Fouard & Co., Bairnsdale.[10]

Although clothing shops were common, Lebanese families tried their hand at other businesses, including warehouses, clothing factories, hotels and farming. For example, in the late 1930s there was a migration from the Lebanese village of Baan to Thornleigh, on the north-western fringe of Sydney. Following in the footsteps of a fellow-Lebanese entrepreneur, the new arrivals purchased cheap farmlets on 2-3 acres of land and applied their farming skills to small-scale fruit and vegetable growing. This led to chain migration and a diversity of occupations with second and later generations. By 1979 it was estimated that more than 1,000 persons from Baan, almost one half of this town's original population, were living in Sydney.[11]

In many cases, young Australian-Lebanese would work in local businesses where they would acquire skills and experiences which they then used to contribute to existing family businesses. Others, from better-off families, entered professions and used their professional knowledge to improve and expand businesses they inherited from their parents.

Having young people working in family businesses held many attractions for Lebanese families. They provided a source of cheap and trustworthy labour. They ensured that the young people had the opportunity to learn the business and perhaps succeed their parents in due course. They also enabled the older generation to maintain a benevolent surveillance and influence over their teenage and adult children. The children of these immigrants sought to achieve more than the economic security that was the objective of their parents. Many family stories tell of the young Australian-born generation succeeding their parents in various businesses and expanding the original enterprises.

The shop-keeping phase was significant for a number of reasons. It provided employment for family members and enabled the Lebanese to continue trading, as in their hawking days, but in a more sedentary form. It involved interaction with the wider Australian community and fostered adaptation to Australian activities and values.

Learning English

Adult immigrants who settled in Australia learnt English through a variety of informal means, including their own efforts at self-education. The young Australian-born children learnt English through attendance at school as well as mixing with other Australians.

The learning of English was one of the pathways to interaction with wider Australian society. The ability of the Lebanese settlers to communicate in English depended on a range of factors that included their previous education in Lebanon and the language spoken at home. Literacy levels in Arabic were a guide to the ability of Lebanese settlers to learn English. Some of the more educated immigrants had been taught some English in Lebanon, while others learned the language in Australia as they travelled around the countryside selling goods.

Queensland historian Anne Monsour (2010) provides several stories of immigrants teaching themselves reading, writing and speaking English through reading newspapers, dictionaries, through conversation with Australians and with earlier Lebanese settlers. For example, Jacob Mirob, settled in Cairns, Queensland:

> Every night after the shop closed, he'd go over the road–there was the School of Arts Building, the Library–and he'd sit there with the newspapers and the books in front of him and he taught himself to read and write English from that...

Joseph Monsour, who arrived in Australia in 1926, was already literate in French and Arabic.

> It didn't take me long to learn English ... on account of the French ... when I arrived here ... [he borrowed books from his cousin] ... I took all his books ... it was in the summertime ... I used to get up four o'clock every morning ... [one book at a time]

The degree of exposure to English-speaking Australians influenced Lebanese settlers to learn English, as the experience of Calile Malouf illustrates:

> They were working with English-speaking people all the time so it [the Lebanese] was never a closed ... community.[12]

Women who were involved in the family business learned English in the same way as their relatives and friends, whereas those who remained in the home learned at a slower pace. For some women, learning the language was achieved alongside running a business and caring for their family.

In this period, speaking Arabic in public was considered a disadvantage as it identified the speaker as foreign at a time when, in the inter-war period, being loyal to Australia, its values and ways, was important officially and also at the local community level. Being foreign was viewed as being un-Australian. Initially, parents spoke to each other and their children in Arabic. The children responded in Arabic and, as the years passed, in English. Once the older children started school, Arabic began to lose its status as the language spoken at home. However, speaking some Arabic was maintained while there were grandparents living in the family home. The Arabic language was also used for Lebanese food and perhaps particular songs or sayings that only carried meaning if expressed in Arabic.

Inevitably the Lebanese-born were required to speak English at school and in business. This use of English as the main language of communication contributed to their transition from immigrant to settler. English became the language of the children. The children of Lebanese settlers were most susceptible to the pressure to speak English in Australia and were confronted with comments such as, 'If you are in Australia, speak Australian or go back to your own country'. Overall, immigrants and their families made many and varied cultural adaptations to life in Australia. These ranged from valuing the ability to speak Arabic and insisting that it be spoken at home while transacting business in English, to insisting that only English be spoken as the future of the immigrant settlers and their children now lay in Australia.

The second generation: schooling and beyond

The children of the first-wave settlers from Lebanon who attended schools during this period made their own adaptations to life in Australia. They were raised in close-knit families, often including three generations in the one house, in the inner suburbs of the capital cities, as well as in country towns of eastern Australia. As the older family members were born in Lebanon, they tended to maintain Lebanese cultural values and practices in their families. This meant that the second generation was brought up in families in which Arabic was spoken by the older generation and understood by their children, Lebanese food was enjoyed, and other family traditions were practised, including religion.

Where the extended families were large enough, with perhaps two or more branches, they provided opportunities for the young cousins to socialise with each other, work together in business partnerships, and provide financial support in times of need:

> Links were established among the cousins who lived close together in the 'urban village' of Carlton, attended the same schools, played together, joined the same groups and who shared the same social situation of being both Lebanese and Australian.[13]

The discriminatory legislation at the national and state levels in the late 19th century and early 20th century made a major impact on the second generation. Their parents were keen to see them identify as Australian and consequently passed on little information about their origins, original language and culture.

> Lebanese immigrants sought to position themselves on the 'white' side of the colour line, emphasised their Christian credentials, and concealed their eastern identity.[14]

The school experience of Lebanese Australian-born children was often their first introduction to the attitudes of the wider society. At school, Lebanese students would encounter other students of predominantly Anglo-Australian backgrounds, some of whom carried the racist attitudes of their parents. Lebanese students were sometimes looked down on because of their skin colour, their strange sounding names and their tendency to stick together. Some children responded by being defensive about their background and sensitive to discrimination while others ignored it altogether or stood up for themselves, even physically. Two children, growing up in rural

Queensland, recount their experiences:

> I always had a resentment about it [being Lebanese] because it was
> always a burden to carry when I was a child... It sort of set you
> apart before anything else... You had no-one else to associate with...
> Discrimination wasn't the word in those days, but you were kind of
> looked down on because you weren't English.[15]

Some families became wealthy through their success in business quite early in their lives in Australia. These families were able to provide a privileged upbringing for their children by sending them to private schools and later universities. In the case of the Callil family from Melbourne, as we noted, the second-generation sons were taken to Lebanon where they completed their education in Church schools. Attendance at Catholic and Protestant schools in Australia may also have been a means of integrating their children into the upper echelons of society.

The first Syrian parliamentarian in Australia, the Hon. A.A. Alam MLC, highlighted the intellectual and professional achievements of two young Syrian/Lebanese in a journal entitled *The Syrian World* in 1927. He described the achievements of Professor Fred Callil of Melbourne and Dr Frank Gaha of Sydney in glowing, and possibly exaggerated, terms.

> Not long ago the Australian newspapers featured the brilliant case of
> a Syrian Australian, Fred Callil, who was acclaimed a prodigy. For at
> the age of seventeen he took his B. A. degree and two years later his
> M. A. from the University of Melbourne. At the age of twenty-four
> he was appointed professor of ancient history and languages. He won
> more scholarships... than any other student of Australia. The father
> of this young Syrian prodigy is Khalil Fakhr, a wholesale merchant,
> originally of B'sharrie [sic], Lebanon.

> Dr Frank Gaha, son of Ibrahim Gaha of Zahle is another example of
> the highly educated Syrian of the second generation. Up to thirteen
> Frank received no education whatsoever, but so outstanding was his
> natural intelligence that when his father, a successful grazier, sent him

to St Joseph's College, in Hunter's Hill, Sydney, he graduated at the
top of his class in nineteen months. He took his degree at the Sydney
University, went to Europe and returned with more degrees than any
other doctor in Australia.[16]

These selected examples give some indication of the pride of
the community in the successes of two members of the second
generation. These comments by A. A. Alam should be understood
in the context of some continuing discrimination against Lebanese
settlers by groups within Australian society. They also convey a
sense of justification that Lebanese are more than worthy of being
accepted as the equal of Australians and that the discrimination and
exclusion of Syrians were clearly misplaced.

Some parents 'edited' the stories they told their children about
life in Lebanon to protect them from the reality of the poverty,
religious discrimination or lack of opportunity they had faced in
Lebanon and the discrimination they encountered in their early
years in Australia. In doing so, Lebanese immigrants attempted to
remove any embarrassment they felt at having come from such a
lowly and foreign background.

The Australian-born Lebanese children addressed different issues
over the span of their lives compared to their parents. Their parents
struggled to attain economic independence through diligence, thrift
and business sense to ensure their survival in their new home.
Depending on where they lived, they mainly, but not exclusively,
interacted within the Lebanese community.

Australian-born Lebanese found it easier than their parents to
interact in the wider community. Their concern was more about
gaining a degree of social acceptance in a post-war society that
experienced tension from the divide between Protestant and
Catholic and between English and Irish and other ethnicities. The
settlement experiences of their parents had an impact on the cultural
and social adaptations made by their Australian-born children.

Many second-generation young people engaged in a range of

sporting and social activities alongside other young Australians. Sometimes they would join mainstream groups such as local football and cricket teams, the Freemasons, Temperance bodies, the Citizen's Militia and local Protestant and Catholic churches. Here they acquired varied skills and experiences ranging from participating in sporting teams, conducting meetings, engaging in different forms of worship and, above all, learning to mix with other young Australians and adapt to their way of life. In some instances, they would experience a degree of conflict between their Lebanese upbringing and the attitudes and behaviour of other young Australians with whom they associated:

> The army was an important experience in the lives of these two third-generation Lebanese-Australians as the camps took them away from home and family and enabled them to compare themselves with young Australian men: 'I never mixed much with them because they were all heavy drinkers.'[17]

9

ESTABLISHING LEBANESE COMMUNITIES

Step by step the ladder is ascended.
Arabic Proverb

During this period there was relatively little migration from Lebanon, with the exception of small numbers of relatives coming to join their families in Australia (see Table 3). Within Australia the major movement of Lebanese during this period was leaving the occupation of hawking in rural areas and moving to larger cities and country towns, where many became shopkeepers and some few owners of clothing warehouses and factories.

Groups of Lebanese established small communities based on their common religion, language, culture and place of origin. This led many to keep a low profile in the wider Australian community as maintaining their language and culture tended to be achieved within the home and their community. These communities provided opportunities for people to work together in business with fellow Lebanese and enjoy a social life based on their common experiences as both Lebanese and Australians. These contacts often led to marriages between children of Lebanese immigrants. In some instances, marriages were negotiated across other Australian states and even across nations such as New Zealand, Lebanon and the United States.

From 1920, those immigrant Lebanese who were eligible to apply for citizenship did so with enthusiasm. They were keen to demonstrate their loyalty to the Australian nation and their public spiritedness.

At the local community level, Lebanese business people and their families donated to charities, joined community organisations, supported the needy, and generally showed themselves to be exemplary citizens. During the 1930s Depression, as we noticed, some Lebanese shop-keepers were able to offer much-needed assistance to the needy and poor in their local districts. This formed the basis for their involvement with, and acceptance by, local communities, especially in country towns. It was as if the Lebanese wished to demonstrate that their earlier exclusion from citizenship was unjustified and inappropriate.

Established Lebanese were keen to express their patriotism in times of war. The Lebanese Ladies War Comforts League held a Ball in the Sydney Town Hall which raised £6,000 for the purchase of four ambulances for the war effort.[18] This was matched by the owners of the Latoof and Callil factory in Melbourne who, as noted earlier, also donated an ambulance to the Australian Army during the 1940s.

Religion

The process of developing major Lebanese churches in Sydney and Melbourne, having started before the Great War, continued during the inter-war period with the consolidation of these few early churches rather than the establishment of new places of worship.

Although the Maronite, Melkite and Orthodox Lebanese each had their own place of worship in Sydney, these churches could not meet the needs of Lebanese living elsewhere in Australia. This meant that the priests would travel throughout New South Wales, to Victoria and South Australia and as far as Dunedin in New Zealand, to minister to the needs of their faithful. Father Nicholas Shehadie from St George in Sydney and Archimandrite Antonius Mobayed from St Nicholas in Melbourne travelled extensively to perform marriages, baptisms and funerals throughout their states and beyond. On these occasions they also celebrated liturgies for their people. Shehadie had arrived in Sydney in 1910 and immediately began conducting Orthodox Divine Liturgies in Arabic, even though the Orthodox had not yet established their church. He also ministered to the Antiochian Orthodox during his travels throughout eastern Australia and New Zealand.

The religious practices of Lebanese settlers in Australia provided different avenues for entering broader Australian society. For those with no access to their own churches, religion became a means of aligning with one of the dominant religions, predominantly Catholic. Maronite Lebanese, who recognised the Pope but who had their own distinctive eastern rite, were able to prove their compatibility with Australian society by participating in Catholic Church services alongside other members of the wider Catholic community. However, attendance at Latin Catholic services did not meet the cultural and social needs of the Maronite new arrivals. For example, in Melbourne some Maronite and Melkite Lebanese attended the Saint Nicholas Syrian Orthodox Church, which had been established as early as 1932. This they did until their own churches were founded, namely, the Maronite Church by Father (later Monsignor) Paul in 1955 and the Melkite Church by Father Dubous in 1976.

Melkite Bishop Clement Malouf from Lebanon during his visit to Brisbane in 1928. (Source: Eileen Malouf)

In a similar fashion, before the Greek Orthodox Church of The Holy Annunciation was opened in Melbourne in 1901 a number of Syrian Orthodox families not only attended the Church but were also actively involved as donors to the Church and serving as church wardens and altar boys. However, this church eventually became a solely Greek Church with the liturgy celebrated in the Greek language. The Syrian Orthodox continued to attend The Holy Annunciation Church, especially on Feast Days, and to celebrate sacraments such as baptisms, marriages and funerals; however, they did not feel that this was their church as they longed to celebrate the liturgy in Arabic and to receive the sacraments in their own Arabic language.

The opening of St Nicholas Church in 1932 came just a year after Archimandrite Mobayed arrived in Melbourne. Six months after the opening, members of the young so-called 'Syrian choir' wrote to him 16 November 1932, thanking him for all he had done for them:

> As it is twelve months since you arrived here, it is therefore twelve months ago since we were brought together as one large and happy family with your reverence as our head. Before you arrived here we were straying as it were from the Orthodox faith, but since your arrival you have brought us together in a manner as a shepherd would gather his flock from an impending danger.

> The choir, which you established from the younger members of the Church, has attained a certain degree of knowledge, which served to show that you have spent much time and patience to bring about such results...[19]

The Orthodox Lebanese split their religious adherence in Australia. Some followed their countrymen into the Catholic or Anglican churches, often through intermarriage with partners from those churches. Others retained their Orthodoxy and contributed to the establishment of their own churches. Some of the Melkite adherents chose to follow the western Catholic religion while others sought to retain their own religious identity.

Differences across the eastern capital cities reflected the work of key community members. This explains why the first Lebanese churches had been established in Sydney by the Melkite Catholics and Maronite Catholics as early as the 1890s. Orthodox services had been held in Sydney after the arrival of Father Nicholas Shehadie in 1913 and St George Antiochian Orthodox Church was opened in Redfern in 1920.

The story in Brisbane was different again. An attempt was made to consolidate all three main Lebanese Christian religions into one church in 1936, ministered by a Melkite priest. However, after the Second World War this arrangement gave way and St Clements became a solely Melkite Church. This led the Maronite Catholics and Antiochian Orthodox in Brisbane to establish their own churches in the 1980s.

Religious identity on a personal level reveals a good deal about the orientation of the children of Lebanese immigrants. Many of the Australian-born children outwardly supported one of the main Anglo-Australian religions. However, within the family a different story was being played out. Lebanese religious identity continued to be important as a means of identifying themselves, especially within the Lebanese community. To conform to an Australian religion, for some immigrants, diminished that identity. The recollection of one second-generation Lebanese-Australian in Queensland underlines the strength of conviction with which religious affiliations were held during this era of deep sectarianism in Australia:

> We were brought up very strict Protestants [in Australia]. My parents, they despised the Catholics. We were supposed to be called Orthodox. We were sent to Protestant schools ... and Protestant church, although I was sent to All Hallows, but I was never allowed, they told me to tell the teacher ... I must not learn anything to do with the Catholic religion.[20]

Parents generally believed that some religious education was important. In some cases, parents insisted that their children attend either Catholic schools or Protestant Sunday schools. Here is another recollection:

> But you see, not to be foreign, we were all sent to Sunday School at
> the Church of England.[21]

After the Second World War the Australian-born children of Lebanese immigrants often helped establish Lebanese churches. These institutions in many ways provided a distinct blend of cultures that expressed their identity as both Lebanese and Australian. The participation of the first Lebanese/Australian-born generations in their own ethnic churches often provided greater satisfaction than participation in wider society bodies:

> Activities in the church were regarded by interviewees as educative
> because the experiences and skills acquired through participation in
> host society groups were extended and developed within the Church.
> Interviewees testified to feelings of security, confidence, achievement
> and personal fulfilment as skills and abilities reached full flowering
> within the more personal and secure setting of the ethnic church.[22]

Contacts with Lebanon

During this interwar period contacts with Lebanon continued to be limited, affected as they were by the Great Depression and the Second World War. These events severely restricted emigration from Lebanon to Australia. In one year, 1933, the numbers returning to Lebanon actually exceeded the new arrivals from Lebanon (see Table 4). The Second World War virtually shut down movement between the two countries and isolated the small Lebanese communities in Australia. This proved to be a catalyst for the almost complete assimilation of the young Australian-born Lebanese. This hiatus in relations between the two countries was only broken when immigration recommenced after the Second World War.

Construction of a tank trap near Tripoli by Lebanese civilians under the
supervision of 2/3rd Field Company Royal Engineers: Lieut A E Baumgarten and
Serg JW Hasse of 2/3rd Field company, 6 June 1942.
(Source: Australian War Memorial)

10

LEBANESE IDENTITY BETWEEN THE WORLD WARS

During and even before the French Mandate, the influence of France over Lebanon was pervasive: economically, politically and culturally. We saw that much of the silk industry was controlled by French companies to the extent that France saw Lebanon as another French satellite. Even after the decline of the silk industry, France envisaged Lebanon as a banker for the region and as a tourist destination. French political control over Lebanon was gained soon after the Versailles Treaty and the founding of the Lebanese Republic in 1926. The economic and political influence of France extended into the cultural domain as French influence was found in the education system, in the language used by the educated classes, and through French support of the Maronite religion. The flag adopted for the Mandate was simply a cedar tree superimposed on the French tricolour.

At the same time, during this period American missionaries were also active, establishing Protestant educational institutions and churches. In the process they sought to educate leaders of society imbued with American and Protestant values. In this period Lebanese were identified as recipients of more powerful western religions and cultures.

To recap the situation in Australia, the period between the world wars was marked by the aftermath of the Great War, the Depression and the looming Second World War. During this time there was an assertion of Australian identity with the need to form a cohesive society to overcome the social and economic hardships confronting the nation. The cultural imperatives of the period to loyally align with British and Australian interests tested the identity of non-Australian and non-British residents, including Lebanese.

Lebanese immigrants and their children suffered as did other members of the lower classes in the interwar years. Employment was hard to come by, food was scarce, and rents difficult to pay. The urgent need for money saw many immigrant children take work where they could find it or experiment with different jobs. In short, these circumstances made it difficult to pursue those elements of identity that defined them as Lebanese. Many Lebanese children underplayed their Lebanese identity because the times demanded it.

In Australia the relationship of Lebanese immigrants with their religion formed a central part of their identity. When there were no available churches or mosques to meet their specific religious needs they would make the necessary compromises. For example, Maronite and Melkite Catholics would attend Roman Catholic churches. Likewise, Orthodox from Lebanon would attend Greek Orthodox churches or Anglican churches and Sunday Schools. Islamic Lebanese would pray in their homes or attend mosques, which were open to Muslims of all nationalities. The Protestant Syrian/Lebanese would attend western Protestant churches. However, in each of these cases, while the religious needs of the migrants might have been fulfilled, other elements of their identity were lacking, including their own language, the involvement of their family, and their common experience of being Lebanese migrants.

Where numbers permitted, Lebanese migrants would attend churches, established by their fellow nationals, to meet their specific religious, linguistic and cultural needs. These migrant churches were almost an extension of home, where extended family members would meet together, attend services, and enjoy social and sporting activities. These religious institutions in this way met both the primordial and constructivist elements of migrants' identity. Those Lebanese migrants who attended mainstream churches and schools as well as their ethnic churches gave expression to a hybrid religious identity.

The identity of Australian-Lebanese was strongly influenced by the Great War. First-wave Lebanese immigrants and their children were keen to present themselves as loyal British-Australians in the aftermath of this war. This they did through enlisting in the armed services and through engaging in patriotic activities as well as public expressions of loyalty. Sometimes they chose to underplay or even deny their Syrian background but at the same time to identify themselves as loyal Anglo-Australians.

Lebanese Ladies War Comforts League NSW Presenting 6 ambulances, undated. (Source: Australian War Memorial. Photographer: Eric Charles Johnston)

During this period hawking had all but declined as a common occupation for Syrian-Australians but they maintained their strong tradition of self-employment. We find them in various businesses such as warehouses, shop-keeping of various sorts and even small farming. Not only was self-employment in one's own business defined as desirable by Australian-Lebanese but it was also recognised favourably by members of the wider community.

NOTES

1   Traboulsi, F 2007, *A History of Modern Lebanon.* Pluto Press. 2nd Edition. p. 75

2   *Ibid.* p. 90

3   *Ibid.* p.101

4   Batrouney, T 2015, *Memoir: Trevor Batrouney*, Unpublished Memoir, p. 4

5   Naff, A 1992, 'Lebanese Immigration to the United States: 1880 to the Present', *The Lebanese in the World*, Centre for Lebanese Studies in association with I.B. Tauris & Co. p. 143

6   Abu-Laban, B 1992, 'The Lebanese in Montreal', *The Lebanese in the World*, Centre for Lebanese Studies in association with I.B. Tauris & Co. p. 229

7   Price, C 1984 'Working Papers in Demography: Birthplaces of the Australian Population 1861 – 1981' Department of Demography, Research School of social Sciences. Australian National University, Canberra. p. 10

8   Chittleborough, J 2000, *Hassan Ali (Harry) Monsour (1884 –1959)* in Australian Dictionary of Biography Vol 15, Melbourne University Press

9   Pascoe, R 1990, 'Raymond Betros: Hawker', *Open for business: immigrant and Aboriginal entrepreneurs tell their story*, Office for Multicultural Affairs. p. 6

10 *Ibid.* p. 6

11 Burnley, I. 'Lebanese Migration and Settlement in Sydney, Australia', *International Migration Review*, vol. 16, Spring, John Wiley & Sons.

12 Monsour, A 2010, *Not quite white: Lebanese and the White Australia Policy 1880 to 1947*, Post Pressed.

13 Batrouney, A 1978, *The Lebanese Community in Carlton, Melbourne 1880–1920*, History Honours Thesis, Monash University.

14 Monsour, A 2009, *Raw Kibbeh: Generations of Lebanese Australian Enterprise*, Lebanese Australian Historical Society. p. 250

15 Monsour, A *Op.Cit.* p. 142

16 *The Syrian World* Vol 2 No, 7 1927 p. 9

17 Batrouney, A *Op. Cit.* p. 16

18 *Sunday Sun and Guardian.* 7 November 1943

19 St Nicholas Antiochian Orthodox Church Archives, 1932

20 Monsour, A *Op. Cit.* p. 140

21 *Ibid.* p. 138

22 Batrouney, A *Op.Cit.* p. 9

PART 3

THE REPUBLIC OF LEBANON 1943-

Significant changes took place in both Lebanon and Australia from the end of the Second World War in 1945 and the establishment of the Republic of Lebanon in 1943. Events in Lebanon and Australia made major contributions to the migration of Lebanese to Australia during this period. These included revolts, sectarian disputes and political instability in Lebanon and elsewhere in the Middle East, all of which acted as 'push' factors for emigration to Australia and elsewhere.

At the same time, in the 1950s and 1960s, Australia began experiencing a post-war economic boom and political stability which supported the arrival of large numbers of refugees and immigrants from a number of European nations. The second wave of immigrants from Lebanon came to Australia when migration was seen as important for national economic, industrial and civil development and for the defence of the country. The Australian Government's attitude towards immigrants was largely determined by their ethnicity and their presumed suitability to become 'new Australians'. British and northern European immigrants were ranked ahead of southern Europeans who were preferred to 'Asians,' a category which, at the beginning of this period, included immigrants from the Middle East.

11

LEBANON:

DIFFICULTIES FACING THE NEW NATION, 1943–1975

The reason the country has fallen so low is precisely because so many of its children chose to leave rather than reform it. I, for one, need to be among my relatives so that they will share my joys when I am joyful and console me when I am in distress…

Amin Maalouf

External political factors included the demographic movements in the Middle East, due to the creation of Israel and the forced exodus of Palestinian refugees. These developments resulted in tensions that simmered throughout the 1960s. Following the 1967 war between Egypt and Israel and the subsequent attack on an Israeli civilian jet at Athens airport in early 1968, Lebanon became a major target for Israel striking at the Arab world. On 28 December 1968, Israeli commandos launched an attack on Beirut airport, damaging or destroying twelve planes. A prominent Maronite politician from this era argued that this attack was unjust and unprovoked:

> Lebanon was] the de facto confrontation state with Israel, though by default and not by a decision made by the Lebanese Government.[1]

Picture taken during the historic announcement of the independence of the
Lebanese Republic, 1943.
(Source: Australian War Memorial. Photographer: Frank Hurley)

Refugees from Palestine in 1948 leaving Haifa, Palestine
(Source: American University of Beirut)

The almost daily Israeli raids into south Lebanon to try to crush Palestinian incursions into Israel created uncertainty and danger in the region and politically throughout Lebanon.[2] The precarious relationship that Lebanon experienced with its neighbours and its target by both combatants made life in Lebanon tense and unpredictable. The different relationships of religious groups and factions within Lebanon with their particular allies in the Middle East amplified tensions throughout Lebanon. External political factors included the rise of pan-Arab nationalism, which provided an alternative vision that challenged the dominant Lebanese Christian view of the nation.

The social, political and economic disruption of the Second World War had brought with it independence for Lebanon in November 1943 and multiple difficulties in establishing the new nation and an effective government in turbulent and uncertain times. During this period Lebanon was struggling with a political structure that reflected a precarious balance between pressures and challenges from political and religious groups within its borders as well as political and religious groups in neighbouring countries. During the post-war period in Lebanon some sectors of society enjoyed a period of relative prosperity with entrepreneurs leading the development of the financial and commercial sectors. The overarching issue in determining the collapse into civil war occurred when 'independent patron-warlords were concerned only with the short-sighted search for political advantage, regardless of the long-term impact such strategies would have on the political system'.[3]

The political structure allowed for the continued dominance of wealthy Lebanese families as had been the case in the *Mutasarrifate* of Mount Lebanon. A group of mainly Maronite, some Melkite, a few Orthodox and other Christian religions as well as six Muslim families formed a 'Consortium' of 24 families that dominated commercial and financial life in Lebanon. Their goal was to manipulate and exploit the political system to maintain and expand the wealth of their families. 'Members of these families were in positions of significant political power and influence, holding controlling positions in all of the country's economic sectors' As the leading families controlled entry to these positions, they exerted major social and political influence over the nation's economy. The Consortium 'established itself as an intermediary between Western markets and the entire Arab hinterland'.[4] During this period Beirut was the focus of trade in gold in exchange for petro-dollars between Europe, the United States and the Middle East.[5]

The income allocation of the Lebanese population shows how a small part of the population generated most wealth compared with other sections of the population. For example, two per cent of the population who were bankers, industrialists and financiers earned 80 per cent of national revenue. In contrast, the lowest sector of society, industrial and agricultural workers, formed 78 per cent of the population and earned 20 per cent of the national revenue. The middle group of workers, bankers, public servants, artisans and agriculturalists included 20 per cent of the population but did not, of themselves, generate an equivalent proportion of national revenue.[6] There was a clear sense of the national wealth becoming more unequal in the period 1943–1975.

In what historian Fawwaz Traboulsi describes as a 'fundamental dichotomy', Lebanon was divided between an idea of 'judicial, civic and political equality of all Lebanese as citizens' and their membership of religious communities which highlighted entrenched inequality because of 'unequal access to political power and public office'.[7] The contradictory nature of the National Pact and the Constitution was aimed at appeasing Muslim communities with promises of power and involvement while retaining the dominant role of Christians, primarily Maronites, in the running of the nation. This tension characterised the challenges to the administrations of a succession of Lebanese presidents from the 1950s to the 1970s which led inexorably to civil war.

Young people, in particular, felt keenly their exclusion from positions of power and influence in the political system and their inability to achieve a good life through economic achievement. Contact with western nations during the Second World War had the effect of presenting a vision of a better life in the countries of the 'new world', including Australia.

Internally, the intra-group events of this period contributed significantly to the collapse of government. The za'im leaders used their power for their own political and financial purposes. In 1973, 41 out of 800 families controlled the majority of shares in joint stock companies, involving some 70 per cent of the turnover. Between 1970 and 1974, the number employed in agriculture in Lebanon declined from 50 per cent at the end of the 1950s to 20 per cent in 1975. This contributed to the emigration of 8,566 persons per year between 1960 and 1970, rising to 10,000 each year between 1970 and 1974. Along with this, émigré remittances increased from 5.38 per cent of GDP in 1951 to 30 per cent of GDP in 1974.[8]

Education played a significant role in challenging the structures of society. Improved access to universities across Lebanon led to young people attending universities where students of different religious groups mixed together and debated the issues of the day. Between 1944 and 1946 the Lebanese Government opened 150 state schools which saw an increased enrolment from 30,000 to 41,000 in a short space of time. However, after 1946 there was little expansion in education with only 21 per cent of Lebanese students attending state schools. Lebanon retained the same proportion of public and private schools, with no alteration to the French style curriculum being taught.[9]

Different sections of society were 'in motion to contest the established order' and confront the policies of the commercial/ financial oligarchy, expressing in one way or another, a deep desire for political, economic and social change. Limited educational and occupational pathways led mainly young Lebanese to consider emigration as a means of changing their social and economic circumstances and to escape the instability of political turmoil.

The instability of Lebanese society was apparent in a number of key events during this period. As early as 1968 students and teachers at the Lebanese University held a 50-day strike, demanding increased wages, better teacher tenure and student amenities. In 1972 16,000 public education school teachers struck for increased wages, the right to join a union and retirement after 25 years of service. The agrarian crisis, where tobacco workers in southern Lebanon campaigned for a better share of crops, resulted in a protest in Beirut in January, 1973. In April 1973, the General Workers Union of Lebanon (GWUL) held a general strike which challenged those with oligarchical power by calling for a limit to their privileges through a reduction of rents and an increase in salaries.

Attempts at political reform from above did not work. 'The Lebanese bourgeoisie and political establishment, in both the Muslim and Christian sectors, were unwilling to surrender any privileges for the cause of reform'.[10] Revolution was made 'in the most vicious and destructive manner from below'.[11] The army became torn between supporting the system of government and the homeland.

The events of this period had a significant impact on the Lebanese people by strengthening their sense of allegiance to diverse religious and political groupings which represented their interests in the face of the ruling group in society. Socially, the events revealed the division between those with wealth and power and those without. The orientation of Lebanon to the west rather than the Arab world and the focus of developing tertiary sectors of banking and finance alienated many industrial and agricultural workers, the most populous group in society.[12]

Those who lived in villages and towns away from Beirut resented the wealth and power of the elite families, which added to their frustration with their own limited opportunities. This group formed many of the emigrants who left Lebanon in this period for economic opportunity with the additional benefit of greater political stability. Their raised expectations, due to the education they received, added to their frustration with the limitations of life in Lebanon.

12

AUSTRALIA AFTER
THE SECOND WORLD WAR

During the first few years after the Second World War Australia was still recovering from the loss and suffering caused by the conflict, including the Japanese bombing of Darwin and other centres in the north, such as Broome. Apart from the material damage, the war led to a sense of vulnerability among sections of the population and the government. Much adjustment to civilian life was needed by soldiers returning from the war and their families. This applied particularly to many women who returned to their traditional roles as wives, mothers and homemakers, after working in a variety of industries and farms during the war.

By the 1950s there were promising developments. Returned servicemen were supported by the Commonwealth Government to upgrade or acquire qualifications, including university degrees. Rationing of food, clothing and petrol was abolished and consumer goods became more plentiful. Goods and building materials, which had been scarce during the war, now became more available. Secondary industries were established or re-established in the capital cities, including manufacturing of Australia's own car by General Motors Holden. The Chifley Labor Government engaged in planning nation-building projects, the most important being the Snowy Mountains Scheme. This was a major hydro-electricity project which not only produced electric power for much of eastern

Australia, but also utilised the skills and labour of immigrants from all over Europe, many of whom later settled in Australia and made major contributions to Australian society.

The development of secondary industries was significant for the nation in that it attracted immigrants and provided them with employment which, at the same time, led to an increase in Australia's population and the industrialisation of the economy. This was significant for those Lebanese immigrants who gained their first jobs in the in the vehicle and other manufacturing companies in the capital cities of Australia.

The Second World War had revealed that Australia was unprepared for global war and unable to defend itself without the aid of powerful friends. It also revealed the need for a degree of self-reliance in terms of the defence of the nation. Consequently, there was a push from Government for an increase in population as a means of filling empty spaces in the sparsely populated continent. This was to be achieved not only through natural increase but also through the acceptance of approved groups of immigrants and refugees. The first preference was to select British, then Northern and Eastern Europeans, then other Europeans. It was only later that immigrants from non-European nations such as Turkey, Lebanon and Egypt were accepted. Even then, many of these immigrants had to pay full fares with borrowed money which they later repaid after gaining employment. The process of broadening the intake of immigrants to include many European and Middle Eastern immigrants had to be managed carefully by the Commonwealth Government, given a degree of antipathy by sections of the population to non-British migration. The approach taken by government during this period was to staunchly uphold the White Australia Policy and, in the first instance, to select Northern and Eastern Europeans who were preferred on the grounds that they were more like British and Australians.

Australian Government migration policies

In the immediate post-war years, Australia embarked on a campaign to achieve a population growth of two per cent per annum, of which a half was to come through natural increase and a half through immigration. The objective of mass immigration in the 1950s and 1960s was to create a labour force which could help to expand manufacturing industries and make Australia more economically self-reliant.

Between 1947 and 1971 the Australian population grew from 7.6 million to 12.7 million, with net immigration contributing 2.2 million or 43 per cent of the total population growth. With the addition of the children of these immigrants, some 60 per cent of the population increase during this period can be attributed to immigration.[13] This post-war migration included not only British settlers but also increasing numbers of immigrants from a diverse range of European countries. The White Australia Policy remained securely in place until the late 1960s and early 1970s when exceptions were made for groups of Asian refugees and immigrants.

Assimilation

The post-war period was a time for welcoming immigrants from around the world to swell Australia's population in order to defend itself from attack and also to develop the industrial infrastructure that a modern society required. There was a clearly articulated official position on the hierarchy of preferred settlers. To recap, immigrants from the United Kingdom were helped to migrate through heavily subsidised assisted passages, followed by fair-skinned Northern Europeans. Italian and Greek immigrants did not all receive assisted passages because of the belief that 'racially' they were different from the British or Northern Europeans. Nor did they share their predominantly Protestant faith. Lebanese immigrants were included in the latter group as settlers and also had to pay for their journey to their new homes.

The initial Government response to the influx of new arrivals was the policy of 'assimilation.' Immigrants, especially those of non-British backgrounds, were expected to abandon their languages and cultures and conform to the dominant Australian values and become citizens as quickly as possible. The major emphasis was on shedding national loyalties and affiliations and adopting the language, culture and institutions of the host society. The motivation was not primarily economic or political but cultural, and the culture to which immigrants were expected to assimilate was essentially British or British-Australian. There was no place for cultural diversity in this definition of Australia.

On arrival in Australia, there were no formal, organised services to aid the settlement of immigrants. The closest that the wider Australian society came to recognising the settlement needs of Lebanese and other non-English speaking immigrants lay in the labelling of them as 'New Australians'. Implicit in this label was the notion that they were to assimilate to Australian ways and therefore they had to sacrifice their former national identity that classified them as non-Australian. Being a 'New Australian' meant that you were to be tolerated by the wider society until you became an Australian, that is, when you could speak English, share Australian values and understand its social customs. All of this was to be achieved through informal support from family members, village friends or leaders from within their ethnic community.

Despite the lack of formal government policies to assist with the resettlement of refugees and migrants during this period, there was an awareness of the needs of the new arrivals on the part of some individuals and church organisations. Chief among these was the Good Neighbour Council, launched by the Commonwealth Government in 1950, to win public acceptance of the immigration of post-Second World War refugees and settlers. This it sought to achieve through enlisting the co-operation of community agencies and volunteers.

Among the earliest bodies to offer practical assistance to needy refugees in Melbourne was the European Australian Christian Fellowship (EACF) which was founded in 1956 on the initiative of St Aidan's Presbyterian Fellowship in North Balwyn. Its first volunteer, David Cox, describes his activities during the period from 1956 to 1963:

> I would meet ships carrying World Council of Churches-sponsored volunteers and assist them with pre-arranged accommodation and a job, and funds to tide them over until their first pay... Church members acted as host families for adolescents while young men were placed in boarding houses. The overarching focus could be described as 'reaching out in fellowship'.[14]

The EACF became the Ecumenical Migration Centre in 1970 and expanded its work among refugees as a precursor to more formal government assistance in the 1970s.

Australia between 1967 and 1975 was moving in a direction markedly different from any time in its previous history. Old ways were being challenged. There was greater confidence in the economy and society of the nation by the late 1960s. The need to cling to Britain was being tested by the younger generation – the children of German, Swedish, Italian or Czech parents among others, who came to Australia after the war to make a new home and to help build a secure Caucasian society still protected by the Immigration Exclusion Act of 1901.

Post-war settlement and reconstruction, and the associated largest mass movement of people in the world, had interesting and unforeseen effects on Australian society. The realities of life in the late 1960s saw some immigrants wanting to share the successes of their lives with those of their family who remained in their homeland, somewhere in Europe or the Middle East. This resulted in increasing travel and communication with their former homelands and the offer to bring relatives to Australia to help reconstruct their family in a different location. Gradually, Asian immigration was also being accepted. This meant that the basis of Australian immigration and citizenship policy was also being challenged.

From an Australian perspective, the period of 1967-1975 represented an awakening of the nation from a period of reconstruction and uncertainty. Australia's cultural ties to Britain and Europe were being challenged by a local intelligentsia that tended to see the nation as independent and neither a British nor an American satellite. The beliefs of a conservative society that had experienced two world wars and an economic depression were being challenged by a generation that had not endured the deprivations of earlier decades.

From the late 1960s and early 1970s the policy of limiting the immigration of non-white applicants began to ease. The success of limited Asian migration programs of the early 1960s showed that when exceptions were made for groups of Asian refugees and immigrants their cultural, social and economic contributions were valuable. By the mid-1960s, the gradual softening of the assimilationist stance began to take hold and non-white immigration would be permitted if there was evidence of 'close family ties'. By 1967, the Minister for Immigration, Billy Snedden, acknowledged that 'it would be more beneficial to the nation to begin allowing more people into the country based on expertise rather than compassionate grounds, as this would help the national economy.' Compared with 1.2 per cent Asian migration in the period 1917-1951, Asian migration had climbed to 11.2 per cent by 1966-71.[15]

The White Australia Policy was eventually abolished by the Whitlam Government in 1973 and replaced by a policy of multiculturalism which recognised the contributions of the many different nationalities and ethnicities to the identity of the nation. The flamboyant Al Grassby, as the new Minister for Immigration, believed that it was essential for a modern nation to acknowledge the realities of cultural life. The creation of the new Citizenship Act of 1973 ended the preferential treatment of British-born immigrants. It also acceded to the United Nations Conventions on Statelessness and Refugees. The co-incidence of multiculturalism as policy with the ending of the Vietnam War also allowed the acceptance of 'boat people' arriving on Australian shores.

Citizenship

A single important value had underpinned Australian citizenship law and practice during this period: the definition of Australia as British. Australia's Nationality and Citizenship Act, 1948, came into effect on 26 January 1949 and created a distinct status of Australian citizen. In addition, it ensured that Australian citizens also retained the status of British subjects. This British link was so durable that it took until 1984 before Australian citizens could no longer be considered as British subjects. Despite the passing of this Act, aliens were confronted with a number of restrictions such as the right to claim certain pensions, access to public housing, and the full range of political rights.

During this period the White Australia Policy continued to hold sway with resident non-Europeans ineligible to apply for naturalisation until 1956. The later passing of the Multiculturalism Act in 1984 was not in response to a demand from the Australian people, but was rather imposed by government, influenced by Canada's moves to create a separate Canadian citizenship. Australian citizenship at this time was expressed in terms of British culture and ethnicity, not in terms of the rights and responsibilities of citizens of the state. The image of Australians defined in the Act was therefore of an Anglo-Celtic people.[16] Thus the Act defines an 'alien' as a person who does not have the status of a British subject and is not a protected person.

On the economic front, the long economic boom that had secured conservative government under Prime Minister, Robert Menzies, through the 1950s and 1960s, was drawing to a close. The election of the Whitlam Government in 1972 saw a number of socially progressive policies aimed at placing Australia on the world stage and modernising the nation. The co-incidence of significant inflation in the early 1970s, in part due to a rise in oil prices from the Middle East, ushered in a period of economic tension and, ultimately, restructuring, in order to minimise costs. The decade following 1973 saw pressure placed on production line manufacturing businesses to restructure and cut costs. This had significant implications for the many Lebanese immigrants who had arrived believing that they would find work in the same industries that required minimal education and skills as did their family members who had immigrated to Australia in the 1950s and 1960s.

Post-war Lebanese immigration

During the period 1947 to 1975 immigration from Lebanon was strongly influenced by regional instability and economic inequality in the country. A major cause of regional instability were the Arab-Israeli wars and conflicts, which occurred every few years from 1948. These culminated in the Six Day War with an Israeli victory. However, this brought neither peace nor political stability to the Middle East and Lebanon.

13

LEBANESE SETTLEMENT IN AUSTRALIA, 1947–1975

The sweetness of success effaces the bitterness of struggle.
Arabic proverb

During the period 1947-1975 there was a major increase in the Lebanese-born population in Australia. Few of these Lebanese immigrants had trade or professional skills which were accepted by local employers or trade and professional bodies. This generally limited their participation in the labour market to low-skilled or unskilled work. The first occupations of the new migrants were in manufacturing plants or smaller factories, mainly in Sydney and Melbourne. Later, many Lebanese opened businesses where family members worked together in shop-keeping, taxi-driving, milk bars and other small enterprises.

The children of the second-wave immigrants mostly attended schools in Australia. When the children reached school leaving age many families expected that they would follow in the steps of their parents and work in factories or family businesses. Other families were able to keep their children at school which enabled them to gain higher educational qualifications and occupations.

As a result of the increase in the numbers of immigrants the Lebanese communities grew in size and complexity, especially in Sydney and Melbourne. With a degree of financial security came the desire to recreate in their adopted home those institutions which were familiar and meaningful to them. This led to the establishment of more Lebanese churches and the first Lebanese mosques, as well as other community organisations. During this period Lebanese communities continued to demonstrate their public spiritedness and loyalty to the nation. This was amply illustrated by their charitable contributions and the numbers of Australian-born Lebanese who served in both wars.

Lebanese-born population in Australia

Australia's Lebanese-born population grew from 1,869 in 1947 to 33,311 in 1976 (Table 5 Pt 2). This number included those born in Syria/Lebanon and who had arrived in Australia before, and in the three decades after, the Second World War.

By 1976 New South Wales was home to 77 per cent of the Lebanese-born, followed by Victoria with 18 per cent. Much smaller numbers were to be found in the other states (see Table 5 Pt 1). The explanation for this increase was, in part, due to the ending of hostilities and the opening up of transport, firstly, by ship and then by plane to Australia. By the 1961 Census, there was a marked increase in Lebanese-born settlers due to the 1958 Revolution in Lebanon. The numbers of Lebanese-born settlers in Australia doubled between the 1954 Census and the 1961 Census.

A common pattern among these early second-wave immigrants was for young men to migrate alone or in the company of others like themselves. While their major motivation was economic improvement, it was often expressed in terms of love of adventure and desire to seek new opportunities. In all cases, they left immediate family in Lebanon such as parents, brothers or sisters and extended families. Over the years these young men would either marry within the Lebanese community in Australia or return home to bring back a bride.

In the years following the Second World War Australia was seen by Lebanese immigrants as a valued destination which was offering jobs and a pathway to economic prosperity. There was congruence between Australia, which was in need of population growth and labour to work in its expanding secondary industries, and Lebanese migrants who were only too ready to fill that need. In general, Australia's political system was slower to adapt to the reality of immigrants from many different nations and cultures. It was not until the late 1970s that there was some recognition by governments of the settlement needs of immigrants.

Settlement

Lebanese settlement around Australia in this period was typical of the pattern of many other immigrants during the post-war period. Their first point of contact upon arrival was a family member, a fellow-villager or a member of the local Australian-Lebanese community. In their initial phase of settlement these second-wave immigrants joined existing Lebanese communities. Suburbs such as Redfern and Waterloo and then Lakemba and Fairfield in Sydney, and the inner suburbs of Carlton, Brunswick and Northcote in Melbourne, were the initial destinations of many of these post-war immigrants.

In their early years in Australia the major means of communication between young Lebanese immigrants and their families in Lebanon were letters and, as one immigrant put it, 'never a letter without cash'. These letters were sometimes accompanied by photographs and, less frequently, by audiotapes. They were invariably sent by mail as the postal service between Australia and Lebanon was entirely adequate during the 1950s and 1960s. Money, clothes and gifts were also sent through people returning to their village or town. In return, the family would send letters and small gifts from Lebanon. Occasionally, audiotapes of special functions such as weddings and christenings were also sent and received by family members. During this period few people communicated by telephone as it was prohibitively expensive.

Sydney's Australian Lebanese Club 1953.
(Source: National Archives of Australia. W Brindle photographer.
Image No. A1200:L16215)

These second-wave immigrants described common feelings of early loneliness as they missed parents, brothers, sisters and friends and complained that letters were 'not enough to keep in touch'. Some single men experienced less loneliness if they had contacts within the Lebanese community or were confident enough to mix socially with Australians in work places or by attending local dances. Over time, the urgency with which they sought information about the place and the people they left behind diminished as the imperatives of their new life began to assume priority. These immigrants described how, over time, they began 'to take an interest in their new life' until they reached a point, after many years in Australia, of recognising it as their home.

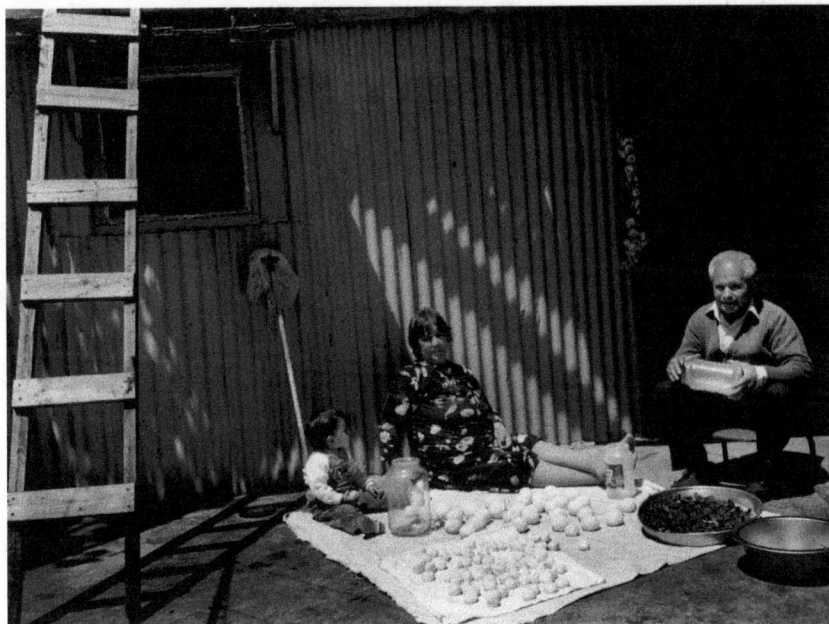

Wardia Jabbour, making and drying home-made traditional cheese 1951 with her
husband & grandson.
(Source: State Library of Victoria)

During the hawking period many of the first-wave immigrants had
plied their trade in country areas which led to considerable settlement
of Lebanese in country towns of New South Wales, Queensland
and Victoria. However, as we saw, hawking declined as the major
occupation of Lebanese immigrant families during the first decades
of the 20th century. This led to internal migration to larger country
towns and, especially, to Sydney and Melbourne. The motives were
to seek alternative employment, often in their own businesses, and
to ensure a good education for their children and grand-children. An
added benefit was to join the larger numbers of Lebanese who had
settled in those cities and who were forming Lebanese communities.
While not congregating in ghettoes, many Lebanese tended to live
in close proximity to each other in inner and middle ring suburbs in
the capital cities. In Sydney these included Redfern and then Coogee,
Kingsford and Kensington and later, in the 1960s, in inner western

suburbs such as Lakemba, Campsie, Marrickville, Hurlstone Park and Croydon. Historians have given a snapshot of these suburbs at that time:

> Redfern was a tough, inner city suburb and although it was the focus of Syrian/Lebanese community life, over time it became a less attractive location for the immigrants and their families. Once people made enough money, they moved to 'better' suburbs. At first this meant places in the Randwick Municipality such as Coogee, Kingsford and Kensington which were just a tram ride away from Redfern.
>
> In the post war period, some wealthier members of the community relocated to more affluent areas like Bellevue Hill and Vaucluse in the east and Strathfield in the West. Randwick Municipality remains a centre of Lebanese settlement in New South Wales, especially for the descendants of the earliest migrants. While a number still owned property in the Redfern area, it is likely to be on the general rental market and although it may allow them to maintain a presence, the area is no longer characterised as Lebanese.[17]

In Victoria, Lebanese immigrants initially congregated in the north-eastern part of central Melbourne and into Carlton which became known as the *koora* (locality). This area housed Lebanese businesses such as clothing factories, warehouses, retail shops of various types as well as their family homes. As we noted, it provided something of a community centre for Lebanese families where they lived, worked and interacted. However, over time, most Lebanese did not remain in this area. Some families moved to what were then more prestigious suburbs south of the Yarra such as Brighton, Elwood and Kew, while others moved into adjoining northern suburbs such as Brunswick and Northcote. Especially after the Second World War, many second-wave families pursued business opportunities, often milk bars, coffee lounges and other small businesses, throughout the metropolitan areas of Melbourne. This led, in turn, to their widespread settlement throughout the city.

Syrian or Lebanese?

The arrival of the second wave of immigrants after the war challenged the self-perception of Lebanese settlers within their communities in Australia. As previously discussed, many initial and early settlers defined themselves as Syrians, due to their classification under the Ottoman Empire as being part of the administrative division of Syria. On many applications for naturalisation dating back to the 1910s, the place of birth is shown as 'Mount Lebanon, Syria'. This was in marked contrast to those migrating after 1920, when Lebanon became a French Mandate. These immigrants saw themselves as Lebanese and quite distinct from Syria. On the other hand, the descendants of the first-wave settlers seemed largely unaware of the change of status of Lebanon as a nation and the term 'Syrian' was generally used until the arrival of the second wave immigrants from the late 1940s.

Now this question of what to call themselves became entangled with the first indications of assertion of their separate identity, as one historian notes:

> In Melbourne, Victoria two important meetings were held in the early 1950s. These informal gatherings proved to be important first steps in establishing in 1951 the first formal body to represent the Lebanese in Victoria – the Australian Lebanese Association. The first was a meeting of members of the Lebanese community in Melbourne in 1950 to protest at articles in the daily newspapers highly critical of Lebanese immigrants who had arrived in Melbourne by ship. The articles expressed outrage at the 'filthy conditions' on board the ships and, in highly emotional and prejudicial language, blamed the Lebanese immigrants who were described as the 'dregs of the earth.' The meeting resolved to write to the newspapers and make personal representations but no retractions were ever printed.

> The second meeting of community members was held at St Nicholas Church Hall in East Melbourne in 1951. The purpose of this meeting was to decide once and for all whether those who came from Lebanon should continue to be called 'Syrians', as the first wave settlers were

known, or adopt the term 'Lebanese', which the new arrivals from Lebanon were adamant was now their correct nationality. This was clearly a political and cultural statement on the independence of Lebanon. Inevitably the new term was adopted and quite quickly became common usage. The name of the only Lebanese church was changed from 'St Nicholas Syrian Orthodox Church' to 'St Nicholas Antiochian Orthodox Church'.[18]

The period of assimilation brought with it a diversity of other Arab immigrants to Australia. Not only was there considerable growth in the numbers of Lebanese immigrants but also the arrival of Egyptians and small numbers of other Arab immigrants. In the early years some of these Arab immigrants would mix with Lebanese and attend their churches and mosques. The settlement of Lebanese during this period was marked by their preoccupation with the practical matters of settling and establishing their families in Australia. The new arrivals would live with their relations and village friends until they could strike out on their own. One particular Orthodox family provided accommodation for their cousins, the fiancé of one of their daughters, and a Druze friend from their village. In this instance, a shared home township was more significant than religion in aiding the settlement of new arrivals.

However, second-wave immigrants were also instrumental in establishing some, and rejuvenating other, religious and community organisations. The involvement of the new Lebanese in these community organisations was not without problems which came to the fore during the establishment and management of these bodies, as shown in the case study of St Nicholas Antiochian Orthodox Church, Melbourne.

St Nicholas Antiochian Orthodox Church has served the Antiochian and other Orthodox in Melbourne for some eighty years. Its significance lies in the fact that, from its inception in 1932 until the mid-1950s, St Nicholas occupied a special place in Lebanese community life. As such, it provided a religious and community centre for many first-, second- and third-wave immigrants from Lebanon and elsewhere in the Middle East. However, by the early 1980s, differences became apparent between the founding families and the second-wave of Lebanese immigrants over the management and control of the Church. The founding families had developed a feeling of ownership and control of the Church which was challenged by a young priest and second-wave Orthodox immigrants. The priest and second-wave immigrants eventually prevailed and gained control of the Church while most of the original families left St Nicholas and established a second Antiochian Church of St Georges in Thornbury.[19]

The second-wave Lebanese continued, under the influence of the descendants of first-wave settlers, to participate in displays of public spiritedness and collections for charity. Sometimes this involved dressing up in traditional dress to attend a Red Cross International Ball or similar event, which stressed the exotic and foreign nature of Arabic culture. Like many other immigrant groups at the time, they established their own ethnic organisations, sought to preserve their own language, religion and cultural practices and, in doing so, rejected the policy of assimilation, but quietly.

Occupations and businesses

Because few Lebanese immigrants possessed trade or professional skills accepted by local employers or professional bodies, and their participation in the labour market was limited to low skilled or unskilled work, their first occupations were in the new post-war industries:

> While the small business tradition continued, many Lebanese men and women found paid employment in factories. Some of these factories, such as the Sunbeam plant, were located near Redfern. When the Redfern Mail Exchange was built in the early 1960s, Lebanese found employment as postal sorters. Lebanese also worked in the ACI Glassworks, the Tooth's Brewery, and the British Motor Works plants at Waterloo and Zetland. From the 1960s to the 1980s Lebanese-born men and women in Sydney were concentrated as manual labourers, production process workers and in trade activities.[20]

Lebanese dignitaries and community members visiting the shop floor and
meeting Lebanese workers at the Fishermen's Bend plant of General Motors
Holden in late 1960s. 1988.

(Source: State Library of Victoria)

Employment in these factories provided the Lebanese with experience
of working alongside Australians from British and other immigrant
backgrounds. While the Lebanese were grateful for the work and,
especially, the working conditions, stories abound of verbal and
sometimes physical conflicts with Anglo-Australian workers, usually
based on racial slurs.

> A young Salem Haddad from Zahle, Lebanon quickly found work at
> General Motors' Holden on arrival in Melbourne. However, his time
> at the factory was made miserable by the racial taunts that he suffered
> at the hands of one fellow worker in particular. Finally, this became
> too much for Salem who one day lost his temper and punched his
> tormenter in the face. Remarkably, after this episode all racial taunts
> stopped and his former adversary became a friendly fellow worker.[21]

Few Lebanese were content to remain as employees, preferring instead to seek self-employment in small businesses where husband, wife and children could work full-time or part-time. The major businesses they entered at this time were milk bars and related small businesses. The advantages of self-employment in small businesses were many. These included opportunities for all family members to work in the one business where they could support each other in many ways. The young would help their parents with the English language while remaining within the family unit and under their parents' guidance. Working in milk bars provided opportunities for interacting with Australians from a range of backgrounds which, in turn, helped the milk bar owners to learn English and something of the culture of the Australian community. Many milk bars had residences attached which provided an economical way for the family to live and work together in the one location.

Lebanese sweet shop Rathdowne St Carlton Melbourne 1951.
(Source: State Library of Victoria)

Another advantage the milk bar offered was the opportunity to purchase foodstuffs wholesale for sale in the shop as well as for their own consumption. Perhaps the major advantage of working in milk bars was that it provided an introduction to doing business in Australia. This encouraged many Lebanese to later own and manage larger businesses in the hospitality industry such as coffee lounges, restaurants and hotels.

Purchasing milk bars had the effect of dispersing the Lebanese throughout the metropolitan areas of the capital cities as they purchased or opened new businesses in suburbs where they saw business opportunities. Later, some chose to purchase houses and settle in those areas. This dispersal meant avoiding too great a concentration of Lebanese in certain areas which enabled them to mix with other Australians and adapt to their ways.

The story of the Haikal family reveals the common themes of family unity and cooperation, entrepreneurial enterprise and educational achievements.

Edward and Marie Haikal and family:

Almazett Lebanese Restaurant

Edward Haikal migrated from Beirut, Lebanon in 1968. The following year he brought out his wife, Marie, and their five children to further the children's education. Edward had been a senior accountant with American Express in Beirut but had to be content with simple book-keeping positions when he first arrived in Melbourne. In the early years the family had to struggle, having to balance the demands of secondary and tertiary education for the children with the need to earn an income for the family.

The family's first venture into business was in 1977 when they leased a Lebanese restaurant, *Abdul's*, in Malvern. On the basis of that experience, they opened the *Almazett* restaurant a year later. The Haikal family was the first to introduce a set price for an open banquet *(mesa)*, a concept that proved a great success with Australians from many different backgrounds.

During this time four of the Haikal children worked in the family business while studying at university. In total, they obtained two medical degrees, a law degree and three science degrees. Following the success of *Almazett*, families related to the Haikals opened the following Lebanese restaurants: *Cedar Tree* in Brighton, *Chateau Lebanon* in Middle Park, *Dunyazad* in North Balwyn, *Sinbad* in Dandenong, *Kanzaman* in Richmond and *Samsara* in Mount Waverley. It was typical for people to work in their relative's restaurant until they had enough capital and experience to open their own. Through family unity and enterprise, the Haikal and related families made a major contribution to the cuisine of Melbourne.[22]

Getting on the taxis

Another major occupation during this period was taxi-driving, which Lebanese ventured into in the 1960s and 1970s. An advantage of taxi-driving was the opportunity it provided taxi owners and drivers to work longer hours than were normally available in factory work, and eventually to purchase their own taxis. It also meant that, in the course of their work, taxi drivers would meet a cross section of the community, learning to communicate with them in English and deciphering the Australian idiom. Many Lebanese taxi drivers purchased their own taxis, with some buying multiple taxi licences and employing drivers, often from within their own community. In this way driving taxis provided yet another avenue for Lebanese to establish their own businesses.

Historian Christine Eid has researched the Lebanese taxi drivers from Hadchit, in Lebanon's Kadisha Valley:

Taxi ventures

John Werden, an early post-war arrival, experienced ongoing dissatisfaction with his factory earnings which motivated him to explore new opportunities. After a short period in Sydney working at the Johnson and Johnson factory in Botany, he established a hawking business. When he noticed a taxi parked in his neighbour's driveway, he recognised his new venture. In 1952 he gained his taxi drivers' certificate and started driving with Green Cabs:

'I picked up night-shift, so there is no way I could spend my money. The first week I earn £25, second week £50, this is good, Jesus, so I had £1000'.

In 1954, John returned to Melbourne, where he obtained his Victorian taxi credentials. He soon became known as the first Hadchit Lebanese taxi driver. John persuaded his cousins, Alamieh and Nadim Hanna, to purchase a taxi:

'A taxi will buy you a house. A house won't buy you a taxi.'

The couple saw great potential in taxi driving. After Nadim bought a taxi in 1959 for £4000, he started to learn to drive, he never drove [a car] before. Werden and Hanna became the first Hadchit Lebanese taxi entrepreneurs in Melbourne, inspiring others to start their own business.

From the 1950s to 1970s, after receiving letters from relatives praising the economic opportunities in Australia, many Hadchitis migrated to Melbourne, including the families of Hanna, Eid, Werden/Warden, Chehade, Sassine, Bazouni, Elia, Hadchiti, Yacoub, El-Khoury, Chukti and Semaan. They all planned to stay for a few years and then return to Lebanon with enough capital to establish businesses. Instead, they settled permanently and can't imagine living anywhere else.

About 14 Hadchit Lebanese men established taxi businesses. They sought to fulfil their hopes of prosperity, independence, mobility and flexible hours. Greater earnings could be made driving taxis than working for a set wage, provided one was willing to put in long hours.

Nadim Hanna nominated his brothers, Youssef in 1956 and Elias in 1963, to come to Australia. He helped them find factory work and then set up their own taxi business. Taxi fever had struck. Once this pattern was established, a succession of taxi businesses followed, inspiring their brothers-in-law, cousins and family friends:

> I used to work [at Bradmill Cotton Mills] from 1963 till about 1965, I started on £8 a week. It was reasonable money back then. That's 40 hours … Then, I didn't count the hours; I'd count the money, that's what I wanted. So, I got on the taxi for Saturday and Sunday, I was making something like £12. I was making equal money. So I said well that's no good, if I can make this money I better get on the taxi and I took the taxi full time and I was doing all right.

Melbourne taxi drivers were required to pass a location test before obtaining a taxi drivers' certificate. After six months, drivers could purchase a taxi licence, allowing them to own and operate a taxi business. Youssef Hanna explains:

In Australia, it was a battle but you could achieve something.
I worked four years in General Motors Holden, then I left
and bought a car off the factory there and I got a bit of a
discount on it, and I put it on the road as a taxi ... I saved
in those four years £3000 because I was very tight with my
money. I came here [when] I was 25 years old. I want to build
myself so I can get married ... Prior to that I studied how
to get the taxi licence—it was very good questions but it was
about over 200 questions, anyway I passed ... I got the car
and got out and I had to work six months before they let me
buy a taxi.

The prospect of greater earnings and 'being your own boss'
outweighed the long hours and personal and financial risks. Popping
home for lunch or coffee became a ritual that reinforced a sense of
freedom. Elias Hanna reflects:

Taxi is good ... I used to go to the milk bar a lot ... if the
man was sick, he was single, he can't afford to be sick, he had
to open the shop. Sometimes his nose running or he's got a
temperature, he's still in the shop. Well I thought the taxi is
all right, you lock it up in the garage and you sleep. You drive
past your sister's [house] you pop in, you have a coffee ...

As another driver says: 'we felt more freedom in the taxi, you could
work any time you want, if you want to work mornings, if you want to
work late, if you want to do more hours when you want more money
for the family'.[23]

Clothing factories

Another way in which Lebanese could work in their own businesses
was in clothing factories. Most were established by first-wave Lebanese
families for whom clothing factories and warehouses were a natural
evolution from the hawking activities pursued by pioneer Lebanese
families. During this period many of these businesses expanded

dramatically as war-time prohibitions were lifted and the population grew, leading to increased demand for consumer goods. After the Second World War some Lebanese new arrivals, especially women, were employed in these factories while some later established their own clothing businesses or purchased existing ones. However, by the late 1970s and 1980s, these businesses ran into major competition from overseas exports and by the 1990s many were forced to close.

An illustrative case study is that of *Salco Pty Ltd,* a clothing factory established in the early 1930s and run by two Lebanese families in succession since that time: the Salamy and Mansour families.

Salco Pty Ltd: 1930-1940s: Fred and Najeebie Salamy

Zachariah Salamy emigrated from Lebanon in the late 1890s from Marjeyoun, Lebanon, with his wife Catherine, and settled in Albury. In common with almost all other first wave settlers, Zachariah was first a hawker and then later a shopkeeper in Albury. After the death of Zachariah in 1913 the family moved to Melbourne where their sons later opened clothing manufacturing businesses.

Salco was established by Fred Salamy and his wife Najeebie (nee Malouf) in Elgin Street, Carlton around 1930. Najeebie looked after the factory, where they manufactured shirts and pyjamas, and Fred opened a warehouse and dispatch centre for the business in Flinders Lane. Fred's brother, Naseeb, was a traveller for the company. The factory employed Lebanese, other new arrivals and, of course, many Australian-born workers.

In the 1940s the factory was sold to Joe Mansour, who later became a prominent figure in the Melbourne Lebanese community. After the sale, Fred and Najeebie continued to manufacture shirts under the label *Stanleigh*. After Fred's death in the mid-1960s, his wife, Najeebie opened a small shop in Elgin Street Carlton where she continued to sell shirts and meet old friends from her earlier manufacturing days.[24]

Salco: Mansour Family 1940s—

Joe Mansour migrated from Lebanon in 1904. After a period of hawking he came to Melbourne in the early 1920s where he became involved in a number of business ventures, including opening a milk bar and later a hotel.

In the early 1940s he bought *Salco* from Fred Salamy and continued to manufacture shirts, pyjamas and school shirts. During this time his son, John, joined the business. The Mansours expanded the business, opening a larger factory on the Elgin Street site in 1954. By 1966 *Salco* had added business and military shirts. All manufacturing was done on site.

John's son, Michael, joined the business in 1966 at the age of 18 years. It was not long after this that the business changed from being a commodity manufacturer to one with up-market fashion designs. For example, *Salco* developed the *Abelard* brand which was at the better end of Australian shirts made from the best linen, silk and Swiss cotton as an alternative to European imports.

The commodity side of the business continued by making police, taxi and ambulance shirts. Over time the commodity side decreased and the fashion side expanded. Major fashion brands of the *Salco* company now include *Gant, Jeff Banks, Geoffrey Bene* and *Thomas Pink*. Products include fashion shirts, fashion sportswear and men's accessories. Major clients included Henry Bucks and David Jones. All manufacturing is now done overseas while design and distribution is still centred in Melbourne.

Three generations of Mansours have run the business since the early 1940s without partnerships but with some family members as employees. The success of the company can be attributed to their decision to specialise in well-known fashion brands, their simple management structure and overseas manufacturing.[25]

The story of *Salco* reveals a number of themes common to Lebanese clothing businesses. One obvious one is that the founders of these businesses had either been hawkers or were the children of hawkers, an occupation which seemed to serve as an introduction to clothing businesses such as warehouses, drapery shops or clothing factories.

Perhaps the major achievements of Latoof and Callil, the first and largest clothing business in Victoria, encouraged other Australian-Lebanese to try to emulate their success. This 'follow the leader' activity was made possible by the small and closely-knit early Lebanese community in Melbourne and their willingness to assist each other.

A further theme is the absolute significance of family involvement in these businesses. Husbands and wives, brothers and sisters, adult children, uncles and aunts and other members of the extended families worked together to establish and run the factories. In particular, many women made major contributions to their family businesses. This applied to the Salamy women, including Najeebie and Queenie.

To a greater or lesser extent each of these businesses reveals what can be regarded as a common Lebanese trait: risk taking and entrepreneurial activity. Some left secure jobs to open or join their family businesses while others seemed to have no alternative employment and yet others seemed to be following a family tradition.

Hamra Furniture Building, West Terrace Adelaide 1954. A family run furniture business that was established in 1928 by two brothers in Adelaide and traded until 2015.

(Source: Library of South Australia)

The people who ran these businesses had to demonstrate adaptability, versatility and resilience as they met and overcame many challenges. For example, during war-time some businesses manufactured army uniforms and other products required during the Second World War. Notable examples in Melbourne were Latoof and Callil, and N. Saleeba and Company, who made uniforms, and Elite Pleaters who made tents for the Australian army. Finally, those businesses which survived and prospered into the 21st century showed great success in monitoring and adapting to the changing business environment.

In addition to these occupations, second-wave Lebanese were to be found in a wide range of other fields, especially those which allowed for the involvement of family and a degree of entrepreneurial enterprise. The Baan case study, to which we referred briefly before, reflects a wide range of occupations, chain migration, adaptation of traditional skills acquired in Lebanon to occupations in Australia and the retention of family and kinship ties in their adopted home.

> In the late 1930s, a migration began of Maronite Lebanese from the village of Baan to Thornleigh on the north western fringe of Sydney. The attraction was the availability of cheap farmlets in an area specialising then in citrus orchards. Here knowledge and skills as part of the peasant garden tradition could be directly applied to economic activities in Australia. A Lebanese entrepreneur bought 160 hectares of land at Thornleigh in 1938 and personally sponsored brothers, cousins and their nuclear families over a 25 year period... Many of the settlers later bought 2-5 acre blocks of this land....
>
> Chain migration resulted in continuing group settlement in this suburbanising district with later settlers being tradesmen, jobbing labourers, carpenters, electricians, stonemasons and the like, some transferring traditional village crafts and a habit of individual proprietorship, and others upgrading qualifications in Australia. By 1960 200 had emigrated from the village of Baan to Sydney, most of whom were in Thornleigh, and small groups in Redfern and in Harris Park, an older western fringe suburb. By 1979 it was estimated more than 1,000 persons from Baan, almost one half of this town's population, were in Sydney.[26]

Lebanese women and employment

Wives, mothers and sisters played a major role in Lebanese families. In addition to caring for their families, through their work they directly contributed to the finances of the immigrant family. As we have seen during the hawking period some women would sew and make garments and other soft goods for sale by the men in their family. A smaller number of women would engage directly in hawking, either accompanying their husbands or striking out alone. This set the pattern for later generations of women who, during the second-wave immigration, would work in a range of factories: food processing, confectionery, clothing and many others. There were also cases of a few women who drove taxis during this period. Christine Eid's research on the Hadchit taxi-drivers disclosed the story of Nour Elaine El-Fakhri, the first and longest-serving Australian-Lebanese female taxi driver in Victoria. It seems that no occupation was closed to Lebanese women since their arrival in Australia and that those who pursued taxi-driving were successful and respected in what was a predominantly male industry.

When a Lebanese family opened or purchased a small business the involvement of women in the family became indispensable. When the family first entered the milk bar business it was common for the wife to assume responsibility for working in the business while her husband remained employed in the factory until the business was fully established. During this period the husband would work in the business in the evening. In almost all cases husbands, wives and children would serve in the milk bars and other retail businesses. This family involvement provided a source of cheap and, above all, trustworthy labour. As we have seen, in this way children would learn the rudiments of small business which would stand them in good stead when some later opened larger business such as coffee lounges, restaurants or hotels. On the other hand, many continued with their schooling and, with their parents' encouragement, gained entry to university and became qualified professionals in a range of fields.

Education

The 1950s to the 1970s was a watershed period in Australian society. Among the major changes was the influx of the children of Lebanese immigrants into Australian schools. At the time, the mono-cultural orientation of Australian schools could be seen in issues such as language, foods, popular culture and ways of behaving. It was in the classroom and playground where cultural differences became obvious. The experiences of alienation felt by Tammy Hayak in the playground encapsulated this experience:

> When I started school at the local Catholic school, there was a mix of cultures. For the first few years my friends were mainly Anglo-Saxon. This was because I was highly conscious of feeling and looking different, and desperately wanted to fit in. However, it was not easy. How would you feel sitting among a group of Australian kids with their Vegemite sandwiches while you pull out a gigantic roll of Lebanese bread and zaatar (an oregano, thyme and sesame seed spread)? My friends laughed saying I was eating birdseed. After suffering this humiliation, I insisted that my lunch from then on was to consist of a neatly cut Vegemite sandwich in a brown paper bag! It is funny to look back on this now, particularly when, due to popular demand, I regularly bring a bag full of *manoosh* of *zaatar* (oregano pizza) to work for my workmates' lunch. How things have changed![27]

The frustration of teachers having to respond to students from different cultural backgrounds became a catalyst for change in the education system. They believed that they were unable to teach effectively in a system that was oriented to a mono-cultural Australia. This was apparent in the role that teacher unions played in support of their members:

> The presence of these new students was considered a real difficulty and, as early as 1954, the General Secretary of the Victorian Teachers' Union (VTU) wrote to the Secretary of the Education Department expressing concern at the problem created for other students by the inability of 'new Australian' students to speak, write and understand English to a satisfactory standard. The General Secretary requested the appointment of specialist teachers, where needed, to benefit the

'new Australian' children, but also to 'enable normal instruction to proceed with the other children'.[28]

By the 1970s, federal and state governments saw the need to address the concerns of teachers in states where there were high numbers of non-English speaking background students. Towards the end of this period the Victorian Government began to respond by creating specialist positions in Migrant English and establishing parallel structures in schools to support learning English as a pathway to educational success.

> In May 1973 the first 60 positions were advertised in primary, secondary and technical schools for assistant teachers with responsibility in migrant education. They were to provide leadership at the school level. Their role consisted of: co-ordinating the work of migrant English teachers, maintaining liaison with other staff members … developing English programs, carrying out pastoral work with migrant children, establishing effective liaison with parent and community groups.[29]

> Most of the 30 positions offered in primary schools were filled, but vacancies remained in secondary and technical schools for a variety of reasons, including the insecure tenure of the frequently temporary, part-time arrangements governing migrant education at that stage, and the general teacher shortage.[30]

The experiences of many Lebanese students in schools revealed the limitations they faced, including the English language, local cultural knowledge as well as limited learning support from home. There was also pressure on older students to contribute to the family income to help pay for a house purchase or rental or other family costs. A number of students were required to leave school as soon as possible and to find work. In some families there were additional reasons for abandoning formal education, including the desire to retain their Lebanese heritage and traditions, and not have them diluted by wider Australian values that promoted individuality:

> A very simple thing is the schools teach the students to be very individualistic and very independent and the parents see independence as moving away from the family and the traditions, and they don't like

that.[31]

Another factor affecting student achievement was the inability of some parents to support the learning of their children. Parents, whose first language was not English and who, in many cases, had little formal education themselves in Lebanon, had limited capacity to help their children with homework problems, reading and, when needed, school intervention.

> Maybe some of the families, they never been at that school even one year or two years. So they have no ideas about the education.[32]

While higher numbers of the second generation attained tertiary qualifications than their parents, the number compared with other ethnic groups was still relatively low. Coming from a background of low English proficiency (and possibly low educational attainment) resulted in many Lebanese second-generation young adults born in this period having a relatively low tertiary attainment compared with other ethnic groups where English language proficiency was higher.[33]

On the other hand, some Lebanese families came to Australia in this period in order to provide their children with educational opportunities and freedoms that had been unattainable in Lebanon. These families devoted their energies to keeping their children at school and free of financial pressures. With perseverance and diligence, a number of the children of 1950s and 1960s immigrants reached high educational standards and went on to major achievements, either in professions or in business.

A significant and potent form of education across the Lebanese communities in Australia was informal and not restricted to school-aged students but open to working adults. As the numbers in the Lebanese communities around Australia grew in the 1950s and 1960s, the informal teaching and learning of skills between adult immigrants became an important form of education. Family members, fellow villagers, members of the same church or mosque and friends all played a role in sharing with others where to find work, how to make money and how to invest their money. This was evident in the experiences of two immigrants in this period.

> Broheim and Hoda Aoun explained how the purchase of a milk bar
> was the result of collaboration between family and friends:

> A friend [Michel Lattoof] said, 'buy a milk bar and I will help you.' He
> used to come and help us clean up and put in stock and everything

> Habib Khoury first started in a milk bar in Fairfield (Victoria). He
> explained: 'A friend of ours recommended me to go into this business.
> My brother had already bought the first milk bar (in our family). I had
> two or three weeks' experience in a milk bar with him. He gave me the
> 'thumbs up' that I can do it'.[34]

Said Sedawi (centre) with cooks at Lebanese House, Russell St, Melbourne 1964.
(Source: State Library of Victoria)

By the early 1970s, there was a growing recognition of Lebanese and
other immigrants not as 'new Australians' but as settlers with their
own cultural ways and values that they brought to the nation. This
can be seen in the story of Assaad and Marie which touches on many
of the themes of this study. It reveals that the Arab-Israeli War and
the conflict in Palestine led to repercussions throughout the Middle

East, including the refugees and stateless persons, such as Assaad, who fled to Lebanon. We see the difficulties experienced by Assaad and Marie in obtaining work, services and education for their children in Lebanon. While the Lebanese Civil War did not commence until 1975, the preceding years were marked by tensions and sporadic fighting which were a precursor to all-out war. This convinced the family to leave Lebanon and join their eldest daughter in Australia. In what was by no means a unique experience, we note the advice and assistance given to this young couple by their landlord and a bank manager.

Assaad and Marie Issa

Assaad and Marie experienced a life in Lebanon that was filled with hardships. This made their emigration in 1972 an easy decision.

Assaad's family lived in Jerusalem, Palestine. In 1948, with the establishment of Israel, they were dislocated and fled to Lebanon. Naturally, Assaad and his parents went to live in El Mina, Tripoli, Lebanon, to be close to his grandparents. As a Palestinian, Assad was 'stateless'. He was unaware of and unable to access services provided by the United Nations in Lebanon to ease the relocation of displaced people. In their early days in El Mina, Assaad worked with crews installing high voltage cabling. He then worked as a taxi driver, but did not have his own car.

There, Assaad married a cousin, Marie in 1952. They were very poor. Assad recalls selling a radio to scrape together money to pay the priest to marry them. He arranged to meet Marie, they went to the church and were married.

Assaad was doing whatever work he could find as a taxi driver. Eventually, he was able to secure work as a driver to Dr Nini, an eminent doctor in Tripoli. By the 1960s he was earning a meagre 275 Lebanese pounds each week. They simply 'did not have enough money to live'.

The vulnerability of their situation is best shown in the experiences of Marie and her daughters, Alice and Georgette. The girls attended a United Nations run school in El Mina (Tripoli). There they were taught the Quran among other topics. This greatly concerned Assaad and Marie who were of the Antiochian Orthodox faith. Keen for the girls to have a Christian religious education, Marie arranged to clean the Antonine Sisters Maronite school each day after classes in return for lessons for her daughters.

Between 1968 and 1972, political tensions in Lebanon were escalating. The shifting alliances and struggle for power of different political groups saw sporadic fighting, attacks and bombings in different locations in Lebanon. Alice remembers being fearful of these events when they occurred. Georgette remembers the family painting the windows dark blue to act as a blackout colour during air raids.

Assaad and Marie's daughter, Katy, had married and move to Australia with her husband. This, together with their poverty and the political unrest in Lebanon, led Assad and Marie to decide it was time to also migrate to Australia. To do so they borrowed 4,000 Lebanese pounds and 1,000 American dollars from Jack, Marie's brother.

Assaad and Marie arrived in Melbourne on the 11th November, 1972 at 11 in the morning of Armistice Day. As they entered the airport, sirens sounded for a moment of silence to commemorate the end of World War 1. Both the sirens and peoples' actions worried Marie and Assaad as they were reminiscent of the Lebanon they left.

Assaad and Marie and their four children were installed in a caravan in Geelong by Marie's brother at the cost of $2.50 per day. Their luggage from Lebanon was temporarily lost. They only had the clothes in which they travelled. Marie would wash every evening and dry the clothes overnight. They had to walk everywhere in Geelong and carry with them whatever they bought. Assaad and Marie decided there would be more jobs to be found in Melbourne. After a week or two they moved to Melbourne.

As often happens in immigration stories, their landlord proved to be an important support for Assaad and Marie. He took them to the Department of Employment and showed them how to search for work. He also showed them how to get around and use public transport.

Assaad found work at General Motors Holden (GMH). Marie worked at a clothing factory and Alice and Georgette worked in another clothing factory in Collingwood. The two boys attended local government schools in Richmond.

Each week the four workers would combine their pay packets. The weekly amount of $152 was used to pay rent, buy food and clothing and repay money borrowed from Marie's brother.

In another fortunate turn of events, their bank manager (of Jewish background) understood Assaad's Arabic, sign language and broken English. He made arrangements to telegraph regular payments to Marie's brother, Jack. After about three years, Assaad asked the manager if he had completed the payment of the debt he owed (through his $80 a week deposit). The manager explained that Assaad had completed the payment some years previously. He now had $3,000 in the bank. Immediately, Assaad wanted to buy car. The manager advised him not to. He said that the money could be used to buy a house with some additional borrowings from the bank as Assaad and Marie had already proved that they could repay a loan. The idea of purchasing a house after such little time in Australia was unbelievable to them. Assaad and Marie were excited and began to look for a house…, eventually settling on the suburb of Essendon where they bought their first house in Vandberg Road. Upon retiring, Assaad and Marie moved to Gladstone Park in 1998 to a more modern house.

Assaad and Marie both realised the importance of speaking English and insisted that English be spoken in the home by their children so that they would better understand how to speak it.

After three years Assaad moved jobs from GMH to become a driver for Australia Post. He regarded this as an important step as it was a 'good, secure, government job'. He remained in this job for some 30 years until he retired.

Assaad and Marie interacted with a cross section of the community. The only time they interacted with other Lebanese people was when they went to church. Their only interaction with Lebanon, since their immigration, has been through return visits. The contact they had

with family members has been over issues to do with the settlement
of inheritance and property.

As their family grew and grandchildren arrived, this occupied much
of their time. On reflection, Assaad and Marie both stated how
wonderful a country Australia is in terms of the opportunities it has
provided them for a secure life. Assaad and Marie and their children
migrated to Australia looking for a new start free of the restrictions
and fears of Lebanese society of the 1960s and 1970s. They are
delighted to have found it in Australia.[35]

14

AUSTRALIAN-LEBANESE COMMUNITIES, 1947–1975

From the 1950s the Lebanese communities in Australia consisted of first-wave settlers and their children, plus second-wave immigrants and their children. Relations between both groups revealed similarities and differences which sometimes led to competitive relationships in community organisations. Where the descendants of first-wave settlers had established community organisations there was a tendency for them to feel a sense of ownership and control over these bodies which, in turn, led to resentment and challenges from those who emigrated after the Second World War. This was one cause of tension within some churches and other organisations.

As the communities grew larger and as places of worship of different religious communities were established, sectarianism provided another cause of some conflict between the Lebanese Christian communities. Although the Lebanese Maronite, Orthodox and Melkite churches developed separately and peacefully in Australia, there tended to be tensions when they were required to work together in welfare or umbrella organisations, such as Australian Lebanese Associations. However, in Australia the tensions and conflicts within the Lebanese community were more muted than those in the home country and tended to be resolved peacefully, if not always amicably.

Relations between the first wave and their children with second-wave immigrants were complex. On the one hand there was an attraction as they shared the same culture, language and, perhaps, religion. On the other hand, there was a feeling among the first-wave settlers and their descendants that the newcomers were not like the pioneer Lebanese. For their part, the new Lebanese remarked on how Australian the original settlers and their children had become and felt that they had lost their Lebanese ways. They were, at times, referred to as 'the old ones'. Nevertheless, there was a degree of co-operation as established Lebanese helped some of the newcomers find jobs and joined them in business partnerships. Friendships and some marriages were also to be found between the two groups. Despite their differences there was a degree of mixing in community organisations and, especially, in social and sporting activities.

Religious communities

As with the earlier Lebanese immigrants, religion played an important role in defining their identity. Religious identity and practice linked immigrants to their original culture and family. It also provided a link to the wider Lebanese community. The impact of post-World War II immigration swelled the numbers of Lebanese settlers in their religious groups. This resulted in sufficient numbers to support the establishment of more Lebanese churches and mosques. At the same time the influx of immigrants led to changed dynamics within the existing churches.

To recap, in Sydney, Lebanese Melkite and Maronite churches were established before 1900 in Waterloo and Redfern respectively. Antiochian Orthodox Church services commenced with the arrival of Father Nicholas Shehadie in 1913. Although Antiochian Orthodox services were held earlier, the first church was established in Redfern in 1920. By the 1960s there were sufficiently large congregations in each of these denominations to justify the development of additional churches closer to where Lebanese settlers were living.

At this time, the numbers of Lebanese Sunni and Shi'ite Muslims were growing in numbers through the 1950s and 1960s. Adherents of Islam began by congregating in private homes for prayer meetings. Many Sunni Muslims settled in suburb of Canterbury, in Sydney. A house in Lakemba was used as a mosque the 1960s. This later became the site for the Imam Ali Mosque on Wangee Rd. By the 1980s and with increasing Lebanese immigration, sufficient numbers of Shi'ite Muslims settled in Arncliffe to enable the building and support for the al-Zahra Mosque, which was opened in Wollongong Rd in 1983.

A study in adaptation: Father George Haydar of St. Nicholas Antiochian Orthodox Church soon after his arrival in Australia in 1948 and Father Haydar in the 1950s, after some years in Australia.
(Source: St Nicholas Antiochian Orthodox Church Archive Photo)

During the period of substantial migration of Lebanese, the churches and their priests, as well as imams and mosques, played a major role in the settlement of Lebanese in the 1960s and 1970s.

These included Father Nicolas Mansour who served at St Georges Church (later, Cathedral) from 1964 to 2004. In Melbourne, prominent religious leaders during this period were Father George Haydar of the Antiochian Orthodox Church of St Nicholas in East Melbourne. Father (later Monsignor) Paul El-Khoury of the Maronite Church of Our Lady of Lebanon in Carlton and Sheikh Fehme Imam of the Preston Mosque. They were always willing to find jobs for new arrivals, becoming unofficial recruiters for the larger car manufacturing companies as they introduced hundreds of young Lebanese migrants to these factories where they were welcomed as diligent employees. While these and later Lebanese clergy were staunch advocates for their own community, they were always willing to help any newly arrived Lebanese, irrespective of their religious or political affiliations. This assistance went beyond employment and extended to finding accommodation, purchasing furniture, assisting in health crises and other necessities of life.

Father (later Monsigneur) Paul El-Khoury inside Our Lady of Lebanon Maronite church on its consecration in 1955.
(Source: State Library of Victoria)

As well as assistance given to immigrants by the priests and imams, other community members would work alongside the religious leaders to assist new migrants in their settlement in Australia.

Islamic Marriage in Melbourne presided over by Sheikh Fehme El Imam. Fehme El Imam migrated to Australia in 1951 and became an Imam in 1974. He established the Preston Mosque in Melbourne and was a founder of the Australian Federation of Islamic Councils. He passed away in 2016. (Source: Department of Immigration and Multicultural and Indigenous Affairs (DIMIA) 1971)

Other Community Organisations

While the Australian Syrian/Lebanese Association operated in Sydney from the 1920s to the 1940s, the longest established organisation was the Australian Lebanese Association which was established in 1949 in Sydney and 1951 in Melbourne. Its function was to be a 'non-sectarian peak organisation to consider the interests of the Lebanese community as a whole'. Until the Civil War in Lebanon it served as an umbrella organisation for the Lebanese communities in Sydney and Melbourne and as a branch of the World Lebanese

Cultural Union. It was recognised by the Lebanese Government as the representative of the Lebanese community in New South Wales and Victoria. However, with its largely Christian membership, it did not succeed in attracting representation from all sections of the Lebanese community.

Australian Lebanese Association Members in Melbourne, honouring Australian Ambassador to Lebanon, William Forsyth 1967. (Source: Andrew Batrouney)

The various political factions in Lebanon had their counterparts in Australia. These included a number of right-wing parties supporting the Christians in Lebanon such as the Kataeb or Phalangist party, the Lebanese National Liberal party and the Lebanese Forces. Left-wing parties include the Socialist Progressive Party, the Syrian Nationalist party, and the Amal or Shi'ite party. The Lebanese Nationalist Movement was non-sectarian and advocated the integrity and independence of Lebanon.

Arabic media

By the 1970s Australian-Lebanese communities were maturing with a range of religious and welfare organisations being established. A major Arabic newspaper, *El Telegraph*, was published in 1970 and the first Arabic radio programs were produced by the Special Broadcasting Service (SBS) in the 1970s. This decade was a watershed in terms of communication about Lebanon and the Middle East and also about the Australian-Lebanese communities in Australia. The growing number of return visits to Lebanon during this time also increased communication about Lebanon and their village or town. Upon their return from overseas, these immigrants would typically be visited by members of their families and fellow villagers during which information about the home country would be relayed and any gifts and letters distributed.

The 1970s brought about considerable changes in the range of media available to Arabic speakers, including Lebanese, in Melbourne. The four major Lebanese newspapers available in Melbourne were published in Sydney with small sections dedicated to Melbourne community news and advertising. The oldest Arabic newspaper, the *El Telegraph*, was politically neutral. *Al Bairak* started as a Lebanese leftist paper and although its prime motivation was commercial, it still retained something of its original orientation. *An Nahar*, although it too originally had a leftist orientation, later had no political line but offered two to three pages of community announcements. The newest newspaper and the one with the highest circulation was *El Herald*. This paper was supported by the Lebanese Nationalist Movement and favoured the national integrity and independence of Lebanon.

A variety of radio programs catered for the Lebanese community of Melbourne. The Special Broadcasting Service (SBS) offered 10 hours of Arabic broadcasting on radio 3EA. It contained news from all Arabic-speaking countries and from around Australia. The ethnic radio station 3ZZZ offered three hours in Arabic from a right-wing Christian political perspective. Community radio 3CR included a number of programs, including *Saut El Shaab* (*Voice of the Masses*) and *Voice of Arab Women*.

Television programs also revealed great diversity due to advances in communications technology and different Lebanese groups seeking a voice. In addition to the occasional Arabic television program on SBS, there was a community television channel as well as cable television ART (Arab Radio and TV) which showed a variety of telecasts from the Arab world such as Arabic films, sports and general entertainment programs. For example, notices about personal events in both Lebanon and Australia were broadcast on Arabic radio programs.

Both before and during the Lebanese Civil War the press and other media became politicised, as they identified with one or another of the warring factions in Lebanon. However, during the later post-war years, there was an increased focus on entertainment and local or overseas news of personal or community importance.

An Noor: An Australian-Lebanese Journal

'An Noor' - Monthly magazine - A Noor was a Lebanese monthly magazine published for the 30000 Lebanese migrants in Australia. It is printed in English and Arabic.
(Source: National Archives of Australia A12111:1965)

This period also witnessed the unique development of the Australian-Lebanese journal *An Noor*.

A major development, during this period, was the publication of a monthly journal in Melbourne, which provided information from overseas and news about Lebanese-Australian communities throughout the country. A small group of community activists published the first edition of *An Noor* (*The Light*) on Lebanon's National Day, 22 November 1963. Its first editorial, 'A New Light is Born,' outlines the aims of this magazine:

> The publishers take pride in presenting Australia's first Lebanese monthly magazine and, unlike any present or past Lebanese publications, *An Noor* is not confined to any one state or section of the Lebanese community or to membership of any association but will be available and on sale to every Lebanese person in Australia.

Over the four and a half years of its existence *An Noor* included regular news and articles about Lebanon and the Middle East as well as news about the Australian-Lebanese communities throughout Australia. It featured items on National Day celebrations; community functions attended by Lebanese consuls and Australian politicians; family events such as marriages, births and christenings; profiles of prominent Australian-Lebanese; and commentary on Australian national events. The aim of representing news and views of the Australian –Lebanese community as a whole was largely achieved and *An Noor* attracted broad support and readership. However, the demands of producing a monthly magazine proved too great for the resources of this volunteer group and, after four and a half years, the *An Noor* experiment came to an end.

Contacts with Lebanon

Second-wave immigrants were the transitional group in that they lived through the communications technology revolution. Upon arrival and during their first years in Australia, their communication was as restricted as that of their first wave counterparts. Towards the end of the period travel and communications made contacts with Lebanon easier than it had been in earlier times.

The need to maintain contact included not only normal filial feelings but also a sense of obligation to assist their family. This often involved assisting family members and fellow villagers to emigrate and settle in Australia. In this way the second wave was following in the footsteps of Lebanese migrants of earlier years who maintained contact and provided assistance to their family and village.

A second reason for maintaining contact was to obtain information about Lebanon and the Middle East. This was particularly important in the period before the establishment of Arabic newspapers and other Arabic media in Australia and before news about the Middle East was widely reported in Australian papers. They gained information through letters from family and friends and through receiving magazines in Arabic or French about affairs in Lebanon and the Middle East. However, this information was usually some months old.

The explosion of information and communication technologies in the 1990s provided immigrants with the opportunity to use cheaper telephone calls, videotapes, email and the internet to communicate with family and friends in Lebanon. These had the advantage of providing direct, immediate and relatively cheap communication and information. On the other hand, as members of this group entered their sixties and seventies, their age and experience limited their use of these more modern media, except through the assistance of younger members of their families.

15

LEBANESE IDENTITY IN AUSTRALIA
1947–1975

Although family, religion and location have always been key indicators of identity for most Lebanese, during the period after independence some chose to highlight the national identity of Lebanon and the Lebanese people as a whole. This led to a duality of identity in their new home. Some Lebanese emphasised judicial, civic and political equality of all Lebanese, while the majority continued to identify primarily in terms of their religious community.

Not long after Lebanon gained its independence, Lebanese associations sprang up to celebrate the establishment of the Lebanese nation and to represent the Lebanese Government in Australia. Support for Lebanese identity was not seen as incompatible with membership of Lebanese churches and mosques. However, more Christian than Muslim Lebanese initially chose to join these bodies, causing Lebanese Muslims to later establish their own organisations.

Yet another distinction in identity was whether migrants should identify as 'Syrian' or 'Lebanese'. The first-wave immigrants typically defined themselves as Syrian, having come from the Syrian province of the Ottoman Empire, while the post-war immigrants identified as 'Lebanese'. This debate was short-lived after the arrival of second-wave immigrants from an independent Lebanon.

Lebanese National Day function in Melbourne in late 1950s.
(Source: Laurence Aboukhater)

Given the size and diversity of the Lebanese communities in the larger capital cities of Australia, a number of non-sectarian, non-political organisations were established, especially to provide welfare services. Although the Lebanese community is not one of the larger immigrant communities in Australia, it can claim to be one of the more diverse. Lebanese immigrants were more likely to join sectional bodies, whether religious, political, cultural or welfare, rather than bodies seeking to represent the total community. This even applied to sectional 'umbrella' or 'roof' bodies, rather than a single one to represent the whole community. The range of Lebanese community bodies in Australia reflected the diversity of Lebanese in their home country. As such, it provided a layer of identity as some people chose to identify primarily in terms of those groups.

Another fundamental distinction was between those who supported a dominant Christian view of the nation while others saw Lebanon as coming under the umbrella of pan-Arab nationalism. The differences even extended to lineage, with some modern-day Lebanese claiming descent from the ancient Phoenicians, who were known for their trading prowess and educational achievements, while others emphasised their Arabic heritage.

During much of this period both the Australian Government and the wider society embraced the policy of assimilation and defined Lebanese migrants legally as 'aliens' or possibly 'new Australians' but they were certainly not recognised as British-Australians. The desire to assimilate provided an incentive among small groups of Lebanese migrants to join host society bodies, such as the Freemasons and Oddfellows or to participate in sporting activities and to follow local and national sporting teams.

Choice of occupations also tells us much about Lebanese identity. While the first jobs of most post-war Lebanese migrants were in manufacturing industries, many were not content to remain as employees but sought opportunities to run their own businesses. This they found in their own milk bars, delicatessens, taxi-driving, shop keeping and, in fact, in any enterprise where they could work for themselves and put in longer hours than in employment. Often shop-keeping involved a succession of businesses in the one industry. The smaller numbers of people of Lebanese descent who became professionals, such as doctors or lawyers, were often recognised and relied upon by members of the community. While for some Lebanese opening businesses was hazardous, for others it provided the basis for their future prosperity and formed an important part of their identity.

NOTES

1   El Khazen, F 1997, 'Permanent Settlement of Palestinians in Lebanon: A Recipe for Conflict' in Journal of Refugee Studies Vol. 10, No 3. American University of Beirut.

2   Fersan, E 2010, 'Syro_Lebanese Migration (1880 – present): 'Push and 'Pull' Factors in *Viewpoints (Special Edition) Migration and the Mashreq*, The Middle East Institute.

3   Khalaf, S 1987, *Lebanon's Predicament*, Columbia University Press. p. 183
4   Traboulsi, F *Op. Cit* p. 118
5   *Ibid.* p. 116
6   Labaki, B 1992, 'Lebanese Emigration during the War (1975 – 1989)' in Hourani, A & Shehadi, N (eds) 1992, *The Lebanese in the World: A Century of Emigration*. Centre for Lebanese Studies & IB Tauris & Co. p. 172
7   Traboulsi, F *Op. Cit.* p. 109
8   *Ibid.* p. 159
9   *Ibid.* p. 163
10 *Ibid.* p. 173 citing Salibi, K 1988
11 *Ibid.* p. 173
12 Gates, C 1989, 'The Historical Role of Political Economy in the Development of Modern Lebanon' *Papers on Lebanon Series*, Centre for Lebanese Studies. p. 5
13 Foster, L et al 1994, *Gender Equity and Australian Immigration Policy*, AGPS.
14 Brotherhood of St. Laurence 2016, *Opening Doors*, Brotherhood of St Laurence.
15 Fairbrother, K 2012, 'Australia's Immigration Policy Following the Second World War' in E International Relations – Students. www.e-ir.info
16 Jordens, A 1995, *Redefining Australians: Immigration, Citizenship and National Identity*, Hale and Iremonger Pty Ltd.
17 Convey, P & Monsour, A 2008, 'Lebanese Settlement in New South Wales: A Thematic History' for The Migration Heritage Centre, Powerhouse Museum.
18 Batrouney, T 2015, *Memoir: Trevor Batrouney*, Unpublished Monograph.
19 Batrouney, T 2007, *Cherishing the Faith: The Antiochian Orthodox Church in Victoria 1989 – 2006*. St. Georges Antiochian Orthodox Church. P. 59
20 Convey, P & Monsour, A *Op. Cit.*
21 Interview S. Haddad. March 2009.
22 ALHSV 2009, *Family, Business and Community* Exhibition Brochure.
23 Eid, C 2018, *Taxi Fever*, Monograph
24 Interview John Salamy, 2009,
25 Interview Michael Mansour, 2009
26 Burnley, I 1982, 'Lebanese Migration and Settlement in Sydney, Australia', *International Migration Review*, vol. 16, Spring, John Wiley & Sons. p. 106 – 7
27 Parker, B et al 2009, *Geography for Australian Citizens, Teacher Resource Book*. Macmillan. p. 43
28 Martin, J 1976, 14–15, cited in Department of Education and Early Childhood Development 2011 p. 7
29 Victorian Education Department Annual Report 1972–73 p. 9
30 Martin, J 1976, *Op. Cit.* p. 15
31 Suliman, R 2003, quoted in O'Neill. S, Stateline (NSW) Broadcast: 4 April 2003
32 Ibrahim, K 2003, President of the P & C at Punchbowl Boys High, NSW, quoted in O'Neill Stateline (NSW) Broadcast: 4 April 2003.
33 Khoo, S et al 2002, *The Transformation of Australia's Population: 1970–2030*, University of New South Wales Press. p. 59.
34 ALHSV Seminar 2013, *Milk Bar Life* 2013
35 Interview Assaad & Marie Issa, April 2018

PART 4

The Lebanese Civil War, 1975–1990, and Syrian occupation, 1976–2005

The 1975-2005 period brought with it times of great change both in Lebanon and in Australia. Lebanon was the focus of many skirmishes and battles in a proxy war between Israel and the Arab world, in particular Syria. The demographic shift in Lebanon, with the arrival of displaced Palestinians, saw growing support from within Lebanon for strong relations with the pan-Arab world in the struggle against Israel. The effect of the sporadic violence of these events was to destabilise Lebanese society and to destroy infrastructure, especially in the south. The associated dislocation of residents was one cause of the increased emigration in this period.

The Civil War had a far-reaching and long-term impact on the nation of Lebanon, on the Lebanese communities abroad and, above all, on the lives of those who lived through the war and fled from it. The loss of Lebanese lives and lack of information during the war led to protests among families on the fate of the disappeared. This was especially prevalent after the Civil War had ended and through the period of Syrian occupation to 2005.

A major outcome of the war was the increase in the numbers of Lebanese-born population in Australia, especially the growth of the Lebanese Muslim community. This was largely due to the Relaxed Entry Policy which lasted five months, from early October 1976 until February 1977, during which time some 1,000 Lebanese were admitted to Australia each month.

Australia was addressing its own challenges in a more moderate way with no external political intervention. The impact on a society that had accommodated many hundreds of thousands of immigrants since the Second World War was the need to find a way to address the social and cultural complexity brought about by immigration. The softening of the White Australia Policy in the late 1960s and its replacement by the policy of Australian multiculturalism in 1978 provided a blueprint for the development of Australian society for the following 25 years.

Australia underwent a number of economic and social changes during this period. These included changes in the economy, which saw the decline in manufacturing industries and rise of the mining industry, both of which had a significant impact on employment, particularly for unskilled immigrants, such as many of the Lebanese immigrants. The education of the children of Lebanese immigrants provided problems for some young people and their families based around cultural differences and lack of family support. On the other hand, children of families with the necessary financial and cultural resources were able to remain in education and obtain educational qualifications and occupational attainments.

16

THE LEBANESE CIVIL WAR, 1975–1990

Myself and my brother against my cousin, but my cousin and I against a stranger.

Arabic Proverb

The descent into civil war is a complex story including a combination of external and internal factors. External political factors included the demographic movements in the Middle East, due to the ongoing conflict with Israel and the forced exodus of Palestinian refugees. These developments resulted in tensions that simmered throughout the 1960s.

External factors that contributed to the de-stabilisation of Lebanon were the heavy financial involvement of foreign banks which, by 1970, owned some 80 per cent of bank deposits in Lebanon.[1] Secondly, the pressure from pan-Arab nationalism galvanised and provided an alternative political vision that challenged the dominant Lebanese Christian view of the nation. A third factor was the rise and development of a powerful Israel that was determined to see off any Arab aggression by bombarding southern Lebanon and testing the resolve of the Lebanese government and army. We already saw that

Lebanon became a major target for Israel striking at the Arab world when, on 28 December 1968, Israeli commandos launched an attack on Beirut airport. The almost daily Israeli raids into south Lebanon to try to crush Palestinian incursions into Israel created uncertainty and danger in the region and politically throughout Lebanon.[2]

The precarious relationship that Lebanon experienced with its neighbours and as a target by both combatants made life in Lebanon tense and unpredictable. The different relationships of religious groups and factions within Lebanon with their particular allies in the Middle East amplified tensions throughout Lebanon.

Socially and politically, the seeds of disruption were laid with the National Pact in 1943 and the retention of control by the elite families who used their political power to maintain and further expand their wealth and influence. Internally, the intra-group events of this period contributed significantly to the collapse of government. The za'im leaders used their power for their own political and financial purposes. In 1973, 41 out of 800 families controlled the majority of shares in joint stock companies, involving some 70 per cent of the turnover.

Between 1970 and 1974, the number employed in agriculture in Lebanon declined from 50 per cent at the end of the 1950s to just 20 per cent in 1975. This contributed to the emigration of 8,566 persons per year between 1960 and 1970, rising to 10,000 a year between 1970 and 1974. Along with this, émigré remittances increased from 5.38 per cent of GDP in 1951 to 30 per cent in 1974.[3]

Different sections of Lebanese society were 'in motion to contest the established order' and to confront the policies of the commercial/financial oligarchy, expressing in one way or another, a deep desire for political, economic and social change. Limited educational and occupational pathways led mainly young Lebanese to consider emigration as a means of changing their social and economic circumstances and to escape the instability of political turmoil.

The instability of Lebanese society was apparent in a number of key events during this period. To recap, as early as 1968 students and teachers at the Lebanese University held a 50-day strike, demanding increased wages, better teacher tenure and student amenities. In 1972, 16,000 public education school teachers struck for increased wages, the right to join a union and retirement after 25 years of service. The agrarian crisis, where tobacco workers in southern Lebanon campaigned for a better share of crops, resulted in a protest in Beirut in January 1973. In April 1973, the General Workers Union of Lebanon (GWUL) called a general strike which challenged those with oligarchical power by calling for a limit to their privileges through a reduction of rents and an increase in salaries.

Ultimately, attempts at political reform from above did not work. When 'the Lebanese bourgeoisie and political establishment, in both the Muslim and Christian sectors, were unwilling to surrender any privileges for the cause of reform', revolution was made 'in the most vicious and destructive manner from below'.[4] The army became torn between supporting the system of government and the homeland.

The events of this period had a significant impact on the Lebanese people by strengthening their sense of allegiance to diverse religious and political groupings which represented their interests in the face of the ruling group in society. Socially, the events revealed the division between those with wealth and power and those without. The orientation of Lebanon to the west rather than the Arab world and the focus of developing tertiary sectors of banking and finance alienated many industrial and agricultural workers, the most populous group in society.[5]

Those who lived in villages and towns away from Beirut resented the wealth and power of the elite families, which added to their frustration with their own limited opportunities. This group formed many of the emigrants who left Lebanon in this period for economic opportunity with the additional benefit of greater political stability. Their raised expectations, due to the education they received, added to their frustration with discrimination and the limitations of life in Lebanon. The limitations of life in Lebanon were worsened by the continual state of tension and threat between Israel and pro-Arab sympathisers, inside and outside of Lebanon. Many attempted to leave to escape these conditions. Lebanese immigration to Australia grew to 3,000 per year between 1967 and 1971.

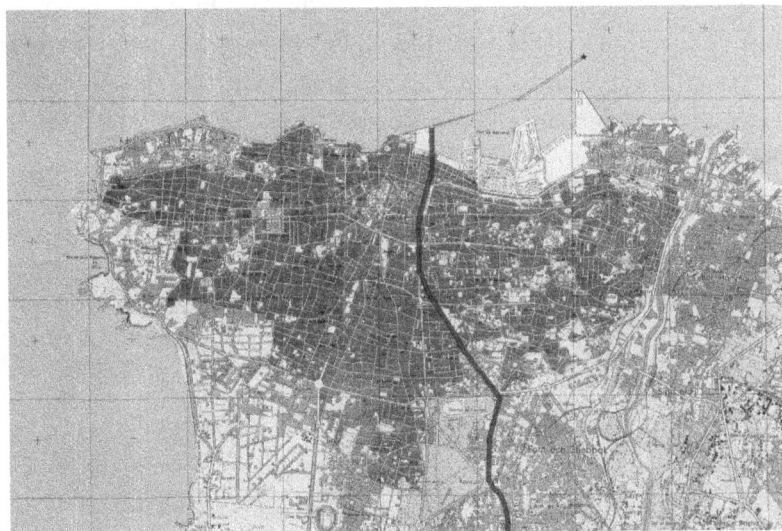

During the Lebanese Civil War (1975-1990), a clear line divided the street battles under the command of religious and ethnic militants. This "green line" passed through the heart of Beirut: from Martyrs' Square, along Damascus Road, separating eastern Christian Beirut from western Muslim Beirut. In Beirut, among the Lebanese, it was known as the Red Line. By foreigners it was called the Green Line because of the green foliage that sprung up along the largely unpopulated line.
(Source: Courtesy of Børre Ludvigsen 2019)

There is no simple explanation for the 15 years of turmoil brought about by the civil war in Lebanon. However, as a result of a range of complex factional alliances the modus vivendi of religious groups was broken, which led to conflict and violence throughout the period; for example, different religious groups which had previously lived together peacefully in villages and towns, now saw each other as enemies. The traditional balance of power, which had existed uneasily before the war, was now in contention because of the politicisation of previously disenfranchised groups and the loss of power by other groups. Different factions controlled different parts of the country as shown by the roadblocks which they used to assert control over their territory.

The war that involved the United States, Israel and Syria in support of factions and factional interests in the Middle East had many complexities that resulted in tragedy upon tragedy. The imprecise estimate of 71,328 dead and 97,184 injured and the three-quarters of a million displaced Christians and Muslims had a devastating impact on the nation of Lebanon and the suffering of those involved.

A woman looking for her children in the aftermath of a powerful bomb that exploded in Tarik al-Jdideh in the mid-1980s. Later she discovered that her children had survived. (Source: Khalil Dehaini)

The Ta'if Accord

After 15 years of fluctuating fortunes, by 1990 all sides in the conflict had exhausted themselves and agreed to an uneasy truce. The war ended after 14 years by 'reconciliation-through-exhaustion' with all sides accepting the principle of 'no victor/no vanquished' and everyone receiving a piece of the pie.[6] This led to the Ta'if Accord in 1991, which produced an agreement that recognised Sunni Islam as the largest group in Lebanon and increased the powers of the Prime Minister who was a Sunni.

Under Syrian mandated power, within the terms of the Ta'if Accord, Lebanon set about developing civil structures to re-establish a functioning society. The most important of these was a constitutional law voted by the Lebanese Parliament on 21 September 1991 to incorporate the Ta'if reforms in a new constitution. In the preamble to the constitution, Lebanon's identity was described as being 'Arab in its belonging' and 'the final homeland for the Lebanese', which separated it from forming a union with other Arab nations, including Syria. In the preamble the law stated that Lebanon would be functioning under a 'system of free enterprise', which was linked to the equitable and concerted development of all regions and to social justice. It was envisaged that Lebanese development was to occur in two phases: the second republic marked by arrangements stemming from the Ta'if Accord and the third republic where political sectarianism would be abolished.

There were some moves to abolish, or at least limit, the influence of sectarianism under these arrangements. The balance of power was altered to one of parity rather than the previous 6/5 Christian/ Muslim ratio. This arrangement was reflected in an increase in the number of parliamentary seats to 128 and in the allocation of cabinet positions. 'Sectarian quotas were abolished in civil service posts, the judiciary, the army and the police, (with the exception of Degree One posts, i.e. Directors-General of Ministries) where parity and rotation were to be applied...'.[7]

The political and social developments under Syrian hegemony resulted in a number of contradictory events that challenged the ideas of reconstruction. The Lebanese army was reconstructed and previous factional members of the military were welcomed back into the newly reformed army. The officer corps was overhauled along non-sectarian lines. Both the Syrian and American armies provided aid to the Lebanese army. However, factionalism was not dead. There continued to be instances of discrimination and persecution for religious and political reasons that were primarily targeted at the middle class who did not have the political connections or wealth of their social superiors to protect them.

Post-war reconstruction of Lebanon

The rebuilding of Lebanon after the war included efforts to repair a fractured society, civil institutions and physical infrastructure. Despite the loss of population through war casualties and emigration, strenuous efforts were made to return Lebanon to a more peaceful society. Depending on commentators' allegiances and perspectives, estimates of the number of Lebanese lost in the Civil War varied greatly. There is much uncertainty and dispute about the exact number of the missing and disappeared. In any event the figures need to be seen in light of the following:

> To date the Lebanese government has made few efforts to examine the truth about what happened during the country's complex past; there has been no serious state-led investigation into the war. As a result there are no official reliable numbers as to the dead, missing/ forcibly disappeared, displaced, injured or physically handicapped— only estimates.[8]

Schools which had closed were re-opened and a range of government services which had been affected during the war were gradually recommenced in some form. During the 1990s educational institutions continued to produce high-quality graduates for a job market that was small and, depending on one's allegiances and connections, limited. In these endeavours, Lebanon sought and obtained financial and personnel assistance from other Arab nations and expatriate Lebanese in the diaspora.

17

THE SYRIAN OCCUPATION OF LEBANON, 1976 – 2005

If you want a country to be ruined pray that is has many leaders.

Arabic Proverb

During the post-civil war period peace in Lebanon was disrupted by three key events which had their origins in regional powers and the weakness of the Lebanese nation. These were the Syrian occupation of Lebanon from 1976 to 2005; the Summer War of 2006 involving the Israeli invasion of south Lebanon and the resistance of the Hezbollah; and the Syrian uprising, commencing in 2011, which produced a flood of refugees and further instability in the region.

The Syrian occupation of Lebanon: 1976 to 2005

Despite some political and social achievements during the post-civil war years, Lebanon continued to experience on-going problems of political instability and conflicts caused by the same political groups, both internal and external, which had been active in de-stabilising Lebanon for the previous 16 years. Syria, Lebanon's larger and more powerful neighbour, took advantage of the chaotic situation and occupied Lebanon from 1976 until April, 2005 during and beyond the civil war.

After the Second World War, Lebanon and Syria had developed

in different directions. Lebanon was moving towards democracy and a free-market economy while Syria came under the influence of the Soviet Union and its totalitarian economic and political systems. Allied to this was the dominant view in Syria that Syria and Lebanon were one country and one people. This was based on the goal of the Syrian Ba'ath Party with its aim to achieve a 'Greater Syria.' This formed the justification for Syria to intervene early in the Lebanese Civil War.

The occupation began when Syria sent in Palestinian units under its control, and later its own troops, to support Christian villagers under attack by leftists in Lebanon. The Arab League was unable to defend Lebanon. It accepted and supported the country's occupation by a large Arab Defence Force, consisting almost entirely of Syrian troops. In this way, the lengthy occupation of Lebanon by Syria was legitimised. An attempt by General Michel Aoun in 1989 to expel the Syrian forces was unsuccessful and their occupation of Lebanon was ratified by a 'Treaty of Brotherhood, Cooperation and Coordination' in 1991, followed by a Defence and Security Pact that same year.

By 1976 it was estimated that there were around 25,000 Syrian troops in Lebanon which, by 1977, had increased to 30,000 troops. By 1990, the Syrian regime had established a hegemonic control over Lebanon. This involved appointing its own proxy government and president in Lebanon, which enabled Syria to occupy the greater part of Lebanon and persecute many thousands of Lebanese who actively opposed the Syrian regime.

The spirit of independence remained alive in Lebanon. University students and professionals started a peaceful resolution to implement the United Nations Security Resolution 520 that called for Syria's complete withdrawal from Lebanon. The decisive period which led to the end of Syrian occupation was 2003-2005 which saw the United States Congress pass a Syria Accountability and Lebanese Sovereignty Restoration Act in 2003. This was followed by France and several other European governments who passed similar legislation.

Amid war-torn Beirut, Um Aziz carries on her chest the pictures of her four sons
who were kidnapped at the beginning of the civil war. She found out later that
they died in Syrian prisons. Um Aziz is one of the thousands of mothers who
lost sons and relatives during the war (Source: al-akhbar.com)

However, this alone did not achieve the withdrawal of Syrians from
Lebanon. In fact, by 2004 there were still 25,000 Syrian troops and
as many as 25,000 intelligence members (*mukhabarat*) throughout
occupied Lebanon. This enabled Syria to enforce a reign of terror
within Lebanon which involved arresting and abducting Lebanese
and subjecting them to imprisonment and summary executions.
As journalist Gebran Tueni stated in June 2005, following the
assassination of colleague Samir Kassir:

> The Lebanese security authorities and the remnants of the Syrian
> system in Lebanon and directly the Syrian regime from top to bottom,
> is responsible for every crime and every drop of blood spilled.[9]

The Syrian occupation of Lebanon lasted until April 30 2005 when
the Prime Minister, Raif Hariri, was assassinated and a public
uprising known as the 'Cedar Revolution' spread through Lebanon
and occupied Beirut. In response, Lebanese citizens opposed to

the occupation formed a coalition which publicly blamed Syria for Hariri's assassination and, once again, called for the withdrawal of Syrian troops. Mass rallies were held in Lebanon and the diaspora until the pro-Syrian government in Lebanon resigned on 14 March 2005. By the end of March 2005, the Syrian government pulled out most of its troops and dismantled its intelligence stations in Beirut and north Lebanon. These developments led to Syria's full withdrawal from Lebanon on 30 April 2005.

The Syrian occupation had dire consequences for Lebanon. It led to a de facto loss of independence as a succession of Lebanese governments and presidents were not able to govern with autonomy but rather in the interests of the occupying power. During the period of occupation Lebanon was little more than a client state.

On the one hand, it led to resentment and opposition by those who advocated a free and independent Lebanon. On the other hand, the occupation was supported by those who advocated close links between the two nations under the rubric of a 'greater Syria'.

Opposition to the Syrian occupation extended beyond Lebanon to include some Lebanese in the diaspora, as shown in a letter from the United Australian Lebanese Movement (UALM) to members of the Australian parliament:

> Our major concern is the continued Syrian occupation of Lebanon and the ensuing denial of Lebanon's independence, integrity and sovereignty. Since 1975 as many as 35,000 Syrian troops have occupied Lebanon on the pretext of the civil war among Lebanese religious factions and Israel's presence in southern Lebanon. However, the end of the civil war and Israel's withdrawal from southern Lebanon has not led to the end of Syrian occupation.

> The Syrian occupation violates international law and hinders Middle East peacemaking. It is contrary to the spirit of the 1989 Ta'if Accord, signed by Syria and other Middle Eastern nations that recognised 'the aim of the Lebanese government to impose its control over all of Lebanese land'. It also flies in the face of the 1982 United Nations Security Council resolution calling for 'the withdrawal of all non-Lebanese forces from Lebanon'.

On behalf of the people of Lebanon and the Lebanese communities around the world, we seek your active assistance in achieving... a free, independent and sovereign Lebanon.[10]

The Lebanese population in Lebanon struggled with their daily lives under oppression from Syria and from the ebb and flow of political and group allegiance in Lebanese politics during the War and the occupation. Sections of the population were threatened at different times by militia and political groups in towns and villages in Lebanon. It was the Lebanese of the diaspora who had the freedom, wealth and love of homeland to raise their voice. Unlike their relatives in Lebanon, they were not involved in the daily struggle to survive or the habitual vigilance of knowing how to negotiate their lives in a war zone.

The peaceful 'Cedar Revolution' achieved its aim of independence for Lebanon through a combination of mass rallies in Lebanon and the diaspora, international pressure, especially from the United States and France, and resolutions of the United Nations.

The Cedar revolution mobilised thousands of Lebanese coming together wanting to see an end to Syrian occupation and intervention in Lebanese life. This rally took place on March 14 2005. (Source: Damir Sagolj)

A major unresolved issue is the number of combatants and civilians who went missing during, and immediately after, the war. In 2000, the Lebanese Government agreed to establish the first commission on the missing and forcibly disappeared. Two more commissions followed: a 2001 commission to investigate the disappeared who may still be alive, and a 2005 joint Lebanese-Syrian commission. These commissions have been severely criticised for failure to take steps to fulfil the government's obligation regarding victims' rights to know the truth.[11]

Despite the efforts of some political parties and large sections of the population, Lebanon remained under Syrian occupation until the Syrian military's gradual withdrawal in 2005. The withdrawal of Syrian troops, while celebrated by many Lebanese, was also a cause of further unrest, especially among those sections of the population which saw close ties between Syria and Lebanon as the better future for Lebanon.

18

AUSTRALIAN SOCIETY 1975–2005

In Australia, these three decades brought rapid changes in many areas. Its population continued to grow and become more diversified with the influx of Indo-Chinese refugees from Vietnam and elsewhere in Asia between 1978 and 1985. The Indo-Chinese refugees from the last years of the Vietnam War led to desperate arrivals coming to Australia. The most numerous of these were the Vietnamese arrivals. In 1976 the first boat arrived in Australia carrying Vietnamese refugees. This was followed by a further 53 refugee boats in the following years. The Vietnamese population increased rapidly: by 1991 there were 124,800 Vietnamese-born people in Australia which increased to 185,000 by 2001. Exact figures are not known, but up to 80 per cent of the boat people might have perished on the high seas.

The Lebanese population in Australia also increased, as a result of relaxed entry requirements for that short period during 1976–1977. During these five months Australia experienced significant economic fluctuations and social changes. These included an influx of peoples from war-torn countries.

Australia was in the grip of an economic downturn in 1976 and the following years. The impact of world-wide fluctuations due to oil shortages saw many Australian markets contract in Europe and the United States. The manufacturing industry, which had survived due to tariff barriers, became less competitive against Japanese and other Asian-manufactured products. It began to decline in the

1970s, while the Australian economy was propped up by primary sector exports. By the early 1980s, farming had given way to mining as the main primary industry while manufacturing was beginning to decline as a percentage of GDP. These developments led to a decline in the numbers of those working in the farming and manufacturing sectors. Given these trends, concerns were expressed in Australia on the viability of accepting immigrants when the economy was undergoing such changes and there were insufficient jobs for Australian workers in traditional industries. At the same time Australia was developing more liberal policies on immigration and citizenship.

Australian government immigration, citizenship and settlement policies, 1975-2005

By the 1970s, after several decades of non-British immigration, Australia was moving from being essentially a mono-cultural society to becoming a multicultural one. Not only was its population becoming much more multicultural than it had been in the 1940s but public policy was also developing in response to this shift.[12] For example, in 1973 the Government proclaimed that future immigration policy would not distinguish between immigrants on the basis of race, colour or nationality. During this period Australia continued its policy of admitting some refugees, with those from Indo-China now replacing the earlier post-war intake from Eastern Europe. Although Lebanese were not officially designated as refugees, special arrangements were made in 1976 to resettle in Australia persons displaced by the Civil War in Lebanon.

The last vestiges of the White Australia Policy were abandoned from 1973 in favour of an immigration policy of non-discrimination on the bases of race, colour or nationality. However, the decisive year in the breakdown of the White Australia Policy was 1976 when the first 'boat people' arrived in Darwin and special concessions were made for Lebanese escaping from the Civil War which had begun in Lebanon.[13]

The policy of assimilation had by now given way to the emerging policy of multiculturalism. By the mid- to late-1970s Australian governments had adopted a policy of multiculturalism. This was based on the idea that membership of ethnic communities is legitimate and consistent with Australian citizenship as long as certain principles (such as respect for basic institutions and democratic values) are adhered to.[14]

Lebanese Folk dancers at Wiley Park, NSW as part of the Canterbury Carnivale 1979 marking the centenary of the municipality of Canterbury.
(Source: Canterbury City Council Library Local History Photograph Collection)

As a result of immigration and the growing diversity of the Australian population, citizenship law and practice were altered progressively from the late 1960s, when the impact of non-British immigration first began to be felt. These changes reflected a general movement from an Anglo-Australian, mono-cultural conception of citizenship to one that recognised the multicultural character of the Australian community. These changes encouraged a broader basis for inclusion and sought to broaden access to all the rights that accompany Australian citizenship.

In these years, the Australian population was becoming more culturally diverse which led, over time, to changes in Government immigration and settlement policies. A major change was the adoption of a non-discriminatory immigration policy which allowed the acceptance of immigrants and refugees from a wider range of source countries than had previously been the case. The second major change was to abandon the policy of assimilation which encouraged new immigrants to adopt the culture and language of mainstream Australia as quickly as possible. Based on policies within both the Galbally Report (1977), and the Report on Migrant and Multicultural Programs and Services (ROMAMPAS 1986), proposed settlement services were developed which recognised and respected the cultural diversity of immigrant groups and ethnic communities. This led to support for ethnic community organisations, including those which employed welfare workers from within their own communities.

In the meantime, from the 1980s the forces of economic rationalism had been exerting a growing influence on immigration and settlement policies and particularly after the election of the Howard Government in 1996. Economic rationalism had an impact on migrant selection criteria, the introduction of user pays and the abolition of cost-free migration. It also supported the sale of government properties and facilities, the outsourcing of services and the abolition of the Immigration Department's research and multicultural policy bodies. These administrative changes after 1996 were accompanied by the government's weaker commitment to the policy of multiculturalism.

From the mid-1990s there was a decline in consensus about migration and immigrant policies among the major political parties in Australia. Previously, policy and decisions about immigration had been politically bi-partisan. They were now based on the down-playing of multiculturalism and the assertion of a crude form of Australian nationalism. This was seen in an increase in negative attitudes to refugees and asylum seekers – attitudes which were taken up enthusiastically by certain sections of society including some politicians, some in the media and some in the general population. The rise to prominence of a few populist politicians influenced the development of government policies and public attitudes against asylum seekers and, to a lesser extent, against other immigrants. The negative attitudes to asylum seekers came to a head in violent confrontations between groups of Australians in 2001.

The 'Tampa' incident, 2001

Two events provided a key turning point in Australia's immigration history. First, Australia's action against the Norwegian freighter, the *Tampa*, in August 2001 illustrated the Australian Government's hardline rejection of 'boat people' and its determination to protect Australia's borders by any means. Just one month later came the destruction of the Twin Towers in New York by Muslim terrorists, causing major loss of life and an uprising of fear and insecurity around the world, including in Australia. The destruction of the Twin Towers was a major international incident which provided reinforcement of the Australian Government's attitudes and actions towards 'boat people,' as illustrated by the Tampa incident and the Pacific Solution.

This involved the Australian Government refusing to accept a large number of refugees who had been rescued by the *Tampa*, after their unseaworthy craft sank in rough seas on their way to Australia. The Government followed this by enacting the Border Protection (Validation and Enforcement) legislation in September which declared Christmas Island, Ashmore Reef and Cocos Island to be outside Australia's 'migration zone.' This was followed by reaching agreements with Papua New Guinea and Nauru to house asylum seekers at Australia's expense.

Although most Lebanese immigrants were not defined as refugees during this period, the introduction of these measures created negative social attitudes to Lebanese and other immigrants from the Middle East. During this period Australian-Lebanese were particularly concerned with vilification of their community as a result of some violent crimes committed by some Australian-Lebanese youth in Sydney.

19

AUSTRALIAN IMMIGRATION FROM LEBANON, 1975–2005

He who wants to eat honey should endure the stings.

Lebanese Proverb

The impact of the Civil War and Syrian occupation on Lebanon's social and economic conditions saw a mass exodus of 894,717 migrants leave Lebanon between 1975 and 1989. About a half of these emigrants left for oil-producing Arab countries and a half emigrated to other parts of the world. Between 1975 and 1980, some 18,000 emigrants made their way to Australia, compared with 32,000 to the United States and 20,000 to Canada. The main occupations of these Lebanese emigrants included workers in industry (32 per cent), construction (30 per cent), transport and communications (20 per cent) and trade (16 per cent).[15]

Patterns in emigration showed that there was a link between the level of economic development and prosperity of the recipient countries and the level of qualifications of emigrant workers. America attracted skilled workers, Europe attracted businessmen and students, the Arab Gulf Countries attracted businessmen and technicians, while Africa attracted workers of lesser skill categories. Qualified Lebanese engineers mainly went to work in the Middle East, in particular in Saudi Arabia and Bahrain.[16] Their professional qualifications, trade training and cultural understanding (including the ability to speak Arabic) ensured a relatively easy transition to their new society.[17]

These emigrants were part of a total number of some 990,000 people, or 40 per cent of the entire population, who sought refuge, either temporarily or permanently, from political conflict in Lebanon. Of these, some 300,000 eventually returned to Lebanon. One half of the remainder went elsewhere in the Middle East and the other half emigrated to Europe, North and South America, Africa and Australia. These emigrants were of different faiths and migrated in family groups. Responding to submissions by members of the Australian Lebanese community and also to international demand to provide a safe haven for those displaced by war, the Australian Government allowed open sponsorship of Lebanese emigrants for a short period in 1976–1977. Community and religious leaders would use their more educated members to fill in application forms, often irrespective of the formal immigration criteria. This period witnessed great growth in the Lebanese community, due in large part to the activities of community and religious leaders.

As we saw, this Relaxed Entry Policy lasted from early October 1976 until February 1977, during which time some 1,000 Lebanese were admitted to Australia each month. In all, between 1976 and 1981 more than 16,000 Lebanese came to Australia. Sponsorship by relatives in Australia was the mechanism for well over 90 per cent of this intake.[18] This influx more than doubled the number of Lebanese-born residing in Australia, which reached 71,349 by 2001.

Many emigrants were initially displaced from their home towns and villages in Lebanon. Given the urgency of their migration and the chaotic nation from which they came, they resembled refugees more than traditional Lebanese migrants emigrating for economic and social improvement. At the time of their arrival in Australia many of these third-wave immigrants were disturbed by the traumatic events of the Civil War and lost in their new setting. Unlike the first two waves of Lebanese emigrants to Australia which were mainly Christian, this third wave of immigrants was largely Muslim (mainly

Sun'ni with smaller numbers of Shi'a and Alawi).

As with earlier patterns of Lebanese migration to Australia, professional emigrants to the Middle East, the Americas, Europe and Australia either emigrated with their wives and children (75 per cent) or joined their extended family (49 per cent).[19] In joining their extended family, Lebanese emigrants fitted into an existing model of chain migration that used known social networks to aid settlement by reducing their sense of isolation. It also aided the transition to a new country by pointing to tried and proven pathways for success. Using these networks reduced the cost of migration and settlement, for both the immigrant and their country of destination, increasing the likelihood of successful settlement.[20] Lebanese emigrants who fled the civil war did not fit neatly into this model.

Those who left to escape the impact of war often did so with minimal preparation and considerable urgency. They paid for passages by air or by sea, depending on their resources. Their need to escape was so great that many journeyed indirectly to their destination, making stops at countries and towns along the way before reaching their destination. Two of the more common locations where emigrating Lebanese waited for migration papers or travel documents were Cyprus and Athens. Whether they intended to return to their homeland was unknown and not fully formulated. However, many were hopeful of returning to their home country once the war ended.

Something of the impact of the war on children is illustrated in the account of a return visit to Lebanon by a young woman, who was wounded as a child during the war. She clearly had mixed feelings about family and country during her five day return visit:

> When I first arrived I was scared... I didn't know whether I would enjoy it. I did like the country but I didn't want to meet my relations...I didn't want family members to plan my agenda... I wanted to breathe the air... I didn't want to be cramped...I felt I had to feel it [Lebanon] like a bird flying.

She also makes clear that the wounds she experienced were more than physical:

> Lebanon did nothing for me. I cannot deny where I came from …
> [but] as a child being forced to leave the country I don't think was fair.
> Someone has a big responsibility …children don't forget pain…why
> should I invest in a country that tried to hurt me? That tried to deny
> my future?

This young woman identified another motivation for return visits of those who were forced to leave hurriedly because of the war:

> We always wanted to know what had happened because we left
> everything behind… had people renting the furniture and apartments.[21]

Inevitably, the Civil War caused an extensive exodus of people from Lebanon to a number of destinations both in the Middle East and the traditional countries of Lebanese migration. At the conclusion of the conflict many, who had left Lebanon, returned to their homes while others left Lebanon permanently. Their decision to settle outside Lebanon or to return home was influenced by their education and occupation as well as the availability of a support network in either place to aid their transition.

Although the Ta'if Accord marked the end of major hostilities in Lebanon, there was much uncertainty about how binding the agreements between warring groups would prove in the future. Those who remained tried to pick up the threads of their daily existence by returning to their homes or settling elsewhere in the country. Those estimated 990,000 who left had to decide if their future lay in joining the Lebanese diaspora or returning to their homeland. It was estimated that nearly three-quarters of the emigrants departing between 1975 and 1990 went to Western Europe, North America or Australia, destinations where migrants typically settled permanently. Those who left for other destinations in the Middle East and North Africa were more able to maintain a home and, in some cases, a family in Lebanon, while commuting to their place of work on a more or less regular basis.[22]

Against the background of domestic and civic disruption and the horrors of civil war, emigration continued after 1990 with some 10–14 per cent of Lebanese citizens leaving between 1992 and 2007. In the absence of any official figures, studies by both Choghig Kasparian[23] and Anis Abi Farah[24] estimated that Maronites, Sunni Muslims, and Shi'a Muslims emigrated in roughly equivalent numbers to their proportions in the Lebanese population.

This group of migrants was diverse in terms of their education and occupation. Many who emigrated had been educated beyond high school and worked in banking or other tertiary industries. A large proportion of men held skilled trade jobs, and a similar number had labouring jobs in Lebanon. Lebanese women, who emigrated with their families, were typically educated to secondary and, in some cases, tertiary level. However, many emigrants possessed skills that did not translate to an industrialised western economy or held qualifications which were not initially recognised in Australia.

Immigration requires significant adjustment to new economic realities as well as social and cultural norms. This applied, in particular, to Lebanese immigrants in the period 1990-2014, coming as they did from a country suffering from the effects of civil war to a nation undergoing economic change and experiencing considerable unemployment. This had an impact on Lebanese men and women in their roles within their families and was the basis for significant identity and even mental health issues. The experiences of many immigrants in Australia, in particular men with families, challenged their self-perceptions as effective members of society at large. Perhaps the greatest difference in immigration to Australia was moving to a nation where the rule of law was paramount rather than the potency of individual actions within the context of family and village.[25] This was especially the case for males who emigrated from a patriarchal society and arrived at one with equal political rights for women and men.

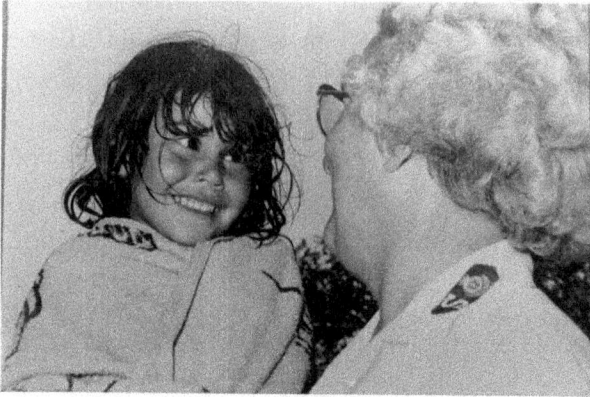

Salvation Army Officer with Lebanese 'refugee' Girl, Maria, 3 years old, in Sydney. 1980s.
(Source: University of Wollongong Archives. Stuart Piggin, Faith of Steel Collection)

There are no official data to give precise numbers of emigrants from Lebanon and their destinations. However, a study of 8,061 Lebanese families in 2001 sheds some light on emigrants and their destinations.[26] The 33,958 people in the sample included 10,000 young people between the ages of 18 and 15 years. Of this group, only a little more than 25 per cent intended to emigrate, mainly for work and better working conditions. The destinations for those intending to emigrate were the USA and Canada (33 per cent), the Gulf States (25.8 per cent), and Australia (12.4 per cent). In numerical terms, of the initial 10,000 young people in the sample, 1,072 intended to emigrate, and of these approximately 128 were intending to make Australia their home. The majority of those intending to emigrate were male: 67 per cent compared to 33 per cent female. The religious breakdown of the intended emigrants was: Shi'ite 27.7 per cent, Maronite 24 per cent, Sun'ni 23 per cent, Druze 7.7 per cent, Greek (Antiochian) Orthodox 4.3 per cent, and Greek Catholic (Melkite) 1.7 per cent.

Further, Lebanese American University sociologist Paul Tabar explores the motivations for Lebanese emigration. He claims that there were two forms of 'push' factors: periods of relative political stability but limited economic disadvantage, and periods of both catastrophic political instability and human displacement. For example, emigration during the period from 1990 to June 2009 was caused by primarily economic push factors, while the period from July 2006 to May 2007 was a period of political disruption, resulting in emigration.[27]

After 1975, Australia received more than 20,000 civil war refugees who were largely poor, sometimes destitute, and over half Muslim. They transformed the character of the Lebanese community in Australia, especially in Sydney where 75 per cent of the Lebanese born population were concentrated: '....an overwhelmingly Christian Lebanese community was confronted with new Muslim immigrants and sectarian identity polarised by war. The older community regretted what they saw as the passing of old values ...'.[28]

The experiences of Faddy Zouky and his brothers and sister illustrate these circumstances. When asked why he left Lebanon to come to Australia in 1984, Faddy replied:

> The civil war in Lebanon became unbearable. It was very hard for us to get any education. [B]asically we were forced to leave because any resemblance of a future was gone out the window because of the war – especially in 1983 – Lebanon was at its worst.[29]

Some Lebanese emigrants between 1975 and 1989 had the social, economic and logistical means to emigrate. Depending on their resources and connections, families might move to safety elsewhere in the Middle East, to Europe, the Americas or Australia.[30] This was no orderly migration as many people fled their homes unprepared for life in a new country. Furthermore, during the Civil War the disruption to education, training and employment of the Lebanese population led to major settlement problems in their countries of migration.

> As a result of the dramatic events occurring in Lebanon, Australia and Canada witnessed an unprecedented increase in the number of Lebanese immigrants. Between 1976 and 1981 more than 16,000 Lebanese came to Australia, which raised the number of Lebanese-born in Australia to 51,371. After ten years (1991) the number had increased to 68,995, with an almost equal number (67,453) of second generation Lebanese-Australians.[31]

Many Lebanese immigrants arriving in Australia between 1975 and 1990 came under an Australian Government Special Humanitarian Program to provide refuge for those displaced by war. The settlement needs of these arrivals from Lebanon were detailed in research undertaken in Sydney and Melbourne by sociologist Michael Humphrey and historian Trevor Batrouney respectively. This was a period when the Australian Government was prepared to respond to humanitarian need and multicultural diversity.

Throughout the 1990s and into the new millennium, Lebanese immigration to Australia slowed markedly, especially after 1991. Between the years 1981 and 1991, the Lebanese-born population in Australia rose from 49,623 to 68,995, representing an increase of 19,372. In the following decade, the Lebanese immigration rate slowed from a national total of 68,995 in 1991 to 71,349 in 2001, indicating an increase of 2,354 over ten years. By the 2006 census, there had been an increase of Lebanese-born to 74,848, an addition of 3,499 people from 2001.

We turn now to the settlement of this group of Lebanese immigrants in Australia.

20

SETTLEMENT OF LEBANESE IN AUSTRALIA, 1975 - 2005

We never used to give a thought to separation and now for us to be together again is beyond our dreams
Arabic proverb

This chapter focuses on the settlement needs of the post-civil war immigrants and the different approaches by the Australian-Lebanese community and government departments in meeting those needs. We also examine the employment patterns and the extent and causes of unemployment among this group. The role of the family and community in providing jobs for the newly arrived is highlighted.

To reiterate, the critical events in the Lebanon region such as the Arab-Israeli War of 1967, the outbreak of civil war in 1975, and the Syrian occupation of Lebanon, saw significantly larger numbers of Lebanese immigrants arriving in Australia than in previous years. The attacks on Lebanese territory and the rising tensions inside Lebanon saw people leave to seek safety and security in other parts of the world.

The fortunes of Lebanese immigrants already settled in Australia had differed from those of earlier times. Some families had opened their own businesses in the food industry while others chose to remain working for employers. As money was accumulated and loans paid off, better quality housing was acquired or investments were made. In addition, the children of the earlier immigrants were completing school or starting work in trades or the professions. Life in Australia began to provide the security and safety for themselves and their families that was their motivation for immigration. This also resulted in the growth of Lebanese communities in each of the capital cities and in some provincial towns.

The Lebanese-born population showed a marked increase between the censuses of 1966 and 1976 even before the Lebanese Civil War. In 1966, the Lebanese-born population in Australia was 10,273; by 1976 it had risen to 33, 434. This represented an increase of 31 per cent over ten years. Australia's population in the same period grew from 10.62 million to 13.54 million, an increase of some 27 per cent. New South Wales continued to attract by far the largest numbers followed by Victoria, with much smaller totals in the other states and territories (see Table 5 Pt 2). By 1996 there were 36,539 Lebanese-born males and 33,685 Lebanese-born females across the nation, revealing a situation of near parity between the sexes.

The increase in Lebanese migration during this period suggests that people felt the need to leave Lebanon, even before the outbreak of civil war. Among the factors causing this migration were escalating fear and concerns about the safety and security of life caused by on-going tensions and sporadic conflicts across Lebanon and the region. The causes of these conflicts were many, including the increase in pan-Arab sentiment in opposition to Christian dominance: Israeli-Arab conflicts in the region, and the Israeli invasion of Lebanon; as well as the on-going economic inequality of the society. Within Australia the easing of the White Australia requirements meant that the nation was now prepared to accept the vulnerable and displaced, regardless of ethnic background.

This period saw a considerable increase in the diversity, complexity and size of the Lebanese community. This led to the proliferation of community organisations: religious, political, welfare and cultural. This made the task of a single umbrella organisation difficult, if not impossible. It led, instead, to the creation of a number of umbrella organisations for different sections of the community.

Settlement patterns of Lebanese immigrants

The demographic profile of Lebanese immigrants to Australia showed a dramatic change compared to those who arrived in earlier times. The majority of those arriving continued to settle in Sydney rather than in Melbourne or the other capital cities of Australia. In contrast to earlier waves of Lebanese immigrants, they were predominantly Islamic in religion, rather than Christian.

> In 1971, 14 per cent of the Lebanon-born population in Australia had been Muslim; in 1981 the Muslim share had grown to 31 per cent. Humphrey (writing in 1988) estimated that Lebanese Muslims in Australia were about two thirds Sunni and one third Shi'ite. Most of the Shi'ites came from the poverty stricken south of Lebanon, but via Beirut. Even though their region of origin was poor, those who reached Australia were from a higher socio-economic bracket than the Sunnis, who came from the North. For example, Shi'ite women were better educated, more likely to have paid work, and lived in slightly smaller households than Sunni women. While most settled in Sydney, especially in the south-western suburbs, the Sunnis established the Imam Ali Mosque in the suburb of Lakemba and the Shi'ites the Al-Zahra Mosque in Arncliffe.[32]

In Sydney, Lebanese settlers concentrated around Bankstown, Liverpool, Ryde and Parramatta.[33] Other suburbs with high concentrations of Lebanese-born were Lakemba, Harris Park, Mount Lewis (18 per cent), Punchbowl (16 per cent), and Greenacre. Suburbs north-west of these, such as South Granville, Old Guildford and Guildford, also had relatively high numbers of Lebanese settlers.

In Melbourne, the location for the third wave of Lebanese settlement followed a similar path to earlier Lebanese settlers. New arrivals initially settled in the inner suburbs of Coburg, Brunswick, Northcote or Preston where cheap housing could be found. Some remained in these areas, eventually purchasing houses. Others moved to outlying areas to the north, to the west and to the south-east for larger, more modern housing on larger allotments. This is evident in Campbellfield,

Dallas, Coolaroo and Roxburgh Park. Lebanese settlers from villages in Lebanon initially tended to live close to each other. However, churches and mosques were not established in outlying areas until several years after Lebanese settlement. Until then, Christian and Islamic settlers would travel to churches and mosques, sometimes many suburbs away.

A characteristic of many Islamic Lebanese, especially the Sunni, in this period, was the large numbers of children in families. Fertility was both a symptom of educational level and, more broadly, of socio-economic status in its impact on immigrants' lives.

Lebanese Muslim households, in the 1990s, had a much lower weekly household income than Lebanese Christians and their lower income had to meet the needs of more members. Indeed, their income per household member was half the national average.

Nonetheless, Lebanese immigrants to Australia were socially and economically advantaged compared to many family members and villagers who remained in Lebanon. This put pressure on them to provide remittances to family members in Lebanon during this period of disruption and crisis. The total value of annual financial transfers to Lebanon between the years 1971 and 1981 increased dramatically from USD 884 million to USD 8,640 million.

Between 1971 and 1981 many Lebanese immigrants came from rural backgrounds where 20 per cent of Lebanon's GDP was produced by 60 per cent of the workforce, mainly from unproductive farms.[34] A smaller number of immigrants came from independent and small factories and enterprises where they worked as skilled or unskilled labour. Those who arrived as immigrants between 1975 and 1990 had few skills that were relevant to the Australian economy of the 1980s and 1990s. With a rapidly declining manufacturing industry in Australia, coupled with their limited educational levels, significant numbers of immigrants experienced difficulties in gaining employment, an essential requirement for successful settlement.

The disrupted lives of those who left Lebanon due to the civil war, led to many settlers who were struggling with their new lives in Australia. The disruption to education and training meant that many young people arrived with little education and few occupational skills. The difficulty of schooling in another language as well as the relative permissiveness of Australian culture challenged the values of some immigrant families, especially those of the Islamic religion. Those who emigrated felt the burden of trying to settle in a foreign country while maintaining their connections with, and support for, their family in Lebanon.

> The third post-1975 wave suffered all the problems that come with refugee status and forced departure while the Muslims among them lacked the pre-existing ethnic institutions of church and community networks that had been established by earlier waves of Christians.[35]

By 1978 there were 50,723 Lebanese-born in Australia which grew to 56,337 by 1986. Just five years later the number of Lebanese-born in Australia had increased to 70,213 by 1991. The breakdown of settlement by state and sex is shown in Table 5 Pt 2. Lebanese-born settlers were mainly concentrated in New South Wales with 75 per cent of the Australian total living there, while about 20 per cent lived in Victoria. This proportion was to become the established distribution pattern of Lebanese settlement in Australia.

This influx coincided with an economic downturn in Australia in the late 1970s and into the early 1980s, which markedly reduced employment opportunities for new arrivals. It also limited the capacity of the Lebanese communities to provide them with much needed settlement assistance. It is against this background that we now examine the establishment of dedicated welfare agencies to meet the settlement needs of the post-civil war Lebanese arrivals. This is followed by a discussion of two major settlement needs facing Lebanese families: employment and education.

Meeting settlement needs

Two case studies follow. The first focuses on Sarkis Karam, a young man who came to Australia in the early years of the civil war. It illustrates the impact of the civil war on his education in Lebanon and his struggle to fulfil his 'childhood dream to be a journalist' in Australia. It also shows that the links with his home village and the Lebanese community in Sydney remained strong after his migration. As a community activist, Sarkis was involved with the Lebanese community in Sydney and, at the same time, he sought to demonstrate his loyalty to Australia and contribute to Australian society.

Sarkis Karam

Leaving his village of Zgharta, 16-year-old Sarkis arrived in Sydney in February 1977 with his siblings and his mother to join his father and uncle. They had collectively made the decision to leave Lebanon during the crisis. He and his family settled in a rented house in Earlwood close to where his mother's brother was living in Canterbury. Sarkis had missed approximately two years of school because of the Civil War. Once he arrived in Sydney, he completed an English language course for four months and went to Sydney Technical College to complete his 'day matriculation' (equivalent to the HSC).

Over the years, Sarkis worked in an assortment of jobs in printing, in clothing companies, taxi driving and owning a café. Throughout this time, Sarkis wrote articles for Lebanese papers in Australia to fulfil his childhood dream to be a journalist. In his forties, Sarkis was able to return to college to obtain an interpreting and translating qualification. Now he works as an interpreter and translator and continues to be a freelance journalist writing articles on Lebanon and Lebanese politics that are picked up by the Lebanese press in Australia. Throughout his time in Australia, he has mostly interacted with Lebanese-Australians, mainly from Zgharta, and with 'Lebanese in general' because of shared experiences and a common culture.

Sarkis has worked voluntarily for Australian-Lebanese community organisations to be part of community-wide activities. He realised, however, that they are limited in the support they provide: 'They do not provide any real help for settling in this country – financially or even guidance. They are lacking a lot in that respect. They organise functions for people from the same village or background.'

The Zgharta Association provided an effective link for members to get to know each other and to attend functions together. In working with these organizations Sarkis stated that 'we always promoted the fact we are Australian and [that we] respect the rules of this country.' Sarkis explained that the function of these associations was to achieve social and political things for Lebanon and for Australia. 'As a village association, we raised funds for Lebanon. We would always send some contributions for the underprivileged or for the village. We always do things on Australia Day – we want to pay something back to this country'.[36]

The second case study is of a community organization, the Australian-Lebanese Welfare (now known as Arabic Welfare, or AW). It identifies the post-war immigrants' range of settlement needs and reveals the different approaches of traditional Lebanese community leaders and Australian Government departments. In particular, it reveals the initiative taken by the Commonwealth Government and the responsiveness of the Lebanese community in the 1980s.

Australian-Lebanese Welfare: the beginnings

By the early 1980s the Australian Government had become aware of the dire situation of the Lebanese new arrivals. In response, the Department of Immigration and Ethnic Affairs (DIEA) took on a proactive role in seeking out community leaders and professionals in Melbourne in order to devise ways of helping with the settlement problems.

The national director of the DIEA, together with the regional director in Victoria, invited a number of Lebanese community leaders to a meeting in Melbourne in 1981 to discuss how the Department might best offer assistance to the newly arrived Lebanese. At this meeting the community leaders presented a traditional approach, asserting that they would be able to look after 'their own people'. This contrasted with the suggestion of a professional of Lebanese background at the same meeting who proposed the government fund and resource a research project to examine the problems and needs of the newly arrived Lebanese in Melbourne and to develop recommendations for the consideration of government.[37]

In the event the DIEA representatives sponsored the research proposal which produced a report entitled *Settlement Problems of Lebanese in Melbourne* (1982). This set out for the first time a detailed analysis of the structure and functioning of the Lebanese community and the settlement problems the new arrivals were experiencing. These included language and communication, childcare, family problems, income security and employment, problems with the law, and health problems.

The report found that there was a need for government-funded welfare workers to work specifically with Lebanese new arrivals. The key conclusion was the need to complement existing traditional support structures with modern professional welfare services:

In moving away from reliance on traditional Lebanese support structures which cannot be expected to cope with the problems of Lebanese settlers in the current economic climate, we must aim to develop a composite service delivery system that is ethno-sensitive and viable within a complex, divided and demoralised community.[38]

It was against this background that a small group of professionals of Lebanese background in Melbourne established a dedicated non-sectarian, non-political welfare body known as Australian Lebanese Welfare, later renamed Arabic Welfare. This body was incorporated on 18 November 1985, which enabled it to engage in welfare work and to undertake other related activities for the benefit of the Lebanese community.

In Sydney, a different model of service provision emerged within the Maronite community, centred around the Eparchy in Strathfield. Australian educated professionals worked with priests to identify and develop counselling services and support networks for community members.

Maronite Counselling Service – Sydney

The Maronite Counselling Service, began in offices at the residence of the Maronite Archbishop in Strathfield, Sydney in the late 1980s. The service represented a model of service provision that acknowledged, and was in response to, the cultural, social and emotional realities of the community attempting to come to terms with the wave of immigrants fleeing from civil war in Lebanon. This wave provided different cultural influences and shifted the community and social dynamic among the Maronites.

A young, Arabic-speaking, psychology graduate, Judy Saba, a member of the parish, was working voluntarily to support Father Michael Kayrouz, an English-speaking priest, in his work in the community. The then Archbishop Abdo Khalife, auspiced what started as a program that included diversity perspectives within new and emerging school-based education programs. Changing demand within the community saw support needed for a wide range of social and interpersonal issues beyond school-based programs.

It was becoming apparent that Lebanese community members went to local doctors for medical attention but resulting referrals to counsellors and psychologists were mostly ignored. The notion of an independent person to whom one would speak of intimate and personal issues was foreign and, sometimes, misunderstood among the community. In fact, many of the Maronite community would seek the counsel of their own clergy when dealing with mental health, relationship, identity and family issues as they believed that the clergy would ensure that confidentiality would be maintained. In those early days, Judy Saba recalls being brought into conversations by the clergy with members of the community desperate for assistance. The many hours of listening to the specific needs of the community led to the creation of a counselling service that worked within a culturally responsive, faith-based framework.

As trust was built, referrals grew. Judy was joined by two additional counsellors: Rony Kayrouz and Debbie Draybe. In parallel, Australian-born Maronite priests, Fr Geoffrey Abdallah was also working with youth and Fr (now Monsignor) Shora Maree, were pivotal in working closely with the growing community. Over time, the reputation of the program as culturally appropriate and relevant to community needs, saw Muslim and other Christian Lebanese seeking assistance.

The success of referrals to counsellors within the Church community began to gain acceptance to the point that the priests themselves saw a need for training. An ongoing training program for priests was implemented to help them identify issues, develop assessment and referral skills and to work with the counselling team to develop an integrated counselling service. It was important to respond to the growing demands placed on clergy as well as to the growing needs of the community.

The issues that were being addressed ranged from presentations of domestic violence issues, drug related issues, gambling addiction and depression, anxiety and identity issues. Many of these issues are still relevant today. The development of a youth service, continued by Fr Geoffrey, saw the recruitment of youth workers including Lisa Makhlouf. Father Geoffrey also ran a program supporting Maronites in prison and their families.

A number of suicides among young Maronite men in the late 1999 – 2001 saw the beginnings of a community-based suicide prevention program. This was the initiative of a community member, George Boutros, who had lost his best friend to suicide. Within the Maronite community, active fundraising for a program also helped draw attention to the issue. The 'Friends of Friends Suicide Prevention Mentor Program' sought to empower interested community members to engage with feelings of alienation and grief among people at risk. The program trained and placed volunteer community members in touch with those identified as at risk and who were either unwilling to attend structured counselling or who simply needed support following counselling. It also provided funding from the community to employ a psychologist, Natalie Moujalli, as project co-ordinator and under her guidance the project flourished.

The devastating loss of lives revealed that some families tended not to understand the signals sent by their son's or daughter's withdrawn behaviour. From their view, any isolating behaviours were seen positively in terms of their own cultural beliefs as 'he's a good boy, he stays at home, he is no longer out partying..' when, in fact, the behaviours may have been indicators of distress and even, what western psychology would term, indicators of suicidality.

By way of illustrating its effectiveness, between 2006 and 2007, the Maronite Counselling Service saw 284 clients between two psychologists and one counsellor, and the Friends of Friends Project trained over 24 mentors and delivered numerous community workshops at church and community venues across Sydney. One of the trained volunteer mentors explains it:

> … my support mentor Selene and I have seen our mentee progress so much and overcome many challenges and we are so proud of him. I have realised that being a mentor basically means providing an ongoing one to one relationship and an opportunity to work more closely with someone to explore their challenges and difficulties.

As was evident in other community initiatives, the cultural capabilities and education of the Australian-born children of Lebanese immigrants provided a new context for the delivery of services. New rules and procedures facilitated new ways of counselling through a cross-cultural lens to make services relevant to clients. This was achieved by working within a community religious structure and engaging cross-cultural psychology skills to gain the acceptance and support of clients, their families and external funding bodies. This was achieved by negotiating confidentiality issues within a small and close-knit community.

In the short term, the culturally-based strategies, outlined above, ensured the success of the Maronite Counselling Service. It attracted government funding and community donations. Over time and with fewer Lebanese immigrants, the need for a specific counselling service diminished. The successor to the Maronite Counselling Service, MaroniteCare, now provides services catering to different community needs.

Occupations

From their earliest arrival in Australia, Lebanese have followed a distinctive occupational pattern marked by high levels of self-employment, particularly in commercial activities, such as hawking and shop-keeping. In 1901, '80 per cent of Lebanese in New South Wales were concentrated in commercial occupations'.[39] By 1947 little had changed, as 60 per cent of Lebanese were either employers or self-employed. However, with the mass migration of Lebanese after the Second World War and especially after the Civil War in Lebanon, the proportion of self-employed steadily declined. Nevertheless, even in the 1991 census, Lebanese men and women were 'noticeably over-represented as self-employed'.[40]

The occupations of Lebanese settlers in the post-civil war period were heavily influenced by two issues: the nature of the Australian economy and the educational and social backgrounds of Lebanese immigrants. In the years immediately following the civil war the Lebanese sought their first jobs in manufacturing industries. However, by the 1980s, production costs in Australia were rising due to oil shortages, reduced tariffs and inflation. This led to reduced demand for unskilled labour that saw high levels of Lebanese settlers facing unemployment. While recent arrivals experienced language and cultural barriers to workforce participation, the major factors in their unemployment were changes in Australia's economy and society which limited opportunities for unskilled Lebanese immigrants.[41]

In the late 1970s and early 1980s workforce participation of recent arrivals from Lebanon showed high levels of unemployment. In Sydney in 1984, the employment rate of Lebanese-born males was 65 per cent and for females 28 per cent. Males between the ages of 20 and 39 years had the highest workforce participation rates. In particular, those with higher education levels were more likely to be in work. Among Lebanese youth aged 15 to 19 years 41 per cent of males and 59 per cent of females were unemployed. The greatest influence on employment was whether the job-seeker was born in Australia or in Lebanon. More than half of the Lebanese-born immigrants did not regain the same occupational status they had in Lebanon. Of note, were the lower participation rates of Sunni Muslim males and females in employment compared with Lebanese of other religions.

The unemployment rate for Lebanese-born in Melbourne was as high as 28.2 per cent in 1984. The unemployment rate in a number of municipalities exceeded this rate: Darebin (30.5 per cent), Hobson's Bay (34.3 per cent), Hume (35.1) per cent Maribyrnong (45.7 per cent), and Moreland (39.1 per cent). This unemployment rate reflected the decline in manufacturing industries that traditionally provided the first jobs for unskilled Lebanese migrants in Melbourne.[42]

Lebanese women experienced significant challenges in participating in the workforce. Their participation in work was dependent on factors such as age, proficiency in English, parental status, educational level and their previous occupation, if any. Women who were employed were mostly involved in unskilled work such as factory or labouring jobs. Most teenage females (71 per cent) were engaged in education while 17 per cent were involved in work. Only 32 per cent of women between the ages of 20 and 24 years were participating in paid work, while between the ages of 25 and 40 years of age even fewer (25 per cent) of the women were working. Marriage and child-rearing may have been contributing factors

Within Lebanese communities in the main Australian cities,

traditional village allegiances and networks emerged as a means of providing employment. For example, expatriates from the Lebanese village of Hadchit, living in the western suburbs of Sydney, employed *wasta*, a form of favouritism based on kinship. The term also refers to networking and building business connections through returning favours, much like the concept of *quid pro quo*. In business, this might mean working together, supporting each other's businesses and giving 'mates rates'. The networks of *wasta* played a significant role in finding work for members of the community, especially within the construction industry.

This extended to a Hadchit telephone directory for community members to use the services of other community members. Reliance on traditional village allegiances became a network of mutual obligations or *wejbet*. This involved initially accepting lower wages and providing help to one's sponsoring family in response to immigration and settlement support. Once the settler married or set up another household, the network continued to provide assistance in finding work and advice and support in the consolidation of capital in investments.[43]

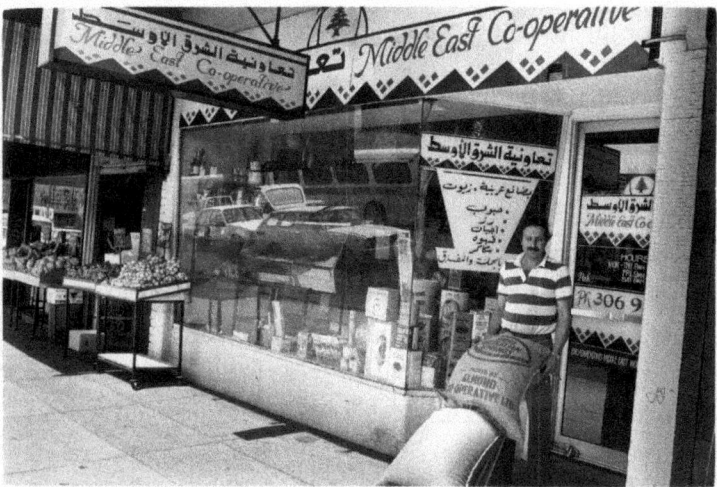

Middle Eastern Co-op in Glenroy Victoria 1988. It was supported by Government funding to address employment issues in Melbourne's northern suburbs.
(Source: State Library of Victoria)

In reflecting on his experiences of migration to Australia, becoming educated and qualified and establishing many successful businesses, Faddy Zouky eventually saw a reason in his father wanting to take the family back to Lebanon after a brief visit in 1969:

> If we did not return to Lebanon, we probably would not have been as successful in Australia. Experiencing the hard life gives you the strength, the ambition, the dream and the vision to do well in your life. You also find that situation in Australian people [who see things] as very hard or tough. We find them to be mere challenges because we've experienced far tougher circumstances or situations. You also learn to appreciate opportunities in Australia. [Following our successes] we were able to look back to Lebanon and to understand and appreciate what Lebanon was all about.[44]

Establishing a new life in Australia also meant families working together as an economic unit. By applying attitudes to family and family closeness that were traditional in Lebanon, many families used the varying abilities, talents and educational levels to grow and develop, in some cases, complex and highly lucrative businesses. Faddy Zouky goes on to explain the way his family worked:

> Siblings became close to work together and to use our closeness to establish a successful business. Each of us has our own talent and way of doing things and we put all of these together. Dad taught us … if you have three sticks together you cannot break them – one by itself you can break. It is important that we stick together and succeed together.[45]

Education

The children of Lebanese settlers arriving between 1975 and the 1990s confronted a number of problems in adjusting to schooling in Australia. In some cases, these limited their success while in other cases they provided the incentive to achieve success in schooling and society.

A major problem was the impact of the civil war on their families and their typically urgent departure from their homes to relocate elsewhere in Lebanon or to seek refuge overseas. Inevitably this had a negative impact on their schooling. At the outbreak of hostilities many students in primary or secondary schools had their education abruptly terminated or disrupted. Families fled their homes as the ebb and flow of war changed the allegiances of villages around Lebanon. The educational experiences of many of the children of Lebanese settlers arriving between 1975 and the 1990s reflected the disruptive effects of civil war on life in Lebanon.

Education was not the highest priority for many families after migration. They often felt the need to have as many family members as possible earn money to contribute to the running of the household. Many children, although eligible to continue their secondary schooling, were unable to do so, instead joining the unskilled workforce.

The educational background and socio-economic status of Lebanese families, often from rural and village backgrounds, tended to limit their children's success in Australian schooling. In particular, the challenges of unfamiliarity with Australian culture and the English language caused stress and dysfunction at a time when Australian schools operated on a model of immigrant assimilation of language and cultural knowledge shared by the wider society.

By 2001, the majority of Lebanese-born males (59 per cent) had no post-school qualifications. Of those with qualifications, post-school diplomas (22 per cent) were twice as frequent as those with degrees (11 per cent) The low level of educational attainment had an impact on household income and often cast the family in a lower socio-economic status than they may have occupied in Lebanon.[46]

The experiences of Lebanese students in Australian schools in the late 1970s and 1980s saw the emergence of a number of issues including cultural unfamiliarity of school and the difficulties students faced in adapting to new ways of learning. In Sydney, Professor Ken

Cruickshank's study of literacy using case studies of students, their school and their families, notes elements of cultural difference that existed between Lebanon and Australia as well as across generations:

> In Lebanon, our parents would tell us if we didn't behave they would tell the teacher. Here the teachers say, 'If you don't behave we tell your parents'. Every week I get asked up to the school. I do not know what to do. My son is a good boy. Why does he get into trouble all the time?'.[47]

The aspirations of students like Ahmad are derived less from their schooling experiences and more from the expectations of parents and the Lebanese community within which they exist:

> Ahmad was attending martial arts classes regularly, something he started at his father's instigation when he was being 'picked on' at school. He had gained several awards at a local club. ... when Ahmad was in Year 10 he was tall for his age and good looking. He had started to take much more time with his appearance... He was studying Arabic through the community school run by the village association. Ahmad was seen as difficult by his parents and as a troublemaker at school. His parents had hopes that he would go to university. Ahmad wanted to be a mechanic or car detailer like one of his cousins.[48]

The experiences of Ahmad, like many other Lebanese students, showed the different sources from which they drew their values about school and education. Ahmad lived most of his life within the local Lebanese community and absorbed its values. He was challenged at school by the expectations of conforming behaviour and by the academic requirements of literacy and numeracy in a language that was not spoken at home. He also gained positive feedback from the awards he received from his participation in martial arts. The achievements that he valued come from within his extended family and community.

The relationship between Lebanese-Australian youths and wider Australian society clearly had an impact on the cultural and educational experiences of these youths. A study of the relationships of Lebanese-Australian young people and the wider Australian culture found that immigrants live not only between their traditional and adopted cultures, but also between segments of society depicted by intellectual, material and social divisions.[49]

This tension contributes to the challenging behaviours of young people as they try to negotiate meaning and identity between the traditional values of their parents and the daily realities they face in their new culture. Evidence of this can be found in the ways that Lebanese-Australian youths would come into conflict with teachers because the instructors would not work in the social and cultural field of these students but impose Anglo-Australian social values. As one student respondent commented about his teacher, 'he gives me no *face*', meaning that his teacher did not acknowledge his importance as a person, balancing the key cultural values of being respectful and maintaining strong cultural traditions while negotiating the values and new culture of the school system. The impact and significance of this related directly to the traditional Lebanese value system where 'communal reputation' (the Arabic *wajaha*) is being threatened among adolescents in the eyes of the individual student and in the face of other students, including other Lebanese students.[50]

Notwithstanding the cultural differences that education highlighted for some Lebanese children, school provided effective pathways for many Lebanese immigrants and their children to gain valued qualifications and occupations. These students responded to parental pressure to achieve highly and exhibit their success in the eyes of their community. Stories of immigrant educational achievement in rising from humble backgrounds, not only among the Lebanese but among other ethnic groups, became part of the folklore of Australian multiculturalism.

21

GROWTH OF AUSTRALIAN–LEBANESE COMMUNITIES, 1975–1990

*Do good and throw it into the sea – if it is not appreciated by an ungrateful
man, it will be appreciated by God*

Arabic proverb

The Civil War had a major impact on the Lebanese in Australia.
The first concern of those with family in Lebanon, especially in the
known war zones, was to seek information and assurances about
the safety of their family. Early in the war the most reliable form of
communication was personal, through family members and village
friends, who were able to return to Lebanon to offer what help they
could. During the war, Badawie Khoury, a well-known and trusted
member of the Melbourne community, went to Lebanon, laden with
letters, money and offers of different forms of assistance which he
distributed.

Lebanese community organisations at this time offered as much
help as they could but their leaders often lacked the knowledge and
expertise to offer professional assistance. Nevertheless, various forms
of help from priests, imams and their congregations, as well as known
community leaders, were welcomed, coming as it did from trusted and
familiar sources. Much of this early assistance tended to be informal
and limited in scope. For example, if a family in need approached a
priest for assistance, a likely response was to send around a plate in
church and give the proceeds to the needy family.

During the height of the Civil War religious leaders travelled to Cyprus or Athens to help arrange passage to Australia through the period of the Relaxed Entry Policy in 1976-1977. In Australia religious and other community leaders cultivated positive relations with officers of immigration departments and obtained help with applications for sponsorship.

From the 1980s special purpose Australian-Lebanese welfare organisations were established with bi-lingual staff qualified in welfare. These bodies were largely funded by governments and were required to conform to government regulations and reporting requirements. Religious bodies also became more professional in their management and organisation. In addition to their religious services, they started to offer a range of activities, social, sporting and cultural, to appeal to their young people and retain them in the faith.

The years 1975-76 marked a watershed in the life of the Lebanese community in Australia. They ushered in a period in which immigrants from Lebanon were fleeing political turmoil and civil conflict and, for the first time, Muslims now began to arrive in larger numbers than Christians. As we are emphasising, these changes in the number and backgrounds of post-Civil War immigrants altered the size and composition of the Lebanese community in Australia.

In many respects the Lebanese community was unprepared to meet the unprecedented settlement needs of this post-civil war wave. While Lebanese individuals, families and organisations struggled valiantly to assist these newcomers, they lacked the resources, expertise and structures to do so effectively. This applied in particular to the Australian Lebanese Association (ALA), rendered largely ineffectual by community divisions. The assistance offered instead came from families, religious bodies, village associations and political bodies.

Furthermore, this immigration wave had an important psychological effect on the established Lebanese communities. For example, it challenged the self-perception of the Melbourne community, which was described in a report as a:

... united, Christian, respectable, upwardly mobile, propertied, business-oriented, community which, through its religious (and lay) leaders had developed links with people thought to be influential in government, professional and business circles.[51]

The Civil War shattered that self-image and caused it to be replaced by power struggles that had reduced Lebanon to chaos, thereby depriving the new arrivals of many of the established leaders and the resources they controlled. Old settlers deserted established Lebanese community organisations, notably the ALA, that had been unable to maintain unity of the Melbourne Lebanese in the face of political and religious divisions.

The Lebanese community not only faced unprecedented settlement needs but also deep political and religious divisions which limited its capacity to meet those needs. Furthermore, sections of the community engaged in blaming the new arrivals for bringing the existing Lebanese community into disrepute and lowering its status in the eyes of the Australian community.[52]

Community organisations

The increase in the Lebanese-born population in Australia during this period led to the establishment of a large number of community organisations to serve the increasing diversity of the Lebanese in Australia. These included churches and mosques, educational and welfare bodies, village associations, political organisations, media outlets, and cultural and sporting bodies. Some of these organisations were solely or predominantly for Lebanese-Australians while others served the wider Arabic community.

The Lebanese in Australia had historically sought to establish 'umbrella organisations' to cover the whole community. However, given the divisions, this has proved difficult to achieve. For example, the Australian Lebanese Association (ALA) was established as early as 1951. Until the Civil War in Lebanon, the ALA served as an umbrella organisation for the Lebanese community in Melbourne and as a branch of the World Lebanese Cultural Union. It was recognised by the Lebanese Government as the representative of the Lebanese communities in New South Wales and Victoria. However, it did not succeed in attracting representation from all sections of the community and it was, in fact, almost exclusively Christian in membership.

The policy of Australian multiculturalism, as exemplified in the Galbally Report in 1978, was significant for the emergence of community organisations. This report proposed a funding and political model adopted by government which led, in turn, to the proliferation of ethnic community organisations. These bodies typically received government grants and the anointing of community leaders to administer funding and to act as spokespeople.[53]

As we already noted, a number of community organisations had been established in Sydney and Melbourne. Each of these bodies was non-religious, non-party political and committed to serve the Arabic community as a whole. Three community organisations are listed in what follows, each with different origins.

The first of these bodies to be established in Melbourne was *Victorian Arabic Social Services* [VASS] (formerly the Victorian Arabic Network) in 1981, with the original aim of bringing Arabic community workers together for support, exchange of information, and joint action. Its activities included monitoring welfare service provision and advocating on behalf of the Arabic community; providing information and cross-cultural training sessions on issues related to the Arabic community; and working in partnership with mainstream organisations, such as schools, to meet the needs of the Arabic community.

The *Arab Council Australia* (ACA) of New South Wales had a different origin. It was established in 1992 as a direct response to the racism experienced by members of the Arabic community in Australia during the Gulf War. The Council engaged in a range of activities to promote Arabic culture and language, eradicate racial vilification, raise public awareness on international human rights issues, oppose negative depictions of Arabs in the media, encourage accurate reporting on Arabs and Arabic issues, engage in educational activities, and respond to government inquiries.

Arab Council Australia

Arab Council Australia began as a grouping of Arabic-speaking community workers in Sydney in 1979 under the name of Arabic Welfare Interagency. They began to meet as a means of supporting each other and sharing strategies in meeting the growing needs of Lebanese who emigrated due to the Civil War. The organisation employed its first staff member in 1983 and by 1990 it had employed a total of 15 staff members. Because of its expanded role, its name was changed in the late eighties to become the Australian Arabic Welfare Council.

The Australian Arabic Welfare Council gained a significant role in the community because it attracted funding and support from the Department of Immigration, the Department of Human Services, the Ethnic Affairs Commission plus large funding from the Department of Community Services. It also attracted funding from the Department of Education for a tutorial program and student support program.

The shift in function of the Arab Council Australia reflects changes in Arabic-speaking immigrants in Australia. In the 1980s the central role of the council was advocacy for the issues of the Arabic-speaking community as a whole. During the next decade the number of Lebanese migrants and refugees declined and communities from other countries in the Middle East grew. In recognition of this, the Council changed its name to the Australian Arabic Communities Council. Through the 2000s the Arab Council Australia played two roles: advocacy on behalf of the community, and providing services for the community. The latter role fluctuated based on government funding. The final change of name happened in 2004 when it became

Arab Council Australia.

Currently, the main activities of the Council are conducted through five Units:

- Administration and Information
- Communication and Events
- Strengthening Communities
- Strengthening Families
- Youth and Leadership

According to long-standing members, the survival of the organisation to date is a miracle, given the internal politics of the community and the fact that the word 'Arab' and 'Arabic' is no longer a unifying term. Its survival is due to its capacity to deliver services above and beyond its funding. It does not have a power base, like a church or mosque or village group. The broad reach and non-partisan nature of the Arab Council Australia has meant that it can attract funding for services needed by the community.

The Public Service prefers to work with Arab Council Australia for its capacity to deliver professional services. On the other hand, governments in New South Wales prefer to fund single identity groups such as religious, political or village groups. These groups may have a greater political influence over their members and can possibly direct votes of their members. This is the challenge that the Council faces going into the 2020s decade.[54]

Religious Organisations

The different historical periods, each with their different 'push' factors, affected the religious composition of the various waves of immigrants. As we have seen, the first two waves were predominantly Christian, while the third wave was predominantly Muslim. By the year 2,000 Muslims constituted 38.6 per cent of the Lebanese-born persons in Australia, with Sunni making up 34 per cent and Shi'ites around two per cent. Catholics accounted for around 40 per cent of

Lebanese-born in Australia, including Maronites (30 per cent) and Melkites (10 per cent). The Antiochian Orthodox constituted at least 11 per cent of the Lebanese-born in Australia. Smaller numbers of Druze (two percent) and Protestants (two percent) were also found among the Lebanese-born.

In Sydney and Melbourne, churches and mosques were the earliest and, for many Lebanese, the most significant community organisations. The motivations for establishing these religious bodies were to reproduce and maintain the religious and cultural practices of the country of origin. In what follows, we outline some of the major developments in these religious communities during this period.

Maronite Catholic Church

An important development in the history of the Maronite Church in Australia took place on 14 July 1973 when Archbishop Abdo Khalife was appointed by Rome to be the first Bishop of the new Diocese of St Maroun in Sydney, Australia. Archbishop Khalife completed his term in 1991 and was succeeded by Bishop Hitti on 4 March 1991. The major achievements of the Maronite Churches in Sydney and Melbourne were the establishment of organisations to meet a range of child care, educational and aged care needs of the Maronite community and others.

The history of the Maronite Community in Victoria dated from the arrival of Father (later Monsignor) Paul El-Khoury in 1955, and the opening of the first Our Lady of Lebanon Church. The second stage was marked by the arrival of Father (later Monsignor) Joseph Takchi in 1982 and his work with the young people of the community. This period saw an increase in those serving the Maronite Community in Melbourne with the arrival of the first Antonine Sisters in 1980. This was followed by the arrival of a small number of Antonine monks in 1998 to undertake pastoral work in the widespread Maronite community.

From their arrival in Melbourne the sisters offered language and religious education classes for children of the parish and beyond. Soon after, the community began to expand its services with the establishment of a child care centre in 1980 and a college with primary and secondary campuses in 1997. A major achievement of the Antonine Sisters was the founding and management of a hostel for the elderly of the parish and others. They built their own convent and they participated actively in the religious, cultural and social activities in the parish. In all that they do the sisters see themselves as 'serving their people in the name of the Church'.

A major milestone in the history of the Maronite parish in Melbourne has been the establishment of Our Lady of Lebanon, a large, modern church in Thornbury, consecrated in March 2008. The church represents a happy combination of modern church architecture and traditional Maronite church items such as the stained-glass windows depicting Maronite saints and the marble altar, both of which were produced in Lebanon.

The larger Maronite community of Sydney houses Our Lady of Lebanon Co-Cathedral in Harris Park, which is the seat of the bishop. They have established some ten parish churches spread around the suburbs. The Maronite Sisters of the Holy Family run two aged care facilities, a pre-school and a college with primary and secondary campuses. Given the size of the Maronite community in Sydney they have been able to offer the same range of facilities as the Church in Melbourne as well as a convent which houses the Sisters.

The Maronites have maintained strong spiritual links with their Patriarch in Lebanon while the monks and nuns of the Antonine Order have links with their superiors in Lebanon. Through these relationships the local Maronite community supports many charitable organisations and activities. For example, during the Civil War, the Parish supported orphan children and poor families.

While the Maronites are an Eastern Catholic Rite, their church has adopted some Latin devotional practices, such as the Rosary and devotion to the Sacred Heart. This has meant that Maronite immigrants were more easily able to adapt to worship in local Catholic churches than were other Lebanese immigrants. Attendance at these churches provided an important means of assimilation into the local Catholic Church and wider Australian society.

Melkite Catholic Church

The Melkite Church is also an Eastern Rite Catholic Church, with its own bishop for Australia. The Melkites were the first Syrian community to establish their own church of St Michael's in Waterloo, Sydney as early as 1897. Additional churches in New South Wales include St John the Evangelist Parish in Greenacre and St Elias Church in Guildford. In Victoria, there are three Melkite parishes: St Joseph in Fairfield founded in 1972; Sts Peter and Paul in Hampton Park founded in 1988; and St Elias the Prophet founded in 2000. The other states of Australia have a smaller Melkite presence, usually a mission or a small parish.

Melkite parishes include not only Lebanese but also considerable numbers of Egyptians and Palestinians. A key figure in the Melkite Church was Archimandrite Aftimos Haddad, who served the Australian Melkite Community from 1964 to 1996. During this time he renovated St Michael's Church and, in 1973, he was appointed Apostolic Vicar overseeing the Melkite community throughout Australia. The first Melkite Bishop of Australia, Bishop George Riashi, was enthroned in 1987, which marked the beginning of the Melkite Eparchy in Australia.

Both the Maronite and Melkite churches have had an ambivalent relationship with the local Catholic Church. On the one hand, they are recognised as Catholic churches with allegiance to the Pope of Rome. As such, they have adopted some of the liturgical practices of the western Catholic Church and have benefited from the financial and in-kind assistance granted by the local Catholic Church. For example, many Maronite and Melkite priests from Lebanon have attended

Catholic theological colleges, especially the Maronite College in Rome, and have generally attained a higher educational standard than has been available to other eastern clergy. The Catholic hierarchy has also helped the eastern Catholics in Australia with the acquisition of Church property for rental or purchase.

On the other hand, both Maronite and Melkite churches have strenuously sought to assert their identity as communities of eastern Christians. For example, the Maronites have retained their Eastern liturgy with its distinctive chanting and iconography. The Melkites share many of the practices of the Eastern Orthodox churches; they have retained their Byzantine liturgy, their traditional iconography, and have not adopted compulsory celibacy for their priests.

Antiochian Orthodox Church

Syrian (later Antiochian) Orthodox were among the first Lebanese to settle in Australia. They were smaller in numbers than the Maronites and did not receive the assistance from established Catholic churches as did the Melkite and Maronite Lebanese. A major development was the appointment in 1969 of Bishop Gibran Ramlawi as the first Bishop of the Antiochian Orthodox Church of Australia and New Zealand. Following the passing of Bishop Gibran in 1999 and the arrival of his successor, Metropolitan Archbishop Paul Saliba, in the same year, there was great expansion of the Church in Australia.

Although Sydney always had larger numbers of Antiochian Orthodox than Melbourne, the histories of their churches in both states were remarkably similar. Both the Sydney and Melbourne churches revealed the influence of the Russian Orthodox Church on the first Antiochian Orthodox places of worship. In both cases the first priests had been trained in Russian Theological Colleges and they brought out icons and other Church items from Russia. The Antiochian churches in Australia also ministered to the Russian Orthodox before the Russians established their own churches. This was particularly the case in Melbourne where the first priest, Archimandrite Antonious

Mobayed, was fluent in Slavonic and familiar with Russian forms of worship.

St Nicholas Church in East Melbourne experienced a period of expansion with the arrival of Lebanese immigrants in the years after the Second World War. The increase in numbers led eventually to the opening in 1971 of a second Antiochian Orthodox Church — that of St George's in Thornbury. Despite a difficult beginning, St George's eventually became a large and flourishing church, which met the spiritual and other needs of the large numbers of Lebanese and other Arabic-speaking immigrants who settled in the northern suburbs of Melbourne in the 1970s and 1980s.

During this period St Nicholas played an important representational role for Orthodoxy in various inter-church forums, while St George's met the spiritual and other needs of large numbers of Orthodox Lebanese. More recent developments have seen the founding of two new parishes: St Paul's in Dandenong (2001) and St Mary's in Kingsville (2004). The Church in Melbourne has also been active in establishing missions, which include The Good Shepherd (2004), St Herman of Alaska (2001), Forty Holy Martyrs in Mirboo North (2005) as well as St Basil the Great and The Holy Transfiguration.

The Antiochian Orthodox Church in New South Wales also underwent great expansion during this period with nine churches being established in Sydney and in the larger provincial towns. These were in addition to St George's Cathedral in Redfern, the Mother Church of the Antiochian Diocese.

Islam

Islam has a long history in Australia which extends back to the early 1700s when Indonesian Muslim fishermen made annual contacts with the Indigenous inhabitants of northern Australia. The second major contact with Islam was with camel handlers from Afghanistan, India and Pakistan known as 'Afghans.'

The Afghan camel drivers were the first Muslims to arrive in Australia in any numbers. It is estimated that during the period 1867-1910 between 2,000 and 4,000 came to Australia to provide transport in the outback. These were joined in the latter part of the 19th century by Indian Muslims who became farm labourers and hawkers…The first mosques in Australia were established in Adelaide in 1890 and Broken Hill in 1891 …[55]

There followed a break in contacts with Muslim arrivals until the great migration from Lebanon, Turkey and other Middle Eastern nations in the post-war years, which led to about 3,500 Lebanese-born Muslims in Australia in 1971. The period following the civil war in Lebanon saw a major change in the religious landscape of the Lebanese in Australia. Unlike the first two waves, Muslims now formed a majority of new arrivals. Just two decades later, the number of Lebanese-born Muslims had increased to more than 25,000. The number grew quickly due primarily to Australia's family reunion policy and the relatively high birth rate of Lebanese Muslim families. By 2016, the total number of Muslims, from all Islamic immigrants, had grown to 604,200 or 2.6 per cent of the Australian population.

The great majority of Muslims in Australia were Sunni with much smaller numbers of Shi'a Muslims. Most Muslim Lebanese migrants settled in south-western Sydney: the Shi'a gathered around the Arncliffe mosque and the Sunnis at the Lakemba mosque. Only a handful of Islamic mosques had been established in Australia before the Second World War. Given the large numbers of Muslims in the third wave, the 1980s and 1990s witnessed a dramatic expansion of Islamic societies and mosques to serve the Lebanese and other Muslims. By 2016 there were as many as 60 mosques in Sydney with the Lakemba Mosque, established by the Lebanese Muslim Association, being the largest and best known.

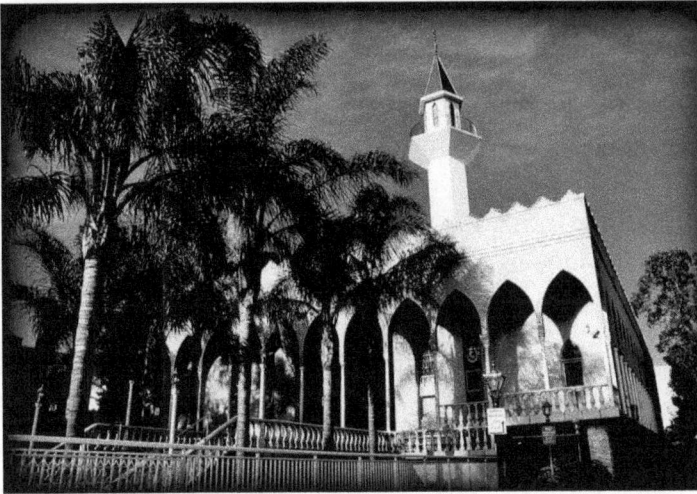

Imam Ali bin Abi Taleb Mosque in Lakemba, opened in 1980
(Source: Lebanese Muslim Association)

Fatima Al-Zahra Mosque, Arncliffe. Opened in 1983.
(Source: J Bar, Lebanese Muslim Association)

By 2016 the number of Islamic societies in Melbourne had expanded to 50 to serve the needs of all Muslims, each of which had a full-time or part-time imam. While Muslims could attend any of these mosques, there were concentrations of Lebanese in the following mosques in Melbourne: Omar Bin Al-Khattab Mosque or Preston Mosque (80 per cent Lebanese); Newport Mosque (all Lebanese); Maidstone Mosque (majority Lebanese); Fawkner Mosque (majority Lebanese) and Dandenong Mosque (around 40 per cent Lebanese).

Depending on their size and length of establishment, the mosques served as social, cultural and sporting centres for their communities by offering senior citizens' groups, women's groups, youth groups and sporting activities. The various Islamic societies came together to form the Islamic Council of Victoria, which in turn came under the Australian Federation of Islamic Councils. The Muslim religious leaders convened as the Board of Imams of Victoria. The Islamic Coordinating Council was founded as a specific purpose body charged with the certification, monitoring and supervision of Halal food exports from Victoria.

The Muslims of Victoria have established six schools, both primary and secondary, over three decades. These include Minaret College which was established in 1992 as the Islamic college of Melbourne South and East, and the King Khalid Islamic College of Victoria in Coburg, an independent day and boarding school founded in 1983 from Prep to Year 12. Werribee Islamic College was founded in 1986 and offers classes from Prep to Year 12. Al-Kamal Arabic School offers language classes on Saturday. Their plans include a community centre for Muslim youth and elderly on the grounds in the northern suburb of Preston.[56]

Smaller groups of Lebanese belong to the Alawi Islamic Association and the Druse Community, as well as various Protestant denominations.

An important contribution to community understanding was made by the Islamic community in Melbourne in founding in 2010 of the first Islamic Museum in Australia. The aims of the Islamic Museum are summed up in its vision statement:

> The Islamic Museum of Australia is a community foundation with
> the vision of establishing a leading cultural institution to showcase
> and preserve the arts, history culture and rich heritage that Islam and
> Muslim societies have brought to the world and, more importantly,
> Australia.[57]

During this period both Christian and Muslim religious leaders were still typically immigrants from Lebanon or other Arab countries with very few Australian-born and trained. This raised issues of difference in language and culture with the Australian-born of Lebanese descent.

Village associations

During the civil war Lebanese in Australia sought to maintain close links with their parent communities in Lebanon. They provided financial and in-kind support to their own religious bodies, their own political parties, their own villages and towns and related charities in Lebanon. This led to the establishment of village organisations with the original purpose of offering assistance to their home villages and towns in Lebanon, either directly or through related church or charitable organisations. Many of the village organisations, which were established during the Civil War, were still in existence during the 2010s. These include, in Melbourne, the village associations of Zahle, B'charre, Hadchit, Miniara, Tripoli and Mena.

These associations produced community leaders, some of whom acted as intermediaries between governments and the community. Occupying such positions accorded community leaders status and recognition both within their own community and sections of the wider Australian community. Especially during times of conflict within Australia or Lebanon, the position of community leaders became conflicted as governments and funding bodies sought to make them accountable for the actions of members of their communities.

A detailed study of one village community around the world revealed an international network of Lebanese who had emigrated from the village of Bichmizzine.[58] These village associations perform a number of functions for their members. First, they provide various forms of support for their home village in Lebanon, typically offered through families, churches or mosques, and other charities. These may involve donations to local charities and support for infrastructure projects in the village such as hospitals and schools. This form of assistance reaches its peak during, and after, times of conflict, such as wars and other periods of civil strife. A second major function is to provide opportunities for social interaction for those from the one village or town. These may include picnics, meetings and, for the larger associations, even national conventions. In this way Lebanese in the diaspora can enjoy the company of fellow-villagers in their countries of migration and also form part of an international network of immigrants and their descendants from the one locality in Lebanon.

Political organisations

During and after the civil war the various political factions in Lebanon had their counterparts in Australia. To recap, these included a number of right-wing parties supporting the Christians in Lebanon such as the Kataeb or Phalangist party, the Lebanese National Liberal party and the Lebanese Forces. Left-wing parties included the Socialist Progressive Party, the Syrian Nationalist party, and the Amal or Shiite party. The Lebanese Nationalist Movement was non-sectarian and advocated the integrity and independence of Lebanon.

Arabic media

The 1990s brought about considerable changes in the range of media available to Arabic speakers, including Lebanese, in Melbourne. We have already noted the four major Lebanese newspapers, all published in Sydney with small sections dedicated to Melbourne community news and advertising. Likewise, the variety of radio programs catering for the Lebanese community of Melbourne continued. The Special Broadcasting Service (SBS) offered 10 hours of Arabic broadcasting on radio 3EA. It contained news from all Arabic-speaking countries and from around Australia. The ethnic radio station 3ZZZ offered three hours in Arabic which adopted a right-wing Christian political line. Community radio 3CR included a number of programs including *Saut El Shaab* (*Voice of the Masses*) and *Voice of Arab Women*.

Television programs also revealed great diversity due to the different Lebanese groups seeking a voice and advances in communications technology. In addition to the occasional Arabic television program on SBS, there was a community television channel. There was also cable television ART (Arab Radio and TV) which showed a variety of telecasts from the Arab world such as Arabic films, sports and general entertainment programs.

During the Lebanese Civil War, the press and other media became politicised as they identified with one or other of the warring factions in Lebanon. The Lebanese and wider Arabic media in Australia became more diverse with particular newspapers and radio stations reflecting the political and religious divisions in Lebanon. However, there has also been an increased focus on entertainment and local or overseas news of personal or community importance.

Numerous other bodies have been established to promote sporting or cultural activities or to provide services for youth and women as well as or other sections of the community.

Contacts with Lebanon

We saw that immediately following the civil war there was a substantial increase in immigration from Lebanon. Some of these post-war immigrants had fled the fighting and turmoil in Lebanon during the last years of the war and were unprepared for emigration. On arrival in Australia some were unsure whether or not they would return to their homeland. Others had decided that their better future lay in settling in Australia. Both groups maintained close contacts with their family in Lebanon. This was achieved through cheaper travel, cheaper international phone calls and, increasingly, through other forms of electronic communication such as the internet, Skype and Facetime.

Playing the Oud and Singing at a Lebanese party at home 1988 Fitzroy.
(Source: State Library of Victoria)

Following the civil war there was an upsurge in return visits to Lebanon for various personal reasons such as visiting family, seeking business opportunities, engaging in political activities, travel and tourism. This ensured that the post-civil war immigrants maintained closer links with their home country than did earlier waves of immigrants from Lebanon.

22

LEBANESE IDENTITY IN A CHANGING WORLD, 1990–2005

In Lebanon, capital and power remained concentrated in the hands of a few wealthy families, while other Lebanese had to engage in industrial action to assert their rights. During this period conflict between religious and political groups in Lebanon sharpened differences and led many Lebanese to identify more closely with their own groups. Lebanese were pushed into stronger allegiances to these groups, especially when conflict led to loss of life and destruction of homes and neighbourhoods.

These decades saw Lebanese national identity shaken to its core. During the Syrian occupation no longer could Lebanese claim to be citizens of an independent nation. The great rallies of the populace in Beirut, Lebanon, revealed two opposing definitions of an independent Lebanon. The first defined Lebanon as predominantly a Christian nation with affiliations to the west. This was opposed by a second rally which saw the future of Lebanon as an independent nation with close links to the Arab world. These opposing definitions of Lebanese national identity were able to be found in the diaspora, including Australia.

To a lesser extent, this conflict was reflected in the Australian Lebanese community as distinctions sharpened between different groups of migrants with connections back 'home'. In Australia, however, there was little open conflict between Lebanese of different religious and political persuasions, but rather separate development as different community groups went their own way and sought government assistance.

The impact of the civil war in Lebanon led early on to some unemployment among Lebanese immigrants and problems in adjusting to aspects of Australian life. Furthermore, the rise of Muslim immigration challenged the prevailing definition of the Lebanese in Australia from a Christian, conservative community to one identified with Islamic fundamentalism and beset by social problems. While this was always a caricature, it took hold within the Australian community, aided by international events and partisan elements of the Australian media.

Within Australia the impact of the policy of multiculturalism in the 1980s led to some support for ethnic communities in the settlement of Lebanese. Lebanese migrants were now defined as one cultural group, among others, who were worthy of Government assistance.

Welcoming the famous Lebanese singer, Feyruz, to Australia in 1984.
(Source: State Library of Victoria)

As we have seen, the stronger part of Lebanese identity, both in their homeland and the diaspora, came from their attachment to family, religion and locality. This suggests that the primordial elements of

Lebanese identity proved resilient in the face of turbulent Middle Eastern conflicts. Evidence for this may be found in the commitment of many Lebanese in the diaspora to retain these links through contacts and multiple return visits to their homeland.

Two events during this period had a major impact on Lebanese identity in Australia: the attack by a Middle Eastern group on the Twin Towers in New York and the Cronulla Riot in Sydney. In both cases there was a conflation of Arab/Muslim/Lebanese into a single entity which was defined by many in government and the media as an enemy of the western world, including Australia. This led to some young Australian-Lebanese being accused of disloyalty to Australia, even though they may have been born and raised in Australia. While this negative definition of identity was imposed on the Lebanese community, some young Australian-born Lebanese chose to proudly identify as Lebanese. And so the wheel had come full circle from some early immigrants denying or underplaying their Lebanese background to some young Australian-Lebanese proudly proclaiming their heritage.

This incense burner had been in the Jabbour family for over 150 years. When their home in Bhamdoun, Lebanon, was destroyed during the war, the incense burner was the only thing they were able to retrieve from the ashes. They carried it from Bhamdoun to Beirut, and then to Melbourne in 1984. The incense burner is a symbol of the rebirth of the faith and culture of this Lebanese family in Australia. (Source: Jabbour Family, ALHSV 2014)

Tapestry of Images of Lebanon from the memories of Lebanese Women.
(Source: State Library of Victoria).

NOTES

1 Traboulsi, F 2007, p. 156
2 Fersen, E 2010
3 Traboulsi, F 2007 *Op. Cit.* p. 159
4 *Ibid. p.* 173 citing Salibi, K 1988.
5 Gates C 1989, 'The Historical Role of Political Economy in the Development of Modern Lebanon' Papers on Lebanon Series, Centre for Lebanese Studies. p. 5
6 Friedman, T 2015, (May 31) *Sunday Age*
7 Traboulsi, F 2007, *Op.Cit* p. 244
8 International Centre for Transitional Justice (ICTJ), 2014, (Jan) Failing to deal with the past: What cost to Lebanon'. https://www.ictj.org/publication/failing-to-deal-past-what-cost-Lebanon
9 Tueni, G 2005, cited in *The Guardian* 2 June 2005. Tueni himself was assassinated in December that year.
10 UALM Papers 2004.
11 International Centre for Transitional Justice (ICTJ), 2014 'The Truth about the missing in Lebanon: An interview with Nizar Saghieh' p. 15

12 Jupp, J 1996, *Understanding Australian Multiculturalism*, Australian Government Printing Service.
13 Jupp, J 1991, *Australian Retrospectives – Immigration*, Sydney University Press.
14 Castles, S & Miller, M 1993, *The Age of Migration: International Population Movements in the Modern World*, Guilford p. 95 - 96
15 Labaki, B 1992, *Op. Cit.* p. 608 - 609
16 *Ibid.* p. 616
17 *Ibid.* p. 616
18 Batrouney, T & Blatt, P 1982, 'Settlement Problems of Lebanese in Melbourne', Report for Migrant Settlement Council for Victoria.
19 Labaki, B *Op. Cit.*
20 Stamm, S 2006, 'Social networks among return migrants to post-war Lebanon' Working Paper, Centre for Comparative and International Studies ETH Zurich Research Collection p. 10
21 Batrouney, T 2005, 'Australian-Lebanese: Return Visits to Lebanon and Issues of Identity', in P Tabar (ed.), *Lebanese Diaspora: History, Racism and Belonging*, Lebanese American University
22 Kasparian, C 2003, cited in Pearlman, W 2013, 'Emigration and Power: A Study of Sects in Lebanon, 1860–2010', *Politics and Society*, vol. 41, no. 1, SAGE Publications.
23 Kasparian, C 2003, 'L'entrée des jeunes libanais dans la vie active et l'émigration, St-Joseph University, Beirut.
24 Abi Farah, A 2000, 'Estimations of the number of Lebanese emigrants in 1999', in As-Safir, December 2001
25 Hyndmann-Rizk, N 2009, 'Balad Niswen – Hukum Niswen: The Perception of Gender Inversions Between Lebanon and Australia', *Palma Journal: A Multidisciplinary Research Publication*, vol. 11, no. 1, Notre Dame University.
26 Tabar, P 2009, *Immigration and Human Development: Evidence from Lebanon*, Human Development Research Paper, United Nations Development Program. citing Kasparian, C p. 10
27 *Ibid.* p. 11
28 Humphrey, M 2004, 'Lebanese identities: between cities, nations and trans-nations', *Arab Studies Quarterly*, Arab Studies Institute p. 40
29 Interview Faddy Zouky June 2016
30 Labaki, B 1992, Op. Cit.
31 Tabar, P 2009, *Immigration and Human Development: Evidence from Lebanon*, Human Development Research Paper, United Nations Development Program p. 5
32 Betts, K & Healy, E 2006, 'Lebanese Muslims in Australia and Social Disadvantage', *People & Place*, vol. 14, no. 1, Centre for Urban Research and Action.
33 Betts, K & Healy, E 2006, *Op. Cit.* p. 30
34 Bureš, J 2008, *Main characteristic and development trends of migration in the Arab world*, Institute of International Relations, Prague.
35 Betts, K & Healy, E 2006, *Op. Cit.* p. 32
36 Interview Sarkis Karam, February 2017
37 Batrouney, T & Blatt, P 1982 *Op. Cit.*
38 *Ibid.*
39 Collins, J et al 1995, *A shop full of dreams: Ethnic small business in Australia*, Pluto Press. p. 54
40 Monsour, A 2008, *Op. Cit.* p. 71.
41 Jayasuriya, L 1991, 'Citizenship, Democratic Pluralism and Ethnic Minorities in

Australia', in R Nile (ed.), *Immigration, Multiculturalism and the Politics of Ethnicity and Race in Australia*, University of London Centre for Australian Studies.

42 Betts, K & Healy, E 2006, Op. Cit.

43 Hyndmann-Rizk, N 2014, 'Migration, Wasta and big business success: the paradox of capital accumulation in Sydney's Hadchiti community' in *Labour and Management in Development Journal*. Vol. 5 p. 5

44 Interview Faddy Zouky, July 2016

45 *Ibid.*

46 Betts, K & Healy, E 2002, *Op. Cit.* p. 33

47 Cruickshank, K 2006 *Teenagers, Literacy and School: Researching in Multicultural Contexts*, Routledge Taylor Francis Group. p. 84

48 *Ibid.* p. 84

49 Portes, A, Fernandez-Kelly, P & Haller, W 2005, 'Segmented Assimilation on the ground: The new second generation in early adulthood' in *Ethnic & Racial Studies*, 28 (6) cited by Tabar et al. 2010, *Lebanon: A Country of Emigration and Immigration*, Lebanese American University, p. 133

50 *Ibid.* p. 64

51 Batrouney, T & Blatt, P 1982, *Op.Cit.* p. 23

52 *Ibid.* p. 25

53 Collins, J et al. 2000, *Op. Cit.* p. 214-15.

54 Interview Hassan Moussa, February 2017,

55 Omar, W & Allen, K 1996, *The Muslims in Australia*, Australian Government Publishing Service in Parker, B, Lancely, K, Owens, B & Fitzpatrick, R 2009, *Geography for Australian Citizens, Teacher Resource Book*, Macmillan. p. 9

56 Henderson, G 2015, '1970s Lebanese Commission led to an Immigration Debacle, *The Australian*

57 Islamic Museum of Australia 2015, *History of Australia's Muslims*, Islamic Museum of Australia. p. 2

58 Nabti, P 1992 'Emigration from a Lebanese Village: A Case Study of Bishmizzine', *The Lebanese in the World*, Centre for Lebanese Studies in association with I.B. Tauris & Co. p. 60

PART 5:
CONTEMPORARY LEBANON

The uneasy peace ushered in by the Ta'if Accord of 1991 was followed by a period of reconstruction and rebuilding of a fractured society, civil institutions and physical infrastructure in Lebanon. However, this fragile peace was interrupted by continuing instability caused by conflict among opposing political and religious groups and by a series of external threats emanating from the region. Chief among these was the loss of national autonomy in Lebanon produced by the Syrian occupation which lasted from 1996 to 2005. This was followed by the Summer War in August 2006 involving the Israeli invasion of the south of Lebanon and the displacement of many thousands from the south of Lebanon to the north. Another external threat to Lebanon was the uprising against the Assad regime in Syria from 2013 which led to 1.5 million Syrians seeking refuge in Lebanon.

The major developments in Australian society during this period included the continuing decline in manufacturing industry and the great advances in computer technology and communications. These technological advances enabled Lebanese in the diaspora to maintain close contact with their families and current events in Lebanon, especially more recent political developments and conflicts such as the Summer War in 2006. Although emigration from Lebanon continued during this period, it did not reach the heights seen during the early years of the civil war. Unlike the first two waves of Lebanese migrants the third wave included a majority of Muslim Lebanese. Substantial numbers of third wave immigrant families experienced unemployment and difficulties with the education system, especially in their early years in Australia.

23

CHANGES IN LEBANON, 2005–2016

To whom can we raise our voice? We have no-one but God to help us.
Syrian refugee in Lebanon, 2015

The years 2005 - 2016 period saw the consequences of the dramatic changes in Australian government policies on immigration and settlement from the mid-1990s, including the treatment of refugees and changing attitudes to immigrants. A major catalyst in changing government and community attitudes towards immigrants from the Middle East was the destruction of the Twin Towers in New York on 11 September 2001. This produced a degree of insecurity among Middle Eastern communities in Australia, including the Lebanese community. Fringe elements among the wider community tended to conflate Arab, Muslim and Lebanese into a single entity which they regarded as a threat to Australia. The Cronulla riots in Sydney in 2005 between some mainstream Australian youth and youth of Lebanese origin was a violent episode which symbolised this conflict.

Syria's withdrawal from Lebanon

To reiterate, the occupation of Lebanon by Syria lasted until 30 April 2005 when the Prime Minister, Raif Hariri, was assassinated. The resulting public uprising known as the 'Cedar Revolution' spread through Lebanon and occupied Beirut. These developments led to Syria's full withdrawal from Lebanon on 30 April 2005. The Syrian occupation had dire consequences for Lebanon. It led to a de facto loss of independence as a succession of Lebanese governments and presidents were not able to govern with autonomy but rather in the interests of the occupying power. During the period of occupation Lebanon was little more than a client state.

Lebanese mothers are still seeking information about their sons who went missing during the civil war.
(Source: Fair Observer, Feb 2015, Photographer: Raha Askarizadeh)

The Summer War of 2006

Perhaps the most damaging conflict following the civil war was the Summer War of 2006 which saw an Israeli invasion of Lebanon and yet again the destruction of much infrastructure and fleeing of civilians as they sought refuge from the conflict. What was the root cause of this war? Both sides defined the war differently with Israel seeing Hezbollah as a terrorist organisation with cross-border ambitions. On the other hand, the Lebanese Government focused on Israel's continuing occupation of the Shebaa farms in the south of Lebanon, its detention of Lebanese prisoners, its refusal to hand over the map for the landmines planted during its occupation of Lebanon and its recurrent violation of Lebanese airspace.

The justification given by Israel and the major western powers for the invasion was outrage over the capture of two Israeli soldiers at the border. The major reason was likely to be the destruction of Hezbollah, the Lebanese Shi'ite militia, which was a strong supporter of the Palestinians. However, this was not achieved. Indeed, a major outcome of the war was recognition of the prominent role played by Hezbollah in confronting and, at times, repelling the Israeli army. This led to increasing respect for this militant group within Lebanon and a more prominent role in the Lebanese Parliament.

The Summer War waged by Israel on Lebanon led to some 1,109 dead, 36,907 injured and 915,762 displaced, approximately 25 per cent of the Lebanese population, according to Lebanese Government figures. The early part of the war saw a concerted attempt by the Israeli Defence Forces to destroy significant parts of Lebanon's infrastructure, including crucially the runways at Beirut airport. Many targets in Lebanon seemed to have little strategic value but can be seen rather as a deliberate attempt to collectively punish Lebanon for failing to control Hezbollah.

The events of this war and the ensuing humanitarian crisis received publicity around the world. One result of this was the mobilisation of support and aid in countries of the Lebanese diaspora. The reaction of the Lebanese community in Melbourne, Australia provides just one example of the response to the crisis:

> This involved the establishment of a group, 'Australians for Lebanon,' in response to the Israeli bombardment of Lebanon, especially south Lebanon. This national group was established after the attack on Lebanon by the Israeli Defence Forces. It mobilised all sections of the Lebanese community in Melbourne and engaged in a range of political and humanitarian activities directed at members of the Australian Government and Opposition.

> One example of Australian-Lebanese community action was the fund-raising dinner held on 30 October 2006 in Melbourne in response to the humanitarian crisis in Lebanon. This was a notable event in that it was supported by all sections of the Lebanese community of Melbourne and many Australians outside the Lebanese community. A number of cultural and humanitarian groups including 'Aid Lubnan', Australians for Lebanon, the Australian Lebanese Historical Society

of Victoria and the Australian Lebanese Youth Association jointly organised this event.[1]

The concern of Australians for Lebanon extended beyond the Summer War to support humanitarian efforts in the immediate post-war years. For example, in January 2007 a delegation from 'Australians for Lebanon' toured the areas in southern Lebanon affected by cluster bombs. It met with the United Nations Mine Action and Coordination Centre which estimated that after the invasion there were around one million unexploded cluster bombs still to be cleared in southern Lebanon. Following the visit, appeals were made to the Australian Government to contribute to the de-mining of Lebanon and the rehabilitation of cluster bomb victims.

The Syrian Civil War 2011-

The Syrian civil war commenced in 2011 as part of the 'Arab Spring' when a disparate group of rebels rose up in opposition to the Assad government. Within four years 220,000 Syrians were killed, over a half of whom were civilians. This uprising quickly became a major cause of instability for Lebanon as Hezbollah entered the war in support of the Assad regime in Syria. This had the effect of dividing Lebanese into pro-and anti-Assad groups which, at times, led to armed conflict. As the civil war widened nearly four million refugees sought haven throughout the Middle East and beyond. Of these, more than one and a half million fled the fighting in Syria and sought refuge in camps within the borders of Lebanon.

> For these refugees there is no money for doctors or dentists, no chance of physiotherapy to correct the most basic childhood disabilities. Teeth fall out, diseases such as diabetes and heart disease go untreated, cancer metastasises.[2]

This presented a humanitarian tragedy for the Syrian refugees who tried to exist on cash handouts of about USD19 a month. Those migrants who reached Lebanon without documentation found themselves living in poverty and unable to access even basic services. Their desperate lives have been graphically depicted in a film entitled *Capernaum* (Chaos) by Nadine Labaki in 2018. This film not only arouses profound sympathy for the children of the refugees but it also depicts the human spirit for survival. At the same time, the situation presented an unprecedented burden for the Lebanese nation with its relatively small population of 4.5 million people.

The year 2014 saw yet another threat to peace and stability in Lebanon. This came in the form of Islamic State and Nusra Front militants who were seeking to gain a foothold in the north, centred around Tripoli, Lebanon's second largest city. In a number of skirmishes the Lebanese Army repelled the militants but the militants' attempts to gain control of parts of the north continued and the threat to Lebanon's autonomy remained.

These developments reveal that Lebanon was in a vulnerable position, located between Israel, which refused to recognise its sovereignty, and Syria, which remained a threat to its complete independence in the region.

Economic and social changes in Lebanon

Economically, Lebanon was experiencing significant hardship in the immediate post-war period. Many factories and much infrastructure situated in East Beirut had been destroyed during the war. This had a major impact on the Lebanese GDP which, in 1990, was only 40 per cent of what it had been in 1987.[3] Under Rafik Hariri as Prime Minister, the company Solidère (of which he was a joint owner) proceeded to rebuild parts of Beirut. To help finance this initiative, public borrowings leapt to extraordinary levels. Public debt in 1993 was 40 per cent of GDP. By 1998 it was 100 per cent of GDP and by 2005 public debt reached 159 per cent of GDP. Lebanon was required to repay almost 60 per cent more than it earned.

Notwithstanding these public borrowing figures, the economy in the mid-1990s was flourishing in the banking and property development industries. Amid this boom, the casualty was public infrastructure and services which continued to be underdeveloped. The wealth derived from banking and property was concentrated in the hands of a few with some 60 per cent of bank deposits belonging to 2.4 per cent of depositors in Lebanon and overseas.

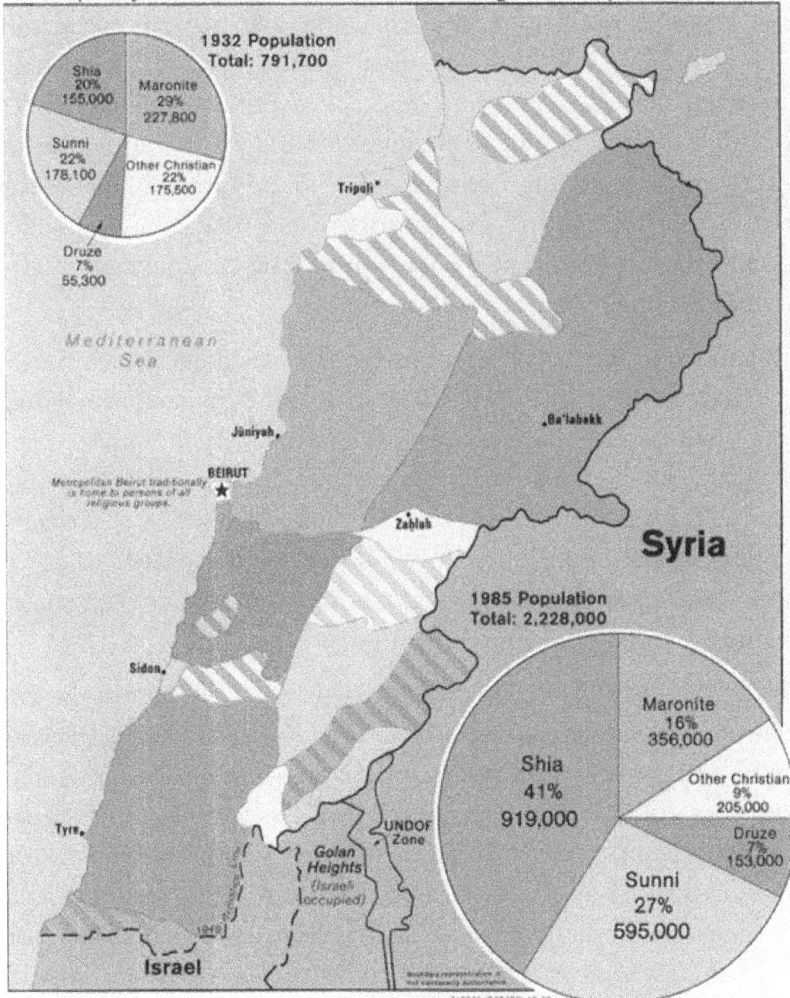

This map represents the changes in the distribution of Lebanon's religious groups from 1932 to the end of the Civil war in 1990. The major changes are the decline in the numbers of Maronites and other Christian groups and the increase in the numbers of Muslims, in particular the Shia, over the period.
(Source: http://www.globalsecurity.org/military/world/war/lebanon.htm)

During this period the economically dominant class in Lebanon, which was traditionally fragmented along communal lines, failed to develop its agrarian and industrial sectors. Instead, it concentrated on the tertiary sector, with particular emphasis on trading, tourism, banking and finance. This trend had been reinforced since 1990 by the commitment of successive governments to neo-liberal economic policies which resulted in a limited and low pay labour market. Politically, the country was organised around the alleged collective interests of the various religious groups. This led to recurrent political crises due to attempts by the communal leaders to reorganise the power structure and improve their share of the national cake. Within this context, local and regional actors would benefit from political instability so that they could use it to improve their bargaining position in relation to their political opponents.[4]

The nature of the Lebanese economy had a significant impact on opportunities for work. According to many commentators, young people had better prospects for work abroad. In the 1990s, some 100,000 Lebanese of working age emigrated. Conversely, to exploit Lebanon's need for cheap labour, Syrian workers in Lebanon numbered some 500,000 by 1995. As they were prepared to accept lower wages than Lebanese workers, they became the targets of resentment among the poorer Lebanese workers.[5]

Some issues that were endemic in Lebanese society before the civil war were still present in the 1990s. There were still high levels of official corruption based on personal greed. One example of such corruption saw two million dollars of foreign aid to pay for electricity generation whittled down to approximately 1.5 million dollars after bribes were paid at different stages in the process. Another issue was the continuing influence of factionalism and sectarianism, both of which impeded much needed industrial development and the equitable provision of government services.

Lebanese society in the 1990s and into the 2000s was unable to address poverty and generate sufficient employment for its populace. It was estimated that 28 per cent of Lebanese lived below the poverty line and 50,000 new job seekers were competing for 35,000 positions.[6] The prevalence of economic factors in the mid-2000s was revealed in the following motives Lebanese gave for leaving their homeland: to obtain work (52.4 per cent); for education (8 per cent); for family reasons (25.4 per cent); and other factors (13.4 per cent).[7]

24

ECONOMIC AND SOCIAL CHANGES
IN AUSTRALIA, 2005–2016

Between the years 2005 and 2016, Australia underwent a series of economic changes. The major development was the continuation of the mining boom which was at its peak during the two decades from 1990 to 2010. This was based on the extraction and export of iron ore, coal and other commodities, particularly from the states of Western Australia, Queensland and New South Wales. Although all states did not participate directly in the mining boom, it did provide the foundation for Australia's prosperity during most of this period.

At the same time, this was accompanied by a continuing decline in many of Australia's large-scale and smaller manufacturing industries which caused the loss of semi-skilled and unskilled jobs. A major cause of this decline was the progressive dismantling of tariff barriers which had provided effective protection for Australia's manufacturing industries. The push for rationalisation under the guise of global competitiveness saw industries lost to overseas markets. This affected a wide range of goods and services which had previously been developed and produced in Australian factories. These included secondary industries which had, in the past, provided many Lebanese immigrants with their first jobs in Australia, such as the car industry.

An associated issue in the post-war period, especially in the 1990s, was the changing role of work and participation in work. Over this period there was an overall reduction in unemployment. This may be explained, in part, by the classification of employment which is one hour of paid employment per week (full time or part-time). There was a reduction in men's participation in the workforce in the 2005–2016 period due to industry restructures and closures. On the other hand, there was an increase in the participation of women in the workforce, mainly in part-time work. During this period, husbands, wives and possibly their children needed to work often in multiple jobs to earn an income to sustain a household.

Another major economic development included great technological advances in communications which meant that immigrants could maintain daily contact with their families in Lebanon and, in a sense, could live in both Australia and Lebanon. This meant that Lebanese in the diaspora could keep abreast of political developments in their former homeland and, to some extent, indirectly participate in them. This period also witnessed cheaper air travel between the two countries which had major implications for immigrants in maintaining contact with their families and homeland.

25

LEBANESE MIGRATION 2005 – 2016

*During my youth, the idea of moving from Lebanon was unthinkable. Then I
began to realise I might have to go, like my grandfather, uncles and others who
left for the United States of America, Egypt, Australia and Cuba.*
Amin Maalouf

In the post-civil war period, a distinction may be made between
those who emigrated in times of stability and those who emigrated
in times of conflict and strife. In times of stability Lebanese
emigrants were drawn from the unskilled and semi-skilled lower
middle class who migrated due to limited wealth and economic
opportunity and in search of a better life elsewhere. In times
of instability and conflict, emigrants were drawn from all social
categories as they mainly emigrated for reasons of personal safety
and for other humanitarian reasons. Many of those who emigrated
left for the nearby Gulf States and Europe while smaller numbers
left for the United States, Canada and Australia.[8]

In summary, between the years of 2005 and 2016, immigrants
from Lebanon settled in Australia mainly for reasons of economic
development but also for security as identified by the years of
their arrival. The uncertain and uneven economic development of
Lebanon in the aftermath of the civil war was of little benefit to
many lower- and middle-class Lebanese and their children. If the

children were educated, they saw more opportunities for fulfilling work outside Lebanon. However, only a small proportion was prepared to leave their native country. Conflict within Lebanon and with Israel saw a small increase in the numbers of Lebanese who arrived in Australia because of security concerns. Similar to immigrants in the civil war period, there were roughly equivalent numbers from religious groups emigrating. Many immigrants who arrived, especially from rural areas, did not possess occupational skills that enabled them to easily find work in Australia. However, by attaching themselves to established communities, especially village groupings, in the large capital cities, they were often able to find work and also receive informal training and advice on developing businesses. Within established communities there was also the infrastructure for welfare and health support should it be needed.

The story of Hany touches on a number of themes common to the experiences of young immigrants from Lebanon in the early 2000s.

Hany

Hany arrived in Sydney in 2005 as a single man at the age of 29 years, aiming to settle permanently in Australia. Hany had completed a law degree at a private university In Lebanon as he felt that would give him a better opportunity to leave the country when the time was right. However, after graduation, he soon realised it would be difficult to find stable employment as he and his family were not aligned with any political group or supported by a particular *zaim*. This proved to be the case when he was employed for some years in Lebanon, Saudi Arabia and Dubai. As a non-aligned lawyer, Hany became frustrated at the limitations he faced in practising law in the Middle East.

After researching potential destinations, Hany decided to migrate to Australia for the opportunities it offered. Upon arrival in Bankstown, Sydney, he looked up a number of contacts he had in the Lebanese community. Consulting these, Hany was advised to drive taxis, as many Lebanese were doing at that time. Instead, he began working with the Arabic Council of Australia (ACA) as he wanted to undertake work that would help people.

Since arriving in Australia, Hany has set about educating himself in ways that help his day-to-day work with the Arabic Council of Australia. He has gained qualifications in English for academic purposes, counselling, management, community service and workplace training and assessment. Arriving as a lawyer qualified in another country, Hany needed to decide whether to pursue a career in Law. This was a challenge as he had to undertake a law degree in Australia as his qualifications were not recognised. Currently, Hany works with the ACA and as a sessional worker with the NSW Attorney General's Department and Department of Justice.

Upon arrival in Australia Hany found that the local Lebanese Arabic-speaking community was much stricter in following Islamic rites than he had been used to in Lebanon and even in Saudi Arabia. As a Muslim, Hany introduced himself to people from the wider Australian community as being of Arabic background and a Muslim. This ended debate or discussion about his background and any assumptions people may make. He found that if one is proud of one's background and heritage and you speak openly about them, people will respect you.

The social and political groups within the Lebanese community in Sydney do not hold any interest or meaning for Hany. He sees them, and the division they bring, as being one of the main reasons for him emigrating. He is very happy to be an Australian citizen for the sake of his children.

Hany's experience with religion in Lebanon has influenced his views of the way that the Muslim Lebanese and Arabic community in Australia respond to their religion. He grew up in El Mina in Tripoli at a time when there was little division between Christians and Muslims and between Sunni and Shi'ite. It was 'a golden age' in his country.

People would visit each other's houses for the different religious festivals and celebrate together. His grandfather and grandmother drank alcohol and his grandmother was not covered with a hijab. Suddenly, after the Islamic 'jihad' in Afghanistan, and through the Saudis in Lebanon supporting a particular mosque or organisation, there is stronger religious identification and behaviour. In the 1980s there were only two lines in the mosque for Eid prayers. Now they put the mats outside and across the road for everyone to attend. Hany sees religion as being used to further political agendas.

Hany believes that the perceptions of Lebanese crime in Sydney are largely activated by the media. They are responsible for fuelling hostility in the wider community towards the Lebanese community as a whole.

Hany's story is but one example of Lebanese immigration and settlement during this period. As such, it cuts across some common stereotypes of Lebanese immigrants held in the wider community.

The numbers of Lebanese immigrants in the 2005–2016 period indicate a reduction in intake compared with the 1980s and early 1990s. The increase in Lebanese-born residents in Australia between 1981 and 1991 was 19,372. On the other hand, the Lebanese-born population in Australia rose from 74,848 in 2006 to 78,651 in 2016, a modest population increase of 3,803 over 11 years.

The age structure of Lebanese-born in 2016 shows an aging community with a median age of 51 years. The age group 0–34 years includes 18 per cent of the Lebanese-born while the age group 35–65 or more years constitutes 82 percent of the Lebanese-born in Australia. As many as 70.2 per cent of the community born in Lebanon were married.

The educational attainment and employment of the Lebanese-born community in 2016 shows that 11 per cent have a Bachelor Degree or above and 7.2 per cent have an Advanced Diploma or Diploma. Some 11 per cent have a TAFE Certificate 3 or Certificates 3 or 4. These qualifications have resulted in 20 per cent of the community working as Technicians and Trade Workers, 15.4 per cent indicated they were managers, 13.5 per cent stated they worked as professionals, 11 per cent were labourers and 10 per cent were clerical workers.[9]

Australian residents born in Lebanon have a very high uptake of citizenship at 88 per cent. This is significantly greater than other overseas-born nationalities which average 59 per cent. This is to be expected, given the strenuous efforts of earlier Lebanese generations to gain Australian citizenship and their enthusiasm to do so when it became available.

The settlement of the post-civil war group is discussed in more detail in the next chapter.

26

SETTLEMENT OF LEBANESE IN AUSTRALIA, 2005–2016

With wealth a foreign land becomes a homeland; and with poverty a homeland becomes a foreign land.

Arabic proverb

This chapter explores some of the settlement issues facing recent immigrants and their impact on existing Lebanese communities. The chapter also touches on some of the responses of community members and how they worked with government agencies to address social problems and issues.

The after-effects of civil war in Lebanon through the 1990s continued to be a push factor in Lebanese migration to Australia. Lebanese communities and the wider Australian society were confronted with increased numbers of immigrants and settlement issues. Coming from a society wracked by a civil war that hindered their education and training, the initial immigrants experienced relatively high unemployment. With the education and training of the second generation the unemployment rate fell during the latter part of this period. By the early years of the 21st century almost as many Lebanese-born were employed in their own businesses as were employees in other businesses.

This period witnessed a dramatic increase in the number of Australian-Lebanese community organisations, reflecting the growing size and complexity of the community. These organisations developed in response to the religious and cultural needs and interests of the diverse Lebanese community as well as changing Australian government policies. In particular, the advent of multiculturalism provided some resources for Lebanese groups to meet their community's needs. At the same time, these policies ushered in competition between Lebanese community groups for both members and resources.

Occupations and business

Between the years 1991 and 2016, the number of Lebanese-born in Australia increased by almost 10,000. (Table 5 Pt 2). As with earlier waves of immigrants, the great majority settled in New South Wales and Victoria, especially in the capital cities of Sydney and Melbourne.

In Sydney, there was a tendency for different religious communities to congregate close to their centres of worship in different areas of the city: the Christian community in Punchbowl and Parramatta; the Sunnis in Lakemba and Bankstown; and the Shi'ites in Arncliffe and Rockdale. As one Sydney interviewee explained:

> Harris Park is for the Kfarsghab, Lakemba for the Sunni Muslims while the Shi'a Muslims are in Arncliffe South. It's like Lebanon, south is Shi'a and north is Sunni. Belmore is a mixture of Christian and Muslim, Strathfield is mainly Christian, Harris Park is all Maronite from the north of Lebanon, including the towns of Kfarsghab, B'sharrie, and Zgharta. Orthodox from Amioun are in Punchbowl and Redfern. Not many Melkites here. There is a very big variety. The Lebanese started spreading out 15 years ago.[10]

The states of Queensland, South Australia and Western Australia had much smaller numbers of Lebanese-born while Tasmania and the two territories were the regions with the smallest numbers (Table 5

Pt.2). However, Lebanese communities also included Australians of Lebanese descent. This still left Sydney and Melbourne as the only places with Lebanese populations of sufficient size and diversity to meet the range of religious and cultural needs of their communities.

The civil war was clearly a major push factor for Lebanese migration to Australia as illustrated in Table 5 Pt.2. This migration took place in the years immediately preceding and during the civil war as well as in the immediate aftermath of the war. However, by the end of the first decade of the 21st century, migration of Lebanese-born had declined to less than 1,000 a year.

The occupational pathways of this wave of Lebanese immigrants were significantly different from the two previous waves. The typical practice of working in an unskilled job until enough capital was made to invest in a business was not always attainable for Lebanese immigrants after 1990. The unemployment problems experienced by significant numbers of third-wave immigrants had negative effects on the settlement of this group.

Some members of the second generation gained access to professional and managerial positions while others worked in family businesses. The 2006 Australian Census enumerated the proportion of Lebanese-born who were employees and those who were owners/managers of their own enterprises in the capital cities (excluding Hobart and Darwin) for that year. Employees accounted for around a half of the Lebanese-born while around 40 per cent were owners/managers. These figures support the view that establishing and working in their own businesses remains the preferred occupation for substantial numbers of Lebanese-born. Again, it must be remembered that those of Lebanese descent were not included in these numbers. Given their length of time in Australia and their familiarity with the economy and society, it is likely that their inclusion would increase the numbers of Lebanese owner/managers of their own businesses.

A common interpretation of these figures would suggest that establishing and working in their own businesses is the preferred and traditional preference of Lebanese. A counter view suggests that the occupational skills and experiences of the Lebanese-born and attitudes of Australian employers tended to exclude a large proportion of Lebanese from the employed workforce, leaving self-employment as an opportunistic alternative.[11]

By the end of the 20th century, a focus on the occupations of Lebanese-born persons in Melbourne revealed a spread across all occupational groups. The professional and managerial groups accounted for 30 per cent of the occupations of all Lebanese-born, which was comparable with the employment pattern for the total Australian population. The group, which included clerical, sales and service workers, accounted for 22 per cent of Lebanese-born as compared to 30 per cent of the Australian-born. The proportions of Lebanese-born in the tradespersons' category and labourers' category were larger than the equivalent figures for the Australian-born.

These data reflect the decline in occupations engaged in manufacturing industries and an increase in service industries and professional occupations, and that those born in Lebanon have a lower proportion of high-level occupations (managers and administrators; professionals; and advanced clerical workers) than those in the same categories for the Australian-born.

A number of accommodations were made to allow immigrants to find a living in their new home. With the limited availability of unskilled employment in large factories like Crown Corning in Sydney or Ford in Melbourne, finding work with family, friends or community contacts helped them earn sufficient money for survival. The informal arrangements surrounding this type of employment may help explain some recorded high levels of unemployment. Working to help out family or friends or to gain experience may not have been considered as employment, even if money was exchanged.

Those who wished to pursue their dream of establishing their own business took significant risks and undertook heavy loans in the expectation that they would be able to meet the repayments. A business agent in Melbourne explained how many opened their first business in the 1990s and 2000s:

> In order to get into their first business, people would borrow 100 per cent or more of the loan. Often they would need to take out a personal loan that I guaranteed for the balance of the business loan. Then they would work hard and pay off the loan.[12]

While food and clothing businesses were common among the first two waves, Lebanese-Australian settlers were to be found in a great variety of other businesses, including hairdressing and construction to cite just two outstanding examples. The Lattouf family of Melbourne became highly successful in hairdressing, opening their first salon in 1987 which grew to 130 salons throughout Australia through establishing a highly successful franchise (Hairhouse Warehouse) selling a range of hair products. Their family-based business is noteworthy in that it gives back to the Lebanese and wider Australian community.

Our second example records the life and times of Tom Hayson, a second generation Australian-Lebanese, who became a major property developer and builder in Sydney. His outstanding contribution was his major role in transforming Darling Harbour into a world class facility for entertainment, cultural and social activities. This was widely regarded as making an important contribution to Sydney gaining the 2000 Olympic Games. Hayson's life and achievements are recorded in Dare to Dream by Kevin Perkins, who gives a detailed account of the many successes of Tom Hayson in property development and construction, with a special focus on his creating the facilities at Darling Harbour.

Unemployment

A number of factors affected immigrant Lebanese employment between 1990 and 2014. First, as we have seen, there was the impact of the declining Australian manufacturing industry struggling to compete internationally. This is in contrast to post-Second World War immigrants who worked in the production lines of clothing and manufacturing industries in the late 1950s and 1960s. These jobs gave them a secure financial base from which to purchase houses, accumulate capital and move into their own small businesses. By the 1990s, this pathway was largely closed.

Secondly, a number of third-wave Lebanese in the workplace had low levels of literacy in Arabic and English, little or no trade training and qualifications, and an accumulation of small-scale agrarian skills gained in their home country, which were not relevant to the urbanised Australian economy. Many Lebanese settlers arriving after 1990 experienced high levels of unemployment, reaching over 30 per cent in some municipalities. This led to some becoming long-term unemployed, who relied on unemployment benefits and other forms of welfare. While this only ever applied to a minority of immigrants, it became, for a time, a defining and negative characteristic of Lebanese among the wider Australian community. Unemployment and low-income employment had a negative effect on household income, especially during the early stages of their settlement in Australia.

Lebanese immigrants experienced higher unemployment rates than Australian residents. In the period 1990–2001, Lebanese unemployment was notably high. Among the 15–24 age group at the 1996 Census, unemployment was 44 per cent and for the 25–44 age group it reached 36 per cent. By 1996 the unemployment rate for Lebanese-born in Melbourne reached as high as 28 per cent. This was exceeded in the municipalities of Darebin (30 per cent), Hobson's Bay (34 per cent), Hume (35 per cent), Maribyrnong (45 per cent) and Moreland (39.1 per cent).

In Greater Sydney, the 2001 Census showed unemployment of a significant number of first-generation and second-generation Lebanese immigrants. Unemployment numbers were greater for suburbs with high concentrations of Lebanese settlers, such as Parramatta and Rockbank. These figures were sufficient to cause alarm among governments. Many employment programs were run by mainstream and newly founded community organisations to provide job training and linking people to work.

For the Sydney statistical district, first- and second-generation Christian Lebanese had an unemployment rate of 22 per cent compared with a 38 per cent unemployment rate among first- and second-generation Muslim Lebanese.[13] Lebanese Muslims earned less per week than Lebanese Christians. This had a marked impact on the capacity of immigrants to settle into their adopted country and establish a home. For example, in the 2001 Census Christians were nearly $150 per week better off than Muslims.[14]

There may be a number of reasons for this disparity. It may be that Muslims, who outnumbered Christians among recent arrivals, had less time to settle in their new country. When first and second generations of Lebanese are looked at separately, the unemployment rate for the second generation falls by 6 per cent for Christian and 14 per cent for Muslim Lebanese respectively. This reveals the impact of education and training, among other factors, on the employability of Lebanese second generation.

Over time, second-generation Lebanese of both Christian and Muslim backgrounds become more educated than their parents and were more likely to hold jobs across many sectors of the workforce, principally retail, transport and professional support. Despite this improvement, by 2006 the Lebanese-born still had an unemployment rate of 12 per cent, almost three times the rate of the Australian-born of 4 per cent.[15]

Education

During this period the educational and employment experiences among the Lebanese-born and their children reflected a polarisation, with some gaining tertiary qualifications, leading to professional and managerial employment, while others experienced intergenerational unemployment and poverty. The educational backgrounds of parents and older siblings, in some cases, served to limit educational aspirations and, in other cases, to enhance them.

Upon arrival between 1990 and 2014 Lebanese settlers were confronted with major challenges. While many migrated to be with family or friends from their home village or town, they still faced the responsibility of finding a home, a job and a niche in the Lebanese and wider community. Education, in particular, presented both problems and opportunities for Lebanese immigrants and their families. The adults who arrived with limited or no post-secondary qualifications experienced difficulty in finding work. Those who had qualifications from Lebanon often had to undergo further training before gaining accreditation in Australia.

A significant number of adult arrivals had been labourers in Lebanon. The 2011 Census showed that for the Lebanese-born residents across Australia aged fifteen years and over, the majority (48 per cent) had less than twelve years of schooling. About 19 per cent had achieved a Year 12 or equivalent qualification. Beyond Year 12, nine per cent had attained a Trade Certificate with six per cent earning a Diploma or an Advanced Diploma. Of the Lebanese-born, nine per cent had completed a Bachelor's Degree or Higher Degree.

Some adult Lebanese migrants made great efforts to improve their knowledge and skills by undertaking training and education courses. In most cases these efforts were directed to improving their employment prospects as illustrated in the following story:

Randa's Story

Randa arrived in Sydney as an 18-year-old bride in 1986. After an arranged marriage with a cousin, she and her husband emigrated from Beirut and lived in Australia with her husband's family. They decided to leave Lebanon because of the unstable situation during the war. For example, there were strikes in Beirut against the government by opposing forces or by Israeli planes. Randa recalled being sent home from school because of military action and how 'There was anxiety most of the time'.

Upon arrival, Randa immediately enrolled in English language classes in Paramatta. At the same time, she worked to complete the final year of her Baccalaureate in English. Following the completion of English language courses, she enrolled in a TAFE course on general education (then Tertiary Preparation Certificate). Her goal was to go to university and continue her education. She enrolled in a Psychology degree which she completed at Macquarie University and later enrolled in a Graduate Diploma in Social Health. When she started working, she completed many work-related courses including those on gambling, counselling, addiction, tobacco control, and intensive family support.

Learning to speak English took her some years. 'My problem with written English may have been because I only spoke Arabic at home with everyone. I could not practise verbal English. Even at University, I did not have many friends. They were mostly younger than me, in their twenties. I had three children when I was at uni. I was really busy. I went to the lectures and I had to go home and pick up my children from child care and then go home'.[16]

Most Lebanese immigrants placed the education of their children as a major priority, especially after the limitations they experienced in accessing education in Lebanon:

> Lebanese always think, first of all, how to educate their children. I bet most of them, 99 per cent, came to Australia, to provide a better future for their families... they wanted their children to learn. This was not available, as it should have been in Lebanon because of... the leaders, if you are not a follower of a certain *za'im*, you cannot provide even your living.[17]

This is confirmed by the positive educational achievements of Lebanese immigrant children before the civil war when compared to their educational achievements during and after the war. A study of the second generation in Australia illustrates the educational and occupational mobility of second-generation Lebanese whose parents arrived before 1981. In this study the Lebanese-born stayed at school and university longer than the Australian-born and higher proportions achieved tertiary qualifications than those with fathers born in Australia, the United Kingdom, or Western Europe. This illustrates a striking increase in educational qualifications and professional occupations across the two generations of Lebanese settlers in Australia.

This finding is confirmed by international studies. In the domain of educational attainment, for instance, the 2001 census in Canada shows that 21 per cent of Canadians aged 15 years and over of Lebanese origin were university graduates compared to 15 per cent being the percentage at the national level.[18]

For children who came from a family background of limited parental education, the value and support for education was limited. Some who came in the aftermath of the civil war experienced difficulty in coping with schooling in Australia, leading to unemployment and underemployment, sometimes across generations. The experience of many families in Lebanon during the previous 20 years had resulted in little formal secondary or post-secondary education. A moderate number had trade skills of a formal or, more likely, informal nature.

Research into literacy practices of immigrant families has revealed a number of challenges that Lebanese families faced in mainstream schools.[19] The socio-economic status of the immigrant family strongly influenced the capacity of students of Middle Eastern backgrounds to acquire English. The low educational backgrounds of many Lebanese immigrants arriving after 1990, due to the social dislocation of the civil war, meant that they had few educational skills to pass on to their children, either in Lebanon or Australia. The cultural distance between the receiving nation and the country of origin has also been found to influence language acquisition. This extends to the ways that families from non-English backgrounds value what is offered in state-run schools. Islamic families frequently value the teaching of

Islamic values, how to be a good Muslim and the memorisation of Koranic verses, which are not offered in mainstream schools.

Speech patterns in the home have also been found to affect student behaviours at school. Lebanese children are viewed as equal participants in the family. They participate by involving in often loud and excited overlapping talk rather than the turn-taking that is the required behaviour of other cultures. This can be interpreted as rudeness or arrogance in the school context. The challenges facing many Lebanese students, particularly those of Islamic background, are whether they assimilate and enjoy some success and happiness at school or whether they reject the education offered and possibly not acquire facility with English.

The language experiences of Lebanese children in the home and school context have implications for identity acceptance and formation. Parents convey to their children what they regard as important from their understanding of their culture, their values, and life experiences in general. When the experiences from the home are challenged by the experiences of the school children are forced to make a decision about the path they will choose.

An Australian study identified areas of similarity and difference between Lebanese-background students and non-Lebanese background students. The study, comparing the motivations to learn, showed that a significant number of students of Lebanese background valued education less.

> Many Lebanese-background students, like others, try hard at schoolwork because they are interested in their work; they need to know they are getting somewhere with their schoolwork; [they] try hard to understand new things at school; and try harder when they see improvement.

> On the other hand, the school experience of Lebanese students highlighted many issues that they had to overcome. These included difficulties with English as a language of instruction and being subjected to, what seemed to them, petty school rules. This was

particularly felt by those who migrated from a war-torn society, where survival and escape were their major imperatives.[20]

The experiences of some Lebanese students in mainstream schools sometimes revealed feelings of victimisation. As one community commentator stated:

> They come into this country and it wasn't ready for them. There is a certain feeling among young people, about their own image in the school... 'They hate us, Miss, they hate us'.[21]

There was also an issue for some male students in having female, rather than male, teachers. This led to situations where Lebanese students, who might not understand or respect the cultural orientation of the school, challenged or insulted teachers and, in particular, female teachers. The issue of parental unfamiliarity with schooling and its values and with the English language sometimes resulted in students' negative views of school. School was often not being respected as a social institution or as a vehicle for social mobility and improvement.[22]

The Lebanese students in Australian schools reveal experiences that they shared with some other non-English background students. Those who spoke Arabic at home were often not proficient in formal, written Arabic that is studied as a second language in some schools.[23] These educational limitations were exacerbated by parents' unfamiliarity with Australian schooling and the values and norms of formal education:

> They [the parents] are having problems. Most of those who came in the 1950s and 1960s and especially during the war were uneducated. They could not follow up with their children or catch up with them. They were busy making money and working.[24]

In this context, the students themselves were sometimes called upon to mediate between the school and home, which required them to translate between the Arabic and English languages. This involved them in being managers of their education and forming a link between their home and the wider, English-speaking Australian society. Steve, the year co-ordinator at Kotara School in Sydney, describes the resultant problems of communication between home and school:

> You know the Arabic translation for lazy, for truancy, for not doing homework is all 'good'. Whenever I sent letters home I know they would be intercepted. 'It's a letter from the school, mum.' 'What does it say?' 'Oh, nothing much. I'm doing good'.[25]

Some parents revealed a degree of shame for their lack of English language literacy in Australia which they contrasted with their family situations in Lebanon where the possession of literacy skills was a source of pride.[26] Some students felt that they did not receive strong support from their parents. It is probable that formal education to the level of senior secondary school was beyond the direct experience of many Lebanese parents. A Sydney interviewee commented that educational disadvantage was due to the gap between the students and the older generation as well as the educational background of the parents.

Lebanese students at times came up against teachers who they felt were culturally biased and who would use their social and cultural position to ridicule, embarrass or intimidate students at large from non-English backgrounds. In situations where students received one set of messages from home and another from school and where personal pride and ego were at stake, conflict with the school can occur. Responses to these issues by mainstream education providers and Lebanese community groups have been intermittent and not always effective.[27]

This resulted in a significant number of Lebanese background youth, often of Islamic faith, who became disenchanted with aspects of the wider Australian society. This is graphically depicted in 'The Lebs' by Michael Ahmad which presents an account of teenage Muslim students at Punchbowl Boys High School in Sydney in the 1990s and early 2000s. We see their resentful attitudes to authority at the school and in society as well as their experimenting with anti-anglo-establishment behaviour, including drinking, sex and drugs. At the same time, these boys have an awareness of their Muslim faith and family backgrounds which together form a counterpoint to their actions and behaviours at school and in the community.[28]

In isolated cases, the limited success and disaffection experienced by some young Muslims have been mobilised by militant, anti-west, Islamic groups who offered an identity and a pathway for those seeking success and meaning in their lives by becoming part of a world–wide radical movement such as Islamic State.

In summary, settling into education in Australia presented a series of challenges for Lebanese young people. Some benefitted from the opportunities afforded them and went on to tertiary studies and became successful in professional fields such as medicine, law accounting, science and education. However, other students' progress in education was affected by their arriving from a socially disrupted country with attitudes, beliefs and practices that were different from those of Australian society in the 1980s and 1990s. This generated issues such as low levels of English literacy, limited family support of schooling, cultural dissonance because of some patriarchal values and a belief by some in the need to be dominant and noticed.

The wrong side of the law

The vast majority of Australian-Lebanese lead peaceful, successful lives in their communities, grateful to be establishing their lives in Australia. However, a small number has been involved in actions and events which could be described as being on 'the wrong side of the law.' In these cases, it is important to distinguish between anti-social behaviour, often associated with young people, and breaches of the law, including organised criminal gangs.

The Setting

The world-wide rise of Islamic fundamentalism in the mid-1990s, culminating in the attacks on the World Trade Centre in New York and other targets in the USA, had a negative impact on the image of Middle Eastern communities, including in Australia. Peaceful, law-abiding Australian-Lebanese were targeted in some quarters as potential criminals. Some Muslim women, who travelled on public transport or in other public places, were vilified and attacked, including having their hijabs pulled off their heads. Islamic youths were abused, pushed and even spat upon. This was all part of the racist attitudes and incidents some Muslims experienced in their daily lives in Australia.

Anti-social behaviour

Against this setting a major event erupted which attracted national attention: the conflict known as the Cronulla Riot, when groups of white surfer youths attacked young people 'of Middle Eastern appearance'[29] using Cronulla beach. The immediate catalyst for the Cronulla Riot was a verbal exchange between these groups which led to physical confrontation. This resulted in a series of clashes and mob violence on 4 December 2005 in the beachside suburb of Cronulla, New South Wales, a location which had been the site of racial and ethnic tensions for some years. Later, this confrontation extended to the suburb of Punchbowl where convoys of men of 'Middle Eastern appearance' sought to get revenge for the earlier riot at Cronulla Beach. Again, there was some violence and property damage but police were able to prevent the violence from getting out of hand.

The media played a major role in escalating the event at Cronulla Beach. While this was by no means an isolated event, it was taken up by sections of the Sydney media, some of whom openly took sides against the Lebanese-Australians. Later investigations revealed that over 270,000 text messages had been transmitted, inciting racially motivated confrontation between the two groups. An underlying issue in these confrontations was the conflation of 'Lebanese', 'Arab' and 'Islamic' into a single 'Other', which was seen as an enemy of Australia.

An obvious consequence of this was the marginalising of many Australian-Lebanese youths from mainstream behaviours. To an extent this drove some to anti-social and disruptive behaviour to assert their Australian-Lebanese identity in the face of Anglo-Australian society. This process seems a common experience for youths of many newly arrived immigrant groups. They attempt to find their place in the wider complexity of Australian society by testing the boundaries of behaviours in their traditional culture and of Australian society.

Criminal Behaviour or Breaches of the Law

There is no demonstrated link between criminality and being of Lebanese background as statistics are not available on the ethnicity of convicted criminals. Unfortunately, this has led to the situation where Australian-Lebanese convicted of crimes have become a focus for some members of the wider community, sections of the media, and some politicians who chose to brand members of the Lebanese community as criminals or potential criminals.

As we noted, the civil war in Lebanon had a lasting impact on some Lebanese immigrants and their families, leading to problems with their access to employment and education in Australia. Social workers in the northern and north-western suburbs of Melbourne reported that, in some instances, these led to their addiction to gambling and even the loss of their homes. At its worst, this involved drug dealing, drug use, and different forms of criminality. The more serious activities of Lebanese criminal groups were involvement in narcotics, weapons trafficking, car theft, and money laundering. In the few worst cases these led to violence in the form of drive-by and pay-back shootings.

A small minority of young Lebanese became involved with extreme

Islamic religious groups, politically rather than religiously. A number of commentators claimed there was a convergence between organised crime and radical Islam. Close family networks, in some cases, aided the transition to religious extremism, including involvement in violence on behalf of Islamic State. On the other hand, there were instances where the young person appeared to be acting alone, having been radicalised without the knowledge and to the distress of their family.

It should be stressed that these forms of criminality did not apply to the vast majority of young Lebanese or their parents. However, as social worker, Leila Alloush testifies this did not prevent them from being subjected to anti-Arab and anti-Muslim racism:

> The level of racism is beyond your imagination. People who used to be very good to their Lebanese or Muslim neighbours – they don't want to talk to them anymore. This is simply because of media and popular representations of race and racial attributes. The City of Hume, which has the highest number of Muslims in Victoria, also has the highest number of racist incidents.[30]

Bassam Maaliki

The following story reveals yet another response to the challenges of settlement from a Lebanese Muslim background. Bassam Maaliki was a 14 year old student whose success in Australia was not confined to academic and professional achievements but involved him in reaching out to other young people from his own Muslim and wider Australian community. He created #uBelong, an organisation dedicated to ensuring that all refugees and migrants, whatever their background, feel a sense of belonging in Australia. This case study represents a positive response to negative experiences on the part of Bassam Maaliki and his extended family to life in Australia. His attitudes and achievements are best expressed in his own words from his acceptance speech when he won the Youth Community Medal at a NSW Youth Community Dinner in 2018. Settlement Services International.

My grandparents migrated to Australia in the 1960s, fleeing instability. Leaving Lebanon with almost nothing, they could speak only limited English and experienced hardships–but were thankful to their new country for extending a hand of assistance. Australia welcomed my grand-parents, providing a safe environment where they were able to retain their culture, their religious background, language and, most importantly,—seek opportunity. As a second generation Australian-Lebanese Muslim I have inherited the heavy burden to educate those who see difference before similarity. I know what it's like to be called a terrorist and to be told to go back to my country. But I was born here. Where would I go?

Throughout their hardships, my grandparents never let go of their roots. They learnt English, adapted to a different culture but shared their Lebanese customs (and food) openly and willingly. I mean, imagine Australia without hummus! My grandparents retained their heritage that would enrich their community and inevitably our country. It's because of them I stand here today, proud to call myself Australian.

27

LEBANESE COMMUNITIES, 2005–2016

Whether you are Muslim, Christian, Druze or Israeli, God protect thee,
remember that religious fanaticism for political goals, or political fanaticism for
religious purposes, is the worst kind of fanaticism.
Ameen Rihani

Community organisations

The 1990s witnessed a consolidation and increase in the number and diversity of organisations that served the community. These included churches and mosques, educational and welfare bodies, village associations, political organisations, media outlets, and cultural and sporting bodies. Some of these were solely or predominantly for Lebanese-Australians while others also served the wider Arabic community.

This period was marked by a proliferation and duplication of organisations to meet the needs and interests of different sections of the whole community. While some were large and prosperous bodies, others were shadow organisations which were little more than vehicles for one or two people with leadership aspirations. Especially during times of conflict in Lebanon, co-ordinated action by the total Lebanese community was virtually impossible. This helps explain the lack of an 'umbrella' body in Australia which could embrace and represent the community as a whole. Instead, a number of 'umbrella' bodies were established to represent different sections of the Lebanese community.

Where there were larger numbers of Lebanese settlers, such as in Sydney and Melbourne, there was a replication of the Lebanese religious, village and political structures. Those interviewed in Sydney explained that the Lebanese community is the same as in Lebanon:

> During the war and after 1975, there was a big migration, mainly from the Muslims. I believe now we are a reflection, a mirror of the society in Lebanon. We have the variety they have in Lebanon. We have Muslims [all sects], Christians all religions. Whatever you see in Lebanon, you see it here.[31]

In this period there were around 200 community organisations in Sydney, most of them village and regional groupings which were often affiliated with larger religious organisations. The community associations included the following 'umbrella' bodies funded by state and federal governments:

- The Australian-Lebanese Association of New South Wales (ALA)
- The Lebanese Community Council of New South Wales (LCC)
- The Arabic Council of Australia (ACA)
- The St George Lebanese Joint Committee

Of greater significance in the Lebanese community of Sydney were the religious institutions which predated and were better resourced than the 'umbrella' organisations. Given the size and significance of the Sydney Lebanese community, Sydney was the home of the mother churches and leading mosques in Australia. The major religious umbrella organisations were:

- The Maronite Eparchy of Australia
- The Antiochian Orthodox Eparchy of Australia, New Zealand and the Philippines
- The Melkite Catholic Eparchy of Australia and New Zealand
- The Lebanese Muslim Association (LMA)
- The United Muslim Women's Association (UMWA)
- The Al-Zahra Muslim Association (AZMA)
- The Al-Zahra Muslim Women's Association Inc. (AZMWA)

The size of the Lebanese community in Sydney allows for the same diversity as occurs in the confessional system of Lebanon. In a community where Christians are numerically equal to Muslims, the issue of Lebanese identity arises. Lebanese Christians continue to mainly identify as Maronite, Orthodox and Melkite. As such, they are aligned with the broader Christian communities of Catholicism and Orthodoxy. Muslim Lebanese (Sunni and Shi'ite) are aligned to the Muslim world, which spans the Middle East, and parts of Africa and Asia. The proliferation of religious bodies and the village associations illustrates the need for each group to gain its own place in the public sphere and to have its own voice to represent the needs and interests of its people.

At the same time there have always been attempts to establish 'umbrella' bodies to achieve collaboration and unified representation among Lebanese community bodies. One example is the Lebanese Community Council of New South Wales (LCC), established in 1983, whose members were drawn from Lebanese organisations and associations. The LCC aimed to strengthen collaboration among Lebanese Community bodies and to enhance the welfare and successful settlement of the community in Australia.

In New South Wales, some politicians cultivated the Lebanese community, because of its size and potential political influence. This led to a reciprocal recognition and relationship between community leaders and politicians that could enhance the status and influence of both parties. On the other hand, it enabled politicians to hold community leaders responsible for illegal activities by their community members, and to attempt to co-opt them in quelling unrest and perhaps violence among the Lebanese. As the CEO of the Arabic Council of Australia explained: 'Politicians and leaders use us to their own advantage at times'.[32]

This was particularly evident in times of community distress in the aftermath of the two Gulf Wars and the tensions generated by the Cronulla Riot. The duress under which the community existed at these times was apparent in the manner in which some politicians from both sides of politics, vilified sections of the Lebanese community, as it suited their political needs.

The effect of this on the Sydney community led to a fracturing of ties between religious groupings, such as they were. This led to 'othering' where sections of the community did not see political targeting as an attack on itself, rather as an attack on a particular section of the community to which they did not belong. This resulted in some religious and political groups distancing themselves from the causes of tension. The unforeseen result of this behaviour was to weaken the cohesion of the total community. As one Sydney interviewee explained, these attacks were not seen as a human rights issue, but rather as an issue where one group tried to prove its loyalty to the wider society by distancing itself from victims of ethnic targeting.

> Discrimination is the major issue facing the Lebanese community in New South Wales today, especially the racism towards the Lebanese because 'everybody is Lebanese'. Everyone is tarnished with the same brush. The nuances are not clearly understood by the general public. The tarnishing of everybody as a terrorist is a massive issue and has been for the last two decades.

> ... Christian Lebanese want to identify as being separate to the Arabs. During the period of the rape stories you would find people coming out who wanted to work around the Lebanese issue, claiming that 'Lebanese' [like them] were not involved. We tried to make it much wider than that, but people don't want to know. They see it as ... defending the Lebanese.[33]

Lebanese Muslim Association in Sydney

The Lebanese Muslim Association (LMA) is the umbrella organisation for three mosques in Sydney. It provides Islamic funeral and burial services and a cemetery in Sydney. In addition, it offers a range of community and social services, an educational college, sports services, and 16 afternoon school classes.

The Lakemba Mosque developed from a group of devout Islamic

Lebanese immigrant families who would pray together and maintain Islamic religious practices, as far as possible. In the 1970s the original families decided to build a mosque for the growing community. The mosque was completed and officially opened in 1975. The LMA, as the umbrella organisation, was behind building the mosque and all other religious activities for the community at this time.

The Muslim community in Sydney has changed over the years. While Lebanese Muslims are still the largest group attending the mosques, other Arabic-speaking immigrants are attracted to the services of the mosques and the LMA. 'Our policy is clear, whoever enters the office we will do our best to meet his or her needs'. Lebanese Muslims today make up about 30 per cent of the service usage. This is an indication of the earlier Lebanese settlement compared with those more recently arrived.

During the 2000s the children of older Lebanese Muslim migrants, as they gained qualifications in different areas, further assisted the LMA. They would bring modern approaches of organisation, strategic plans and policy development to the delivery of services.

One example of the contribution of the LMA was to protect the cultural practice of Muslim burial rites. This involved the LMA applying for a special licence to prepare the body for immediate burial. The mosque at Lakemba has three imams. The imams work together with the LMA to meet with families and deal with marriages and divorce from a religious point of view. This service is important for older Lebanese immigrants who, together with the LMA, pushed for the need to practise traditional Islamic burial.

The recent initiatives of the LMA cover many areas. They run youth programs; in the late 2010s they established a mental health clinic to address issues that for a long time had been ignored. They also set up an office to deal with the registration of marriages divorces and births in Lebanon. The LMA gained approval for the development of a residential aged care facility of 112 beds. They also set up foster care facilities for some 100 Islamic children who had become the victims of marriage breakdown due to failed marriages because of inter-cultural reasons, drug or alcohol abuse or gambling debts. The foster care facility is to help children maintain a strong cultural and religious identity. Plans were underway in the late 2010s for home care to help maintain elderly Lebanese in their homes. There were also plans for community housing.

The LMA in Lakemba has joined with other Christian and Islamic groups who work together on committees to speak on behalf of the Lebanese community in Sydney. Although one of the LMA roles is to advocate on behalf of the Sunni Lebanese community, it also has taken an active role in defending the wider Lebanese community, by providing services and working to improve community relations.

Sydney Sunni Muslims gather for Eid-al-Fitr Prayers at dawn at the Lakemba Mosque in Sydney to celebrate the end of Ramadaan.
(Source: Lebanese Muslim Association, NSW)

Issues in the Lebanese Muslim community

Emerging issues in the Lebanese community focus around the provision of health care. The Lebanese Muslim Association (LMA) has sought to provide services that include an understanding of cultural background but at the same time acknowledge that second-, third- and even fourth-generation immigrants are Australian. The LMA saw over 1,800 refugees (Syrian, Afghani, Myanmar, Iraqi) in just 18 months late in the 2010s.

A key issue in the Lebanese community has been the provision of care for aged parents. Traditionally, the oldest son was expected to look after his parents. The economic realities mean that husband and wife may both have to work to make ends meet. This puts pressure on families where appropriate care of the elderly is a struggle. Sometimes the provision of basic care is not possible. The resultant family tension can lead to mental health issues and divorce. The LMA tries to ease this burden by providing aged care support in the home.

Similarly, children rejecting the values and traditions of parents are also a cause of some social discord. This has led to second-generation parents to seek to blend Islamic faith with life in the Australian community.

In terms of community relations, the 'Lebanese of Muslim faith bear the brunt of discrimination and racism'. The global reaction against Islam has been just as present in Australian cities like Sydney as it has been elsewhere. There has been a negative focus on the Muslim community because of the link between Islam and terrorism. Islamic people who dress differently have become obvious targets for attacks. The lens of security and terrorism has cast Islam as a danger to society. The criminality of some groups in the wider Lebanese community can be seen as caused by a breakdown in communication and understanding between generations. The cultural clashes between the Lebanese and members of the wider Australian community have also led to anti-social behaviours and some criminality within families and community life.

The Lebanese community is changing. The increasing number of educated professionals who are the children of earlier immigrants from unskilled or uneducated backgrounds, means that the community is now led by some members with high-level skills. It is only the negative stories that are looked at by current affairs programs whenever a news issue emerges. Criminality that is attached to the very small number of Lebanese involved gives the whole community a bad name.

> This makes advocating on behalf of the Lebanese Muslim community difficult. Whether it is consulting with government departments on anti-terror legislation or advocating for the needs of particular sections of the Islamic community, the public servants you are talking to may have no detailed understanding about the issues facing the community. We try to bridge the gap between departments and the community by opening our doors and inviting policy makers and public servants to see the issues our community are facing.[34]

The Lebanese umbrella organisations, which focus on community and welfare issues, have remarkably similar values, irrespective of differences in religious faith and practice. Each organisation professes to offer its services to any Lebanese and Arabic-speaking client and to cooperate with other bodies for the benefit of the total community.

Religious organisations

Traditional religion has historically been a key marker of identity among Lebanese immigrants. There has often been a close relationship in Lebanon between religious identity and village identity. If the inhabitants of a village share a particular religion then the village identity is linked to that religious community.

While churches in Sydney may have members of their congregations from many different villages, there is a reciprocity where the village supports the church and the church supports the village. Churches which are more closely aligned with Lebanese national identity, such as the Maronite Church, work hard to support religious identity as well village identity. As one Sydney interviewee put it: 'all groups – village groups – act under the religion umbrella'.[35]

Our Lady of Lebanon Chruch, Melbourne, was opened on 8 March
2008. The planning, construction and furnishing of this church
involved the commitment and contributions of priests and lay
people from the Maronite parish in Victoria.
(Source: Trevor Batrouney, *Living our heritage: the Maronite Church in
Victoria*).

The adherence of the second generation to the religion of their
parents is more variable. The churches and mosques in Sydney
attempt to develop an identity for the children of immigrants. They
provide meeting places for the younger generation and explain the
relevance of religious teachings to their daily lives:

> Only the churches and the mosques bring the new generation together.
> Even at university there's no group at university, they all go their own way.[36]

Most Christian churches provide English services, including bi-lingual
services on Sunday. These are supported by social activities such as
sporting events or jointly watching important rugby league matches,
camping trips and other similar events that have cultural significance
in both Australian and Lebanese communities.

We have a football game especially for the young ones a couple of times a year. They play football among themselves; some are from here, some are from Punchbowl. There are 30 – 40 of them and they organise a sports day.

The best thing which has happened for us is our Sunday School... We are trying to get to those under 18 [years]... once they get attached to the church... they come for more.

...on Thursday night we have a mass for the younger generation. They are all very Christian. It's about identity. It's more the feeling of belonging. Their parents don't feel as if they belong so much.[37]

There is also an element of inculcating the traditional doctrines of the different religious communities. This represents an attempt to establish links between the religious culture of their parents and the realities that their Australian-born children face on a daily basis:

What [the churches] are doing well is attracting the younger generation through a range of different activities, for example, camping.[38]

St Nicholas Antiochian Orthodox Church, Punchbowl, NSW
(Source: St Nicholas Church, Punchbowl)

Village associations

Village associations support the traditional identity, values and worldview of the village. The size of the Lebanese community in Sydney allows for many Lebanese villages to have their own well-developed organisations. In the more organised communities, the associations provide community centres which include meeting places for immigrants and their families. Men will play *taouli* or cards while women enjoy talking among themselves.

Some community groups have a directory of village members and of tradespersons from the village that can be used for various services. This is apparent in the directories of the Hadchit and Zgharta communities to name two.[39] In the case of the Hadchit community, this has been taken a step further in the development and maintenance of traditional village obligations or *wasta* to provide mutual aid and support for those seeking to establish their lives in Australia. The village groupings become social, economic and educational agencies for their members. As such, they are important to the communities they serve, whether Muslim or Christian.

Village associations seek to preserve and promote traditional local identity and relationships as they were in Lebanon. Some groups are supported by substantial numbers, in some cases larger than the populations of the original villages in Lebanon. The extent to which these links occur is evident through many contributions made, not only to families in villages, but also to the well-being and welfare of the village itself. The expatriate Lebanese from the village of Tannourine, provide an example of support for their home village:

> The people from Tannourine built a hospital in their town up in the mountains. There is a government hospital there, it was very poor, and they [the Australian Tannourine village organisation] built a big section on the hospital – it is called 'Australia Ward'. They have all the latest machinery for the heart, for whatever – the latest technology.[40]

Other communities fundraise in Australia through local community events to provide necessary hospital machinery or appliances, such as wheelchairs or ECG machines. Most villages survive from money sent from Australia or America. The same settlement drive that helped immigrant families establish their lives in Australia also helped village groups to purchase houses in Sydney and Melbourne to provide a social focus for their members.

A major challenge among the village associations is their ability to reach into the Australian-born generation of earlier immigrants. The more successful village bodies realised that, to survive and be relevant for the next generation, they needed to survey their members to determine their interests and needs; to run sporting events; to conduct 'heritage' events where people can trace their ancestry. Some groups also organised trips back to the village in Lebanon.

The effectiveness of the associations in maintaining relevance, cohesion and future orientation is dependent on its leadership. Those that are led by Lebanese immigrants wanting only to maintain their links with their village or to gain a personal power base, tend to struggle for relevance among the young. It is only where there is the involvement of some members of the Australian-born generation, including those with tertiary qualifications, that village organisations are able to be more responsive to the needs and interests of the Australian-born Lebanese.

A community worker, who arrived in Sydney in 1986, claimed that the divisions in the community have become sharper over time as a result of conflicts in the Middle East:

> Since her arrival in 1986 Randa indicated that the groupings of the community have become more pronounced. When she first arrived, there were not many divisions between villages or religions and sects. Within the Muslim religion, there was a less pronounced division between Sunni and Shi'ite. The divisions extend beyond how one prays. Now it is huge: people seem to hate each other because of the differences – not in Australia, but what is happening in Syria. In her professional capacity, Randa is frustrated by the way some people

living in Sydney, support their own sect, just because it is their own sect – even if they are doing bad things [overseas].[41]

These divisions are not only political but have an impact on social life within the community, whereby people prefer to interact with those who share their views or are members of the same organisation:

For example, in Marylands there is one street of people from the same village. They visit each other but they don't visit other people. They like to go to the same concerts. My opinion is that they feel safe; they feel happy to be with persons from the same village. It's about being comfortable.[42]

Another community worker provided an insight into the community in Sydney:

In Sydney, there is not simply one Lebanese identity. There are multiple identities. If you live in the south of Sydney, say the St George district close to the airport, you are more likely to have come from the south of Lebanon. If you live in Bankstown or Auburn you're most likely to have come from the North. If you live in Parramatta you are most likely to come from a Christian sect. People seem to gather around other people like them. There is also informal behaviour within communities that questions why people wish to move away from other members of the small community. Certain villages like to stay close to each other. In Arncliffe, there is a village group called Yaroun (a mix of Shi'ite and Christians) and every person who comes from there has to live in Arncliffe, not Bexley or Bankstown or Rockdale. That's where the employment was and where people would find jobs. In the early days [in the 1970s] there would be three or four or more families staying in one house and they would work together. Now the mentality has changed.

Some village organisations contribute to, and help develop, Lebanese identity. Which village you come from in Lebanon provides you with your community DNA in Sydney: they will know your name, your religion, your sect, your politics and your family history.[43]

Social workers in the northern suburbs of Melbourne have noted that there are about five Lebanese villages whose members have only migrated to Melbourne and nowhere else in the world: Mish Mish, Ain El Taheb and Duneer, among others. They live within the same geographical area and tend to marry within the community.[44]

However, in Australia a number of factors have begun to work against divisions in community and loyalty to a particular za'im. First, although the notion of the community leader or *za'im* is prevalent in Lebanon, it loses much of its force in Australia as qualifications, laws and regulations cover many aspects of economic and social life. Secondly, members of the community, who have achieved educational qualifications and professional positions, tend to reject membership of political groupings and loyalty to a za'im.

Welfare organisations

The Melbourne Lebanese community has maintained a similar spread of community organisations as Sydney. These include religious, political, cultural and welfare bodies. As we saw, the welfare organisations were mostly established in the 1980s at a time of dire need to support recent arrivals fleeing the civil war. Over time, these evolved into agencies providing different services for the Lebanese and wider Arabic-speaking community.

Taking Arabic Welfare as our first case study, we can observe this process of adapting to the changing needs of their communities. To recap, Arabic Welfare (formerly, Australian Lebanese Welfare) is a not-for-profit organisation established in Melbourne in 1983 to meet the urgent welfare needs of Lebanese immigrants and refugees who fled Lebanon before and during the Civil War in Lebanon. The original vision of the founders of Arabic Welfare conceived it as a non-political, non-sectarian and professional body dedicated to serving the welfare needs of the Lebanese and the wider Arabic-speaking community.

Over the years, Arabic Welfare expanded its range of services. Initially, it focused on casework to meet the needs of those who came through the door on a daily basis. In a logical extension to individual casework, Arabic Welfare established groups for women, the elderly and young people. In 1995, Arabic Welfare gained funding and encouragement from government to enter the field of employment services.

While these services were initially located in the northern suburbs of Melbourne with its large concentration of Lebanese, Arabic Welfare later extended both its casework and group work services to multiple locations throughout the Melbourne metropolitan area. Over the years the range of services offered put Arabic Welfare in contact with many thousands of Lebanese and their community leaders.

During the 1990s, Arabic Welfare took a leading role in initiating a number of community projects. These included a Lebanese festival, achievement awards for services by prominent Australian-Lebanese, citizenship ceremonies, and functions to raise funds for mainstream local charities. During this decade, Arabic Welfare became a leading Australian-Lebanese community body in Melbourne, recognised favourably by the Australian-Lebanese and wider Australian community.

By the first decade of the 21st century, Arabic Welfare presented as a complex organisation funded by Commonweath and State governments and supported by significant sections of the Australian-Lebanese community. It sought to meet the needs of Arabic-speaking immigrants and their communities and, at the same time, to meet the governments' requirements for accountability and changing priorities. Through its welfare and employment activities, it complemented the work of mainstream organisations and acted as an intermediary with them for Lebanese and other Arabic-speaking migrants.

In a second case study we can trace its Sydney counterpart, the Lebanese Community Council (LCC) which was established in Sydney in 1983. Its origin was similar to that of Arabic Welfare in Melbourne. Both were established at the initiation of the Immigration Minister to help meet the needs of the increased number of Lebanese who emigrated due to the civil war.

As a community worker, Louay Mostapha has an insight into the ways in which the LCC meets the needs of the Lebanese community in Sydney:

> Currently, the LCC is a collective of about 33 community organisations that might represent a village or a town in Lebanon. The LCC is funded for settlement services it provides to recent arrivals with an Arabic-speaking background. The current clients of the LCC are mainly Lebanese and Iraqis. The key settlement issues addressed by the LCC include housing, employment issues and education.

> Louay helps people to link in with different community organisations to find temporary accommodation, to find short term housing, or to be put on a waiting list for public housing. Processing and finding permanent accommodation in public housing can take between 14 and 18 years. His clients are unable to purchase a house because of housing prices in Sydney.

> To find employment openings for new arrivals the LCC works with a number of service providers. But it takes many, many calls to find any available positions. It is extremely difficult to find employment. The community networks include friends or friends of family; any link is used to try to find work. Some clients are able to find work for a day or two some not at all.

The educational background of many LCC clients shows increasing levels of education among the recently arrived, young immigrants, compared with older immigrants. A small number of young immigrants have tertiary education from Lebanon while older immigrants may be able to read and write but are usually not formally educated:

> In Sydney, right now, education is a main issue within the Lebanese community. Around the time of migration from the Civil War, we lost a whole generation due to lack of education. Now there is an emphasis on education. For families now with young kids the main focus is on educating

the children. This is having an impact on birth rate. The need
to educate their children is now resulting in smaller families,
so each child can be given the best opportunities and have a
proper education.

As a peak organisation the LCC helps address community relations
issues that emerge within the community and between the Lebanese
and other communities.[45]

28

Lebanese identity in the new Millennium

The after-effects of the attack on the Twin Towers in New York and the Tampa event in Australia, both in 2001, provided a watershed in terms of relations between Middle Eastern migrants, including Lebanese, and sections of the wider Australian community. In the eyes of some, Lebanese, Arabs and Muslims were conflated into a single group, which was identified with terrorist activity and defined as a danger to Australia and its way of life. Negative community attitudes led to violence and racist attacks, in December 2005, between Lebanese and wider Australian groups during the riot at Cronulla Beach and, later, in Punchbowl, Sydney. These events, and the negative publicity they attracted, affected communal attitudes to Lebanese during this period.

The loss of Lebanese national autonomy during the Syrian occupation was followed by the Summer War when Israel invaded Lebanon, seemingly at will. Again Lebanon was subjected to a neighbouring power defining Lebanon and the Lebanese as a subordinate people. And yet the Summer War led to mobilisation of the Lebanese in the diaspora as they provided various forms of assistance to their former homeland. This revealed that the Lebanese may also be identified as an international community spread throughout the Middle East as well as in Europe and the new world.

The ongoing Syrian civil war with its continuing impact on the Middle East as a whole also confirmed in Australia the negative views of the Middle East and its people. To some extent this was tempered by the humanitarian tragedy caused by the war and the agreement of Australia to accept some Syrian refugees.

During this period Australia's immigration and settlement policies became more narrowly focused with their emphasis on economic rationalism as a touchstone for its treatment of migrants and refugees. These developments reflected and amplified the more negative social attitudes in the economy and society. This had a major impact on the continuing unemployment and some poverty, even criminality, among sections of the Lebanese community. Although Lebanese migrants were to be found in all sectors of Australian society, elements in the media emphasised negative definitions of recent Lebanese migrants in Australia. This contributed to some discrimination against them.

The size of the Lebanese communities in Sydney and Melbourne led to a proliferation of community organisations—religious, welfare and cultural. While each of these bodies had their own mission, clients and membership, they were willing to provide their services to all those who approached them, irrespective of their country of birth or religion. In this way these organisations became multi-purpose bodies which were supported by those Lebanese immigrants and their children who wanted to retain some parts of their traditional identity, whether religious, cultural or political.

In 2011 Amna Karra-Hassan and Lael Kassem set up the Auburn Giants, the first women's AFL team in Western Sydney. The team is made up of second and third generation Australians.
(Source: Auburn Giants Football Club)

NOTES

1   Australian Lebanese Historical Society of Victoria, 2006. Report of the ALHSV.
2   Pollard, R 2015, 'For families of Lebanon's missing, the war goes on'. *The Age*.
3   Traboulsi, F 2007, *Op. Cit.* p. 245
4   Tabar. P 2009, *Op. Cit.* p. 10
5   Traboulsi, F *Op. Cit.* 2007, p. 245
6   Fersan, E 2010, *Op. Cit.*
7   Kasparian, C 2009, *Op. Cit.* p. 24
8   Tabar, P 2010, p. 6
9   ABS 2016 Census Country of Birth – Lebanon.
10   Interview Marie June 2016.
11   Monsour, A. 2014 *Op. Cit.*
12   Interview Salem Haddad September 2016
13   Betts K, & Healy, E 2006, *Op. Cit.* p. 38
14   *Ibid.* p. 29
15   Australian Census 2006. Table 11.5
16   Interview Randa September 2016
17   Interview Marie June 2016
18   Statistics Canada, retrieved from statcan.ca
19   Markose, S 2007, *Home Literacy Practices of Immigrant Families and Cultural Discontinuity: Two case studies*, Australian Association for Research in Education
20   Suleiman, R & McInerney, DM 2006, 'Motivational goals and school achievement: Lebanese-background students in south-western Sydney', *Australian Journal of Education*, vol. 50, no. 3, Australian Council for Educational Research.
21   Interview Randa June 2016
22   Cruickshank, K 2006, *Teenagers, Literacy and School: Researching in Multicultural Contexts*, Routledge Taylor Francis Group. p. 65

23 *Ibid.* p. 65
24 Interview Marie, June 2016
25 Cruickshank, K 2006, *Op. Cit.* p. 69
26 *Ibid.* p. 69
27 *Ibid.* p. 69
28 Ahmad, M M 2018, *The Lebs*, Hachette.
29 Castles, S et al. 2012, *Op. Cit.* p. 18
30 Interview Lebanese Social Worker in Melbourne, April 2017.
31 Interview Marie, June 2016
32 Interview Randa, June 2016
33 Interview Randa, June 2016
34 Interview Almeddine, K & Malas, A May, 2018
35 Interview Ghassan, June 2016
36 Interview Ghassan, June 2016
37 Interview Fr. Nabil, June 2016
38 Interview Shadia, June 2016
39 Hyndmann-Rizk, N 2010, 'Migration, Wasta and Big Business Success: The Paradox of Capital Accumulation in Sydney's Hadchiti Lebanese Community', *Labour Management & Development Journal*, Vol. 14,
40 Interview Marie, June 2016
41 Interview Randa, September 2016
42 Interview Randa, September 2016
43 Interview Louay, September 2016
44 Interview Leila, October 2017
45 Interview Louay, Sepember 2016

PART 6

Contacts between Australia and Lebanon, 2005–2016

In this part we examine four dimensions of Australia-Lebanon contacts: the impact of travel and communications technology; economic links between Australia and Lebanon; political links and the re-opening of the Australian Embassy in July 1995; and the increase in return visits to Lebanon following the end of the civil war. While this discussion is not exhaustive, it includes examples of these various forms of contact between Australians and Lebanon during this period.

29

THE TIES THAT BIND: LINKS BETWEEN AUSTRALIA AND LEBANON

We constantly wear two faces: one to ape our ancestors, the other to ape the West.
Amin Maalouf

Travel

The impact of modern forms of travel on the links between families and other groups in Australia and Lebanon can hardly be overestimated. Since the 1980s we have seen how quicker, easier and cheaper travel has made the world a smaller place, and diminished the time and cost of travel between Australia and Lebanon. In particular, it has facilitated contacts between family members in both countries as testified by Randa, who came to Australia in 1986:

> Randa keeps in contact with her family in Lebanon. She visits her mother in Beirut every year and sometimes goes up to Berlin to see her sister and to Belgium to see her brother. 'We have a house in my father's village, Ali Al Nahri, near Rayak which I love. In summer, we spend most of the time in Ali Al Nahri. There, I see my family from my father's side.' In addition to visits, she communicates with those in Lebanon by phone and skype. Communication is much easier now. Sometimes she speaks to her mother on Skype so that her mother can see her and feel assured that her daughter is well by seeing her face. Equally, Randa is able to see her mother and, if she says that she is well, check she actually looks well.[1]

Representatives and leaders of community organisations have visited Lebanon to attend meetings and conferences and to accompany delegations and tours. These have been complemented by frequent visits to Australia by significant figures in the parent organisations. This two-way travel has reduced isolation and strengthened knowledge and understanding between various groups in Australia and their counterparts in Lebanon.

Efficient and quicker travel has reduced the isolation of immigrant churches and mosques and ensured that they are aware of developments beyond Australia. For example, Church leaders were able to travel to their mother churches in the Middle East and to sister churches around the world. Reports on these visits are then disseminated to all parishes in Australia. The internet also made possible worldwide involvement in significant religious events wherever they are held. This has proved to be especially helpful to the clergy and lay people of an immigrant church or mosque where the centres of authority and religious life of the churches are overseas.

Communications

The means by which migrants maintained contacts with family in Lebanon and other countries in the diaspora has changed over time. By the 2000s the revolution in communications technology meant that immigrants had access to a range of media which provided direct and immediate communication with their family as well as current information about Lebanon.

Third-wave immigrants, with their urgent need to keep in touch with family and developments in Lebanon, took advantage of an extensive range of media with which to communicate speedily and to obtain 'real time' news and entertainment from Lebanon. The difference between the experiences of first- and third-wave migrants lies in the speed, immediacy, versatility and cost of communications, which has collapsed distance and brought the 'here' and 'there' so much closer.

Cable television, the internet and related technologies have been of even greater significance in disseminating news and information throughout Lebanon and Australia. One example was the speed and efficiency with which Lebanese in Australia became informed about the Summer War in Lebanon in 2006. This enabled mobilisation of support and resources in various Australian cities.

The revolution in communications technology and its impact on links between Australia and Lebanon have taken a number of forms. These include the access of Lebanese in Australia to Lebanese and Arab television programs including LBCI, FTV, TL and OTV, which are readily accessible to the diaspora via satellite. Four Lebanese newspapers have continued to be published in Sydney with branch offices in Melbourne and no fewer than ten radio stations. Of even greater importance has been the communication between families in Lebanon and Australia through 'skype' and 'facetime'. This has enabled family members to witness events and activities instantaneously in both countries.

During periods of conflict in Lebanon the activities of the leaders of different political groups revealed the powerful influence that modern forms of travel and, especially, communications exerted on their activities. The activities of leaders of the United Australian Lebanese Movement (UALM) provide a clear example. From the 1990s the leadership and representatives of the UALM made multiple trips to Lebanon to see the political situation at first hand and to offer moral and practical support from sections of the Australian-Lebanese community. Over the years cable television has brought to the homes of members of the UALM in Melbourne the struggles and conflicts in Lebanon, whether these took the form of vigorous debate, demonstrations or armed conflict.

Modern forms of travel and communications have been especially helpful to UALM's continuing interest in Lebanese politics as some members seek to live in both political worlds. However, apart from voting in Lebanese elections, it may be that this 'nationalism at a distance' will eventually wane over time as local Australian issues assume greater significance to those living in Australia.

Economic and political links

Economic links between the two countries have taken a number of forms over the years. The Lebanese in Australia have contributed to the Australian economy through a great variety of occupations, businesses and professions.

Lebanese abroad have always sent remittances to Lebanon to support their families and certain charities, often in their home villages and towns, particularly in times of need. The economic contributions of the Lebanese diaspora include investments of migrant capital, the opening of businesses in the homeland, fostering of trade between the two countries and return visits to Lebanon. Further evidence is clearly indicated by the percentages of money transferred to Lebanon by the total Lebanese diaspora around the world over the last three decades, which ranged from 17 per cent to 46 per cent of Lebanon's Gross Domestic Product (GDP). This was equivalent to one third of the Lebanese GDP and was not a transient phenomenon but rather an historical one.[2]

Since the civil war, the Lebanese Government and other Lebanese institutions, such as business groups and universities, have actively sought to expand the economic contributions of the diaspora to Lebanon. This has involved arranging meetings and conferences in Lebanon to encourage business and cultural links between Lebanon and countries of the diaspora. An example in 2010 is an organisation known as Lebanese Diaspora Energy which has the following mission statement:

> The Lebanese Diaspora Energy (LDE) seeks to showcase the success stories of select Lebanese residents and expatriates, and motivate them to stay connected, while celebrating the Lebanese heritage and promoting the positive image of Lebanon around the world. LDE represents an occasion for emigrants to return to their roots and develop a valuable cultural and social connection with their homeland. The event also enables influential Lebanese residents to meet thousands of Lebanese key players and decision-makers from the Diaspora.[3]

Lebanese organisations are dedicated to raising the international profile of Lebanon and to enlisting successful and prominent people from the diaspora to assist in supporting and strengthening their homeland. The initiatives by civic organisations such as LDE may also be seen as attempts to regain the status of Lebanon among the world community after the trauma of the civil war and invasion and occupation by foreign powers.

Village of Kfarsghab welcomes Australian visitors during Australia-Lebanon week in July 1995 (Source: Trevor Batrouney)

This has been matched by business groups in Australia, such as chambers of commerce, which have supported business links between Australia and Lebanon. One example is the Australian Lebanese Chamber of Commerce and Industry (ALCCI), which was launched in 2011 with the following mandate:

> Charged with the responsibility of enhancing trade links and providing a networking platform for forward-thinking entrepreneurs, we are currently working hard to develop solid relationships with the many communities that make up the wider Australian business community in order to maximise the benefit of two-way opportunities in trade,

tourism and investment at both a local and national level for Australia
and Lebanon.[4]

The membership of the ALCCI was made up of representatives of
business and community as well as professionals and tradespeople.
The Board of Directors included leaders of industry and commerce
while the patrons of the ALCCI included mainly politicians with a
particular interest in commercial and cultural links between Australia
and Lebanon.

Two important events took place in Lebanon from 12 to 20 July
1995 which revealed the strengthening relationship between Australia
and Lebanon. The first was the Australia-Lebanon Week, hosted by
the Ministry for Emigrants, which included meetings with Lebanese
political and religious leaders as well as tours and entertainment for
the visitors to Lebanon. The second occasion, which formed the
centrepiece of the week, was the reopening of the Australian Embassy
in Beirut, hosted by the Australian Government on Tuesday 18 July
1995. These events were attended by a number of Commonwealth
and State parliamentarians known for their interest in, and support
of, Lebanese migrants. In addition to these events, many members
of the Lebanese community in Australia participated in some or all
of the activities of Australia-Lebanon Week. These included leaders
of Australian-Lebanese community organisations, business people,
academics and many representatives of the press.

Throughout the Week, there were meetings with the President, the
Prime Minister, the Speaker of the Parliament, as well as leaders of
the major religious communities. One major event was a reception
at the Carlton Hotel addressed by the Minister of Emigrants, the
Ambassador of Australia and Dr Trevor Batrouney representing the
Lebanese community in Australia. The re-opening of the Australian
Embassy in Beirut was a celebrated occasion hosted by representatives
of the Australian Government.

Australia-Lebanon Week was an endeavour by the Lebanese
Government to declare that Lebanon was entering a period of peace

and prosperity and to seek assistance from other governments and expatriate communities around the world. Unfortunately, events in the decades following hindered Lebanon's pursuit of these lofty aims.

Over subsequent years, local elections in Lebanon provided another political link between the two countries when large numbers of Lebanese Australians with dual citizenship returned to their home village to exercise their voting rights. This had a noticeable effect on the school attendance of Lebanese children in the northern suburbs of Melbourne.[5]

30

RETURN VISITS TO LEBANON

If you come back from a journey, offer your family something though it be only a stone.

Arabic Proverb

Return visits after the Civil War grew exponentially, with multiple visits common. The major purposes were introductions of family members and family reunions, including reunions of 'global' families. A latent function of return visits was the transfer of cultures across both country of adoption and country of origin. While most valuations of Lebanon were positive, some visits were affected by timing, for example, during the civil war, and by conflicts over family property.

The first delegation of Lebanese leaving Sydney to attend a world conference of emigrants in Lebanon, 1964. (Source: Andrew Batrouney)

A comparison of second- and third-wave migrants reveals changes over time in attitudes and feelings towards Lebanon. Second-wave immigrants present a mixture of positive valuations and criticism of Lebanon which indicated that they were now beginning to see their former homeland from the perspective of their adopted country. They offered criticisms of corruption in government, human rights, and peoples' values. In doing so, they revealed their assimilation into the Australian way of life and the lag between their perceptions of the Lebanon they left and the Lebanon they visited. Third-wave immigrants were, in general, more ambivalent, expressing positive feelings about life in Lebanon but a growing awareness that Australia was becoming, or had become, their home.

The period following the Civil War saw a major movement of Lebanese-born and their families back to Lebanon. There had been relatively few permanent departures with, for example, no more than 155 in 1991/92, 126 in 1992/93 and 183 in 1993/94. However, departures of the Lebanese-born living in Australia of a short-term kind (defined as less than 12 months) steadily rose from a low of 5,666 in 1991/92 to a high of 18,755 in 1998-99. To these figures must be added the second-generation Australian-born who also visited Lebanon. While numbers for the latter group are not readily available, it is likely that their inclusion would, at least, double the number of short-term departures of Lebanon-born and their descendants. The proliferation of Middle Eastern travel agents bore witness to the size and significance of return visits to Lebanon.

The purposes stated by Lebanese residents for short-term visits were dominated by the categories of 'visiting friends/relatives' and 'holiday'. These covered a number of activities such as attending family weddings, becoming engaged or married, baptising a child, and visiting the migrants' ageing parents. These visits often included activities such as visiting parts of Lebanon with family and friends. In comparison, short-term visits for business were much less common.

The purpose of most visits was to reunite with family and introduce new family members:

- To see my parents before they died.

- I took my son to introduce him to his relations and where his father was born.

- To see family and what happened to the country [after the war].

The visits of a second-wave migrant, who had been in Australia for over 50 years, revealed the different purposes of visits at different stages in a person's life. After living in Australia for four years, his first visit in 1969 was to spend time with his parents and to marry. Three years later he returned to baptise his first child and to bring his parents to Australia. In 1978 he took his wife and three children to visit the other grandparents. The main purpose of his 1984 visit was political: to engage in fact-finding and to support a particular political party. In 1995 he visited family briefly but spent most time touring Lebanon, Syria, Jordan and Egypt with his elder son. A year later, in 1996, he took his two sons and daughter to again visit family and also to show them Lebanon.[6]

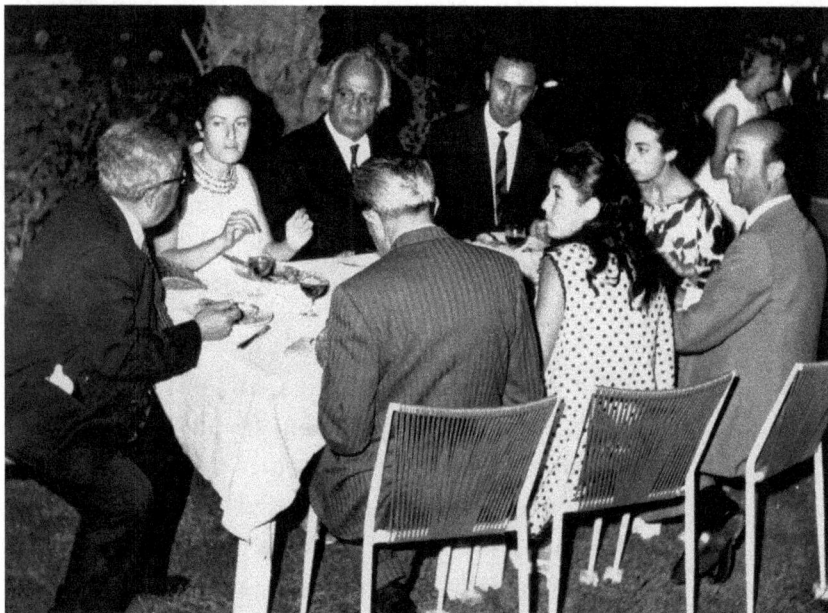

1968 - Sue Khyat eats in the open, Lebanese style with family and friends at a Rotary Club evening function in Tripoli, Lebanon.
(Source: State Library of Victoria)

The desire to visit Lebanon and show children the sights of their homeland proved to be a common theme as many migrants had left Lebanon without seeing the country. There was much joy, especially during the first return visits. A respondent from a village in south Lebanon declared 'my heart was dancing. I was born in this country and I do love it from my heart'.[7]

Another dimension of family contacts were reunions in Lebanon of family members from around the world. One occasion was the fiftieth anniversary of the marriage of the grandparents of a young Lebanon-born Australian, attended by family members from Melbourne, San Francisco, New York, Toronto and Saudi Arabia. Another respondent reported that every second year she has a reunion in Lebanon with her sisters who come from Zahle in Lebanon, Damascus in Syria, Sao Paulo in Brazil, and Miami in the United States of America. These global Lebanese families were able to keep in touch through modern communications media and, more importantly, to meet each other on a regular basis.

Some return visits were undertaken 'to gauge the possibility of returning permanently... to have a future plan to return to Lebanon'. Another respondent returned with her whole family, placed the children in schools with the intention of selling up in Australia and returning to Lebanon. However, conditions in Lebanon just before the war prevented this from happening. Another pattern was to send part of a family, perhaps a single child, back to Lebanon to be cared for by a grandmother, while the parents in Australia both worked. Testimonies about returning to Lebanon reveal an unwillingness to give up the possibility that one day they might return and resume past lives.

Return visits often raised the issue of family property, which had been left behind in migration. In some cases, family members who had migrated lost their connection with their family's properties, which were eventually taken over, with or without compensation, by family members who had stayed in Lebanon. This has been the cause of some conflict between families in both countries. In other instances, emigrants would return to Lebanon, build houses and, after a time, return to Australia, leaving their properties to be cared for and used by other family members. In cases where Lebanese in Australia had tenants in their properties in Lebanon, it sometimes became difficult to evict them and the properties over time became the de facto property of the tenants.

Different attitudes to domestic property in Lebanon and Australia lie behind conflicts over property. In Lebanon, family homes tend to be handed down through the generations and are inextricably bound up with the extended family, whereas in Australia a more functional attitude to property exists where original family homes are sold and second-generation members typically establish their own homes. The great majority of respondents felt that their visits had changed their feelings about Lebanon. On the other hand, some claimed that visiting there did not affect them one way or the other: 'I love to be in both places'.

The Australian-Lebanese revealed a range of attitudes and feelings towards the country in which they were born. Second-wave immigrants, after many years in Australia, expressed generally positive feelings about Lebanon:

- After 46 years in Australia I am still close to my family [in Lebanon] and still close to the village. I am proud of Lebanon as a nation and get upset at what happens.

- For me, I never lost my passion for Lebanon... a major influence on my life is there... I don't think going back ever changed that. I've remained positive.

A third-wave immigrant, who fled Lebanon because of the war, described the intense emotion of homecoming on her first return visit in 1986-87:

Although there was still fighting, it was like going to heaven... we were so excited so happy that we were able to see it... we cried a lot when we arrived at Beirut International Airport, we got emotional, we felt like we went home. I wouldn't believe I was in Lebanon... this is where I belong.

However, the same respondent was less enthusiastic the second time: 'I felt I belonged there and here.' During her third visit in 1991, her views had begun to change:

> I was planning to go for good. I lived in Beirut but it was a big disappointment. No one was happy. All our relations and friends had worries... lost family members. People over there had different worries and problems to us.

These comments map the changes over time in her feelings towards Lebanon with a change of identification apparent as she now came to see herself as different from the people and their worries in Lebanon.

A number of second-wave respondents were profoundly disillusioned with Lebanon, which they now saw through the prism of many years of living in Australia. They claimed they could now see Lebanon in context:

> There were a lot of changes in my understanding about Lebanon... before I didn't know the differences between Lebanon and Australia. In Australia there is a social security system, law and order and no big man/small man. Why don't they do this in Lebanon? You could see the bad things in Lebanon, could feel corruption in government.

A second-wave respondent identified what she saw as a change in people's values due to the war and the differences that were now apparent between her and them:

> My last visit in 1995 disappointed me. Everything had changed. People's values and mentality had changed. War has affected the value of being alive. People don't feel things to a large extent after the war. Their actions now are less charitable—they think we are not practical.

Other respondents compared the present Lebanese with those that they had left at least a generation before:

> People have changed a lot ...they are not like the generation we left... we used to be satisfied... the last few times (I felt) people were becoming greedy.

Some claimed that their feelings for their family in Lebanon were still strong but less so for the village or the country: 'the village has no attraction if my family is not there'. Others were outspokenly critical of aspects of Lebanese life. One young woman, who claimed her parents gave her a rosy view of Lebanon, was profoundly disappointed:

> I thought I had never met such pretentious people. I hated its treatment of people… 45-year-old women who had to prostitute themselves for money… break their backs.

A young Australian-Lebanese man, who could be described as a political activist, stated that 'the visits strengthened my beliefs and strengthened my stand'. Coming from Australia he claimed that he could see what was missing in Lebanon: freedom of speech, foreign occupation and human rights.

The visits of second wave immigrants seemed to strengthen their feelings of attachment to Australia and to support the sentiments in the proverb, 'He who wants to eat honey should endure the stings'. Their satisfactions derive from the standard of living in Australia, the fact that Australia has given them educational and business opportunities, and a more benign and private social life. Second-wave immigrants had spent more of their life in Australia than Lebanon and, importantly, they had children and grandchildren living there. Something of their feelings for Australia are revealed in the following:

> - Australia is my home. It gave me opportunities. This is home, this country.

> - Thank God I was living in Australia. I couldn't wait to get back home… the second time turned me off Lebanon and on to Australia.

These comments reveal that some Australian-Lebanese conceived of Lebanon and Australia as opposites, as extremes from which they had to choose. They contrast with those of a second-wave migrant who described Australia's contribution to his personal development without his losing interest and involvement in the affairs of his former homeland:

> Australia became very quickly very interesting to me. It gave me

freedom and a broader outlook on life. I live comfortably here [Australia] but not cut off from there [Lebanon]. I suffer with them [the Lebanese] and work towards the dream of an independent Lebanon and I feel satisfaction.

The attitudes and feelings towards Australia of third-wave immigrants were more mixed. A young third-wave immigrant changed in her valuation of Australia over time. After her first return visit to Lebanon in 1986, she felt disappointed when she came back to Australia. Others reported on the emptiness of Australia and lack of a rich social life compared with that in Lebanon:

> On my return to Australia I remember feeling numbness for six months… [I] felt a profound confusion…lack of social life in Australia … no cultural life… people in Lebanon are more talkative … lead a richer life.

> - I hated Australia when I returned at the age of eight. I missed my family, Lebanese freedom, so many people around… [I] came here and experienced nothing except parents working.

To summarise, most second-wave immigrants felt strongly that the visits had strengthened their attachment to Australia. On the other hand, third-wave migrants were more ambivalent, being more willing to criticise elements of their life in Australia and compare some aspects unfavourably with life in Lebanon. However, most recognised that their futures lay in their adopted country.[8]

NOTES

1 Interview Randa, September 2016
2 Migration Policy Institute – Lebanon Remittances Profile
3 Lebanese Development Network: Newsletter, June 2016.
4 Australian Lebanese Chamber of Commerce and Industry (ALCCI) website, 2016 p. 2.
5 Interview Leila, October 2017
6 Interview Salem, July 2001
7 Interview Anis, July 2001
8 Batrouney, T 2005, 'Australian-Lebanese: Return Visits to Lebanon and Issues of Identity', in P Tabar (ed.), *Lebanese Diaspora: History, Racism and Belonging*, Lebanese American University.

PART 7:

THE LEBANESE IN AUSTRALIA:

A CHANGING MOSAIC

Lebanon has a long history of migration to many countries around the world. The story of each of these migrations is unique in terms both of the Lebanon the immigrants left and the country to which they came. Our focus has been on one of these migration stories: the history of Lebanese migration and settlement in Australia from the late 19th century to the 2010s.

The Lebanese presence in Australia has been achieved through four successive migration waves and smaller migrations across 130 or more years. We examined the unique characteristics of each of these waves and the impact of both Lebanon and Australia on the settlement of Lebanese in Australia. In this final part we record some of the major contributions of Australian-Lebanese and identify some themes in the story of the Lebanese in Australia over the total period.

Over the last 130 or more years Australia exerted a number of 'pull' influences on Lebanese migrants, the volume and strength of which varied over time but were invariably related to economic opportunities, religious freedom and the absence of civil strife. Likewise, the 'push' factors from Lebanon represented variations on these themes: the famines and Druze-Maronite conflicts in the late 19th century; the periods of civil strife in Lebanon in 1958 and 1967; the Civil War and the disruption of the society and economy in the 1970s and 1980s; and the subsequent occupations and regional conflicts, including their impacts on Lebanon.

31

SOME CONTRIBUTIONS OF

AUSTRALIAN-LEBANESE

The story of the Lebanese in Australia reveals the many and varied contributions of Lebanese to the evolving story of Australia. In what follows we have selected four different types of contribution: the varied lives of some distinguished Australian-Lebanese; Lebanese cuisine; Australian-Lebanese involvement in the armed services; and Australian-Lebanese achievements in sports.

Distinguished Australians of Lebanese descent

In preceding chapters we identified a number of people who have made major contributions to the Lebanese community and to the wider Australian community. This chapter includes those who have achieved eminence and national recognition in their respective fields, listed alphabetically. We recognise that this is not an exhaustive list and that other Australians of Lebanese descent may well be worthy of inclusion.

Alexander Alam (1896–1983)

Alexander Alam was born in Wallsend, New South Wales in 1896, the son of immigrant Lebanese shopkeepers, Joseph and Mary Alam. He had an extensive and varied business career and was a director of Mala Homes Pty Ltd, Zebra Motels Pty Ltd and A. A. Alam Pty Ltd.

Alexander Alam was born in Wallsend, New South Wales in 1896, the son of immigrant Lebanese shop-keepers, Joseph and Mary Alam. After an extensive and varied business career, he represented Labor in the New South Wales Legislative Council for a total of 43 years between 1925 – 1958 and then 1963 -1973. He and his wife, Therese, were leading figures in the Lebanese Community in Sydney and active in its many charitable activities
(Source: ALHS Collection)

Alam represented Labor in the New South Wales Legislative Council for a record total of 41 years. He and his wife, Therese, were active in many charitable efforts for the Maronite, the Lebanese and the wider Australian community. These included the purchase of ambulances to transport Australian troops and others injured during the Second World War. He was recognised for his charitable works by the award of the National Order of the Cedar (Lebanon), the Legion d'Honneur (France) and the Order of the Phoenix (Greece).

Dame Marie Bashir AD CVO (1930–)

Marie Bashir was born in 1930 in Narrandera, New South Wales to Lebanese-born parents, Michael Bashir and Victoria Melick. Marie gained the degrees of Bachelor of Medicine and Bachelor of Surgery in 1956 at the University of Sydney. Then followed an eminent career across a number of fields best summed up in the citation she received when she was made a Dame of the Order of Australia in 2014:

> For extraordinary and pre-eminent achievement and merit in service to the administration, public life and people of New South

Wales, to medicine, particularly as an advocate for improved mental health outcomes for the young, marginalized and disadvantaged, to international relations, through the promotion of collaborative health programs, and as a leader in tertiary education.

Marie Bashir was Governor of New South Wales from 2001 to 2014, making her the state's first female governor and the first governor of any Australian state of Lebanese descent. Throughout her career Marie Bashir has received awards from the Australian and Lebanese Governments and a range of community organisations in Australia.

Stephen Bracks AC (1954–)

Steve Bracks was born in Ballarat, Victoria in 1954. His paternal grandfather came to Australia from Zahle, Lebanon in the 1890s. He graduated in business studies and education from the Ballarat College of Advanced Education and became a commerce teacher at Sacred Heart College in Ballarat. In 1994 he was elected as the Labor member of the seat of Williamstown in the western suburbs of Melbourne.

Steve Bracks AC, Premier of Victoria 1999 – 2007
(Source: Alan Barber, Barefoot Media)

Under Bracks's leadership Labor gained office in the 1999 election. This was followed by two more election victories before he resigned as Premier in 2007. Among his many notable achievements were increased support for provincial cities in Victoria and electoral reform of the Upper House in 2002.

Steve Bracks has remained active in public life. He served on company boards and in a number of pro bono positions. In 2010 he was appointed a Companion of the Order of Australia for services to the community and to the Parliament of Victoria.

Major General Peter Haddad AO

An exemplary achievement was that of Major-General Peter Haddad AO who had a distinguished and specialised role in the Australian armed services. Peter Haddad was born in Albury in 1947 of Lebanese ancestry. He graduated from the Officer Cadet School in Portsea, Victoria and enlisted in the army in 1967. Then followed a long and distinguished career as a logistics officer in the Australian Army.

His career included a number of senior positions, both overseas and in Australia, culminating in his final appointment as Commander, Joint Logistics Command in 1998. His career was marked by academic achievement related to his specialisation. Following retirement from the Army in 2005 Peter Haddad accepted a number of government advisory positions. He was awarded an AM in the 1998 Australia Day Honours and an AO in 2002.

Fehmi Naji El-Imam AO (1928–2016)

Fehmi El Imam was born in Lebanon and migrated to Australia in 1951 at the age of 23. Soon after arrival, he organised prayers in people's homes and the first weekend school to provide Islamic teaching for Muslim children in Melbourne. He then formed the first Islamic Society in Victoria.

Fehmi Naji El-Imam , Mufti of Australia speaking in Brisbane
(Source: Crescents of Brisbane)

Following this voluntary service to the Islamic community, he became an imam in 1974. He was a largely self-educated Islamic scholar who developed great insight into Islam in Australia.

Sheikh Fehmi was a founding member of the Islamic Centre in Preston and later Head Imam of the Preston Mosque, Melbourne. In 1963 he played a major role in establishing the Australian Federation of Islamic Councils. He served as a board member in 2005-2006 on the Muslim Community Reference Group established by the Howard Government.

Sheikh Fehmi became a respected mentor and leader of the Islamic community as Grand Mufti of Australia. He was a staunch supporter of cultural diversity in Australia until his death in 2016.

Jacques Nasser AC (1947–)

Jack Nasser was born in Amioun, Lebanon on 27 December 1947. At four years of age Nasser migrated to Melbourne with his family. In 1968 he graduated from the Royal Melbourne Institute of Technology with a business degree.

In the same year he joined the Ford Motor Company as a financial analyst. This was followed by a number of senior and international positions in the company, culminating in his appointment as CEO and member of the Board of Directors of the Ford Motor Company from 1999 until his retirement in 2001.

In 2010 Nasser was elected chairman of BHP Billiton, a position he held until 2017. Nasser also served on the boards of other companies and was an active philanthropist, especially supporting university programs in business and entrepreneurship.

Nasser received national awards in Australia, Lebanon and the United States. These included Officer of the National Order of the Cedar in Lebanon; the Ellis Island Medal of Honour in the United States; Companion of the Order of Australia and Centenary Medal for 'his contribution to Australian industry, as an adviser to Government and for education in the areas of technology'.

Sir Nicholas Shehadie AC, OBE (1925–2017)

Nicholas Shehadie was born In Coogee, New South Wales in 1925, the third child of Father Michael, an Orthodox priest, and Hannah Shehadie. He grew up in Redfern and attended Cleveland Street Public and later Crown Street Commercial Schools.

Nicholas was a gifted sportsman who played rugby for Randwick for 16 years, and New South Wales and Australia for 30 years. He followed this with a successful business career, selling a range of products for information technology departments in corporate Australia.

His life in public office commenced when he became an alderman of the city of Sydney in 1962 and Lord Mayor of Sydney in 1973. Then followed a number of leadership positions including Chairman of New South Wales Rugby Union in 1979, Chairman of the Sydney Cricket Ground 1990-2001, and Chairman of the Special Broadcasting

Service from 1981 to 1999.

Sir Nicholas Shehadie was honoured for his outstanding achievements across a number of fields, for service to the media, to sport and to the community.

A Taste for Success:
Lebanese Food and Hospitality Businesses

One of the most significant contributions of Lebanese immigrants has been in the food and hospitality businesses. Whether they had a milk bar or delicatessen, a take-away food business, a food production business, a café, reception centre, or restaurant, Lebanese food and hospitality have become well-known and well-accepted in Australian society. From the 1950s onwards, the lessons of hospitality learned within the family from a young age, became assets in food businesses. 'The Lebanese take pride in their hospitality'.[1]

The move into a small business was a goal for many Lebanese migrants who came in the 1950s and 1960s. Lebanese-owned businesses in the form of milk bars or delicatessens were popular in the suburbs of Sydney, Melbourne, Brisbane and Adelaide in the 1960s and 1970s.

These businesses required much effort and time by the owners and their families. The hours demanded in running a small business involved sacrificing leisure time and community activities. Conducting businesses of this nature brought Lebanese into contact with the wider community. This relationship became an important training for the shopkeepers and their children. It allowed them to establish strong links with their regular customers from all nationalities, who enjoyed the warmth of their greetings and their interest in what was happening in their lives. This was to stand the Lebanese in good stead when they opened larger businesses in the hospitality industry.

Broheim and Hoda Aoun took pride in keeping their milk bar open on hot evenings in summer in West Footscray, Melbourne, as they could provide a service for those in the working-class suburb to cool down with drinks and ice-creams.[2]

The inhospitable hours of milk bars and constant demands of 'shop please' placed a strain on family life. Very few families worked in milk bars or delicatessens for longer than five years at a time when they took an extended break before they re-doubled their efforts in another milk-bar or similar business. Some moved into cafés, take-away shops or pizza restaurants where the family did not live on-site and the hours were friendlier and less taxing.

Some Lebanese settlers, with the experience of successful cafés and milk-bars behind them and with an ambition to develop a larger and more lucrative business, opened restaurants or reception centres. In some cases, this enterprise was undertaken with a partner and often with members of the family. The move into these types of business and the employment of chefs and cooks, wait staff and bar staff meant moving into roles as employers rather than working only with family members.

In Sydney, one of the early Lebanese restaurants, Wilson's, was established in Pitt Street, Redfern in the 1950s:

> After Wilson's was established, it rapidly grew in popularity. Many Lebanese came to live in the Redfern/Waterloo area when they first arrived, including Sir Nicholas Shehadie and members of the family of Her Excellency the Governor of New South Wales, Marie Bashir. Wilson and his family bought a house in Great Buckingham Street. Quite quickly, other people living around them also came to enjoy the Lebanese food. Family members opened a second restaurant in Cleveland Street and later in Randwick.[3]

Around the end of the 1960s, many Lebanese restaurants emerged in the inner suburbs of Sydney, just south of the city. These restaurants grew where the original Lebanese community was located in Redfern and Surry Hills. These businesses included: Emads and Salindas, Abduls, Fatimas, Nadas, Omar Khayyams, Almustafa, the Prophet, Girne Pide and Erciyes. Many of these were still operating in 2010s, although with different owners.

The business model developed by Lebanese shopkeepers, who moved from milk bars into larger takeaway businesses and cafés and then restaurants, provided a valuable training for their children. Many children, whose first business experience was serving in milk-bars and cafés, moved on to their own businesses in restaurants, catering for a more modern clientele. Restaurants in the inner city such as Nour, Le Souk and Zaida in Surry Hills, among others, exemplify this trend.

In Melbourne, some individuals and families became synonymous with the development of successful restaurants. In the 1950s and 1960s, Louis Fleyfel had a succession of milk bars and cafés in Geelong and Melbourne until he opened The Walnut Tree in West Melbourne and then the well-known Le Chateau in Queens Road, South Melbourne. In the mid-1970s Louis Fleyfel opened The Left Bank in Malvern. These restaurants helped introduce fine dining to Melbourne in the 1960s and 1970s.

In recognition of these achievements and his contribution to the Australian-Lebanese Community as Honorary Consul, Louis Fleyfel was awarded an Order of Australia in 2014. Among his major benefactions were his generous donations to the Maronite Church of Our Lady of Lebanon in Melbourne. His Order of Australia citation reads:

> For distinguished service to the Lebanese community in Australia, to the identification and implementation of bilateral trade and investment opportunities, and to philanthropy.

Fleyfel's dedication and generosity to his church was rewarded in 2015 when he received a Papal Knighthood in the Order of St Gregory the Great.

Edward Haikal migrated from Beirut, Lebanon in 1968. The following year he brought out his wife, Marie, and their family of five children to further their education. A senior accountant with American Express in Beirut, Edward had to content himself with simple book-keeping positions when he arrived in Melbourne. During the early years, the family struggled, with Edward and Marie always trying to balance the demands of secondary and tertiary education for their children with the need to earn an income for the family.

The family's first venture into business was in 1977 when they leased a Lebanese restaurant, Abdul's, in Malvern. On the basis of that experience, they opened the Almazett restaurant a year later. The Haikal family was the first to introduce a set price for an open banquet (*mesa*), a concept which proved a great success with both Lebanese and other Australians. During this time four of the Haikal children obtained tertiary qualifications, including two MBBS, an LLB, and three science degrees. They each worked in the family business while studying.

Following the success of Almazett, families related to the Haikals opened other Lebanese restaurants. These included The Cedar Tree in Brighton, Chateau Lebanon in Middle Park, Dunyazad in North Balwyn, Sinbad in Dandenong, Kanzaman in Richmond, and Samsara in Mount Waverley. It was typical for people to work in another family's restaurant until they had enough capital and experience to open their own. Through family unity and enterprise, the Haikals and related families made a major contribution to the Melbourne cuisine experience.

One of the best–known Lebanese restaurateurs in Melbourne is Abla Amad, who was born in Lebanon in 1935 and migrated to Melbourne in 1954. In 1979 Abla Amad opened a traditional Lebanese restaurant in Melbourne's inner suburb of Carlton. As well as providing a meeting place for Lebanese migrants, this highly popular restaurant introduced Lebanese cuisine to thousands of other Australians.

Abla Amad has been a highly successful publicist for Lebanese food, producing two popular editions of her cookery book: *Abla's Lebanese Kitchen* in 2001 and 2010. In recognition of her life's work, Abla was made a member of the Order of Australia in 2015 'for service to tourism and hospitality... and the Lebanese community'.

In Brisbane, Antoine Ghanem and the Ghanem Group has developed a number of restaurants. He has a Byblos restaurant in Brisbane and one in Melbourne that each serve Lebanese cuisine in attractive riverside locations. The Ghanem Group has extended into other cuisines and state of the art themed bars and dining establishments close to the Brisbane River waterfront at various locations. These outlets cater to a wide range of contemporary food tastes. Like many other Lebanese entrepreneurs, the Ghanem Group provides employment for many in the wider community in their many food businesses.

A newer type of food business emerged with Faddy Zouky and the Zouki Group. The Zouky brothers came to Australia in the early 1990s and soon established cafés and reception centres. With larger plans they were able to secure the rights to the hospital cafeteria in many of the hospitals in Victoria and in other parts of Australia, as well as other select cafés. There are some 60 Zouki café outlets around Australia and spreading into the Middle East. Faddy Zouky became a well-known philanthropist and convenor and president of the Australian – Lebanese Chamber of Commerce and Industry (ALCCI) supporting Australian-Lebanese charities and wider Australian community groups. In recognition of these achievements he was awarded an Order of Australia Medal in 2013.

Lest We Forget

Australian-Lebanese have always been proud of their family members who served in the two world wars and later conflicts. They fall into two groups: those born in Lebanon who migrated to Australia and those born in Australia of Lebanese ancestry. However, it was not until the 1980s that their stories began to be consolidated on a community-wide basis. This was brought about by the community research carried out and sponsored by Australian-Lebanese Historical Societies in New South Wales and Victoria. It was also aided by the research undertaken on Lebanese identity and the Australian armed forces by Geraldine Khachan towards a doctoral thesis.[4]

The Australian-Lebanese shared the same experiences as other Australians who served in the wars of the 20th century. Problems in identifying those of Lebanese heritage who served in the armed forces include the Anglicisation of names and those with names common to other nationalities. However, in 1914 at least 80 young Australian-Lebanese joined the Australian Imperial Force and fought in the various battlefields of the Great War. They joined in the ill-fated Gallipoli campaign; they fought in the battlefields of the Western Front, including France and other European countries; and they fought in the deserts of the Middle East, including the charge of the Light Horse at Beersheba in 1917.

Among many others, these included George Saleeba, Leslie Doblie, Aneese Jabour and James Callil from Victoria; Richard Lahood, John Mansour, Edward Shalala, Michael Aziz from New South Wales; Walter Abotomy, Harold Gabriel and Michael Antony from South Australia. In a reflection of the pattern of early Lebanese settlement, relatively large numbers came from country areas around Australia.

During the Second World War Australian-Lebanese fought against the German enemy in the European battlefields, in the deserts of North Africa, in Palestine and in other Middle Eastern countries. They stood up against the invasion of Japan across south-east Asia and, with the aid of their allies, repelled the Japanese from islands of the Pacific, including, importantly, New Guinea.

> Significant numbers of Lebanese-Australians served in the armed forces during the Second World War. The Australian War Memorial records show around 80 people who served in Australian forces, who were actually born in Lebanon. Many more descendants of earlier Lebanese settlers also served...They served in the three armed services, in overseas conflicts and in Australia and included women as well as men. And if they were too old for regular service their names appear on the rolls of local defence units.[5]

Among the many hundreds of Lebanese-Australians who served in the Second World War were several sets of brothers. Mick and Albert Batrouney, Mick and Jack Aboud, Nicholas and Joe Antees among many others.

Leila Fleyfel (nee Ganim) served as an army nurse in Greece and New Guinea during the Second World War. Australian-Lebanese also served in peacetime, including Jack Rawady, Joseph and Michael Batrouney who served in the citizens' militia between the wars. Australian Lebanese also participated in the Korean and Vietnam wars.

Inevitably, some were killed in action, some were taken prisoners of war, and some returned to Australia with physical wounds and psychological damage.

Australian-Lebanese were not only loyal in war and peace but the community also proudly supported their sons who served in the Second World War. This can be seen in a khaki-bound copy of the New Testament with the Royal Insignia on the cover which was given to every serving member of St Nicholas Church in World War Two.

The research undertaken suggests that the participation by Australian-Lebanese in Australia's defence force in both a civil and military role during the Great War and the Second World War was an important means of integration into wider Australian society:

> ... the Australian Armed forces was the institution that gave them the opportunity to prove themselves as Australians, and for those who did not enlist, their patriotic actions was a means to contribute to the war effort and be counted as patriotic Australians.

> After their wartime experiences many Australian-Lebanese veterans felt more confident in reinforcing their loyalty to Australia through their active participation in civil society.[6]

Australian-Lebanese in Politics: A Voice for the People

The early Lebanese, many of whom who settled in the rural areas of Australia, often became significant members in their local communities. This was invariably based on their activities as shopkeepers and owners of other commercial enterprises. As their businesses prospered they sought to become involved in their local communities. Some chose to work within their church and ethnic community while others chose to join wider community bodies. Some even became active in both Lebanese community organisations and wider society bodies. The case study of the early Lebanese in Albury (p. 28) provides examples of their range of business ventures and community activities, both of which were also in evidence in other provincial cities.

By the end of the 20th century and into the 21st century elected representatives of Lebanese background had joined local councils and sat in both upper and lower houses of state and Federal parliaments. In common with other members of parliament, they represented a range of political parties. The following selected examples convey something of the variety of their contributions to politics in Australia.

Two well-known local government representatives of Lebanese background included Sir Nicholas Shehadie, lord mayor of Sydney (1973–75) and George Joseph, lord mayor of Adelaide (1977–1979).

In New South Wales a number of politicians of Lebanese background have represented their electorates. As far back as Alexander Alam (1925–1958) Lebanese background politicians have held various role within their parties and within government. Barbara Perry (nee Abood) held several ministerial positions in her long parliamentary career between 2001–2015. John Ajaka is the President of the NSW Legislative Council and previously he also filled a number of ministerial roles between 2013–2017. Hon. Shaoquett Moselmane, is currently a member of the Legislative Council. Jihad Dib, a former school principal of Punchbowl Boys High School between 2007–2014, when he was elected to the lower house of NSW Parliament in 2014.

In Victoria, Steve Bracks was elected as a Labor member of

Parliament in 1999 where he served three terms as Premier, until resigning in 2007. Some current members of the Victorian parliament include Marlene Kairouz, Nazieh Elasmar, Kallil Eideh and Cesar Melhem.

Jackie Trad is the member for South Brisbane in the Queensland Parliament. She is also the State's Treasurer and Deputy Premier. Jackie Trad is a local to South Brisbane where she and her Lebanese- born parents lived and worked. In the Federal sphere Daryl Melham and Michael Sukkar were members of the House of Representatives.

A current member of the Federal Parliament is Bob Katter. The Katter family established something of a political dynasty in North Queensland. Their origins include the Arida family who were successful merchants, owning many stores throughout north and west Queensland. The Aridas were also highly regarded as benefactors in the communities where they had businesses. Bob Katter Snr served in the Australian Parliament from 1966–1990, representing the National Party of Australia, followed by his son, Bob Katter, who was elected to Federal Parliament in 1993. Bob Katter first represented the National Party of Australia until 2001 and then stood as an independent until 2011 when he founded Katter's Australian Party. The third member of the Katter family to enter politics was Robbie Katter who won the seat of Mt. Eliza in the 2012 Queensland state election.

The contributions of Australians of Lebanese backgrounds to politics in Australia are marked by a range of varied positions and achievements. Some were councillors, mayors and lord mayors in local government. Others were members and ministers in state and Federal parliaments, with Steve Bracks reaching the position of Premier in Victoria and Jackie Trad becoming Deputy Premier in Queensland. Their adherence to party politics is similarly varied and covers the political spectrum: the Australian Labor Party, the Liberal Party, the National Party and a host of smaller parties.

In all, their contribution to politics in Australia is a mark of their adoption of Australia and its values and their desire to contribute to the nation. At the same, their involvement in politics proved to be of benefit to their particular community and to the Lebanese community as a whole.

Sporting Australian-Lebanese

A glance at the popular press and television programs or listening to mainstream radio, especially on the weekends, reveals the widespread popularity of sport in Australia. This is particularly the case for sports with mass entertainment value such as Rugby League and Australian Rules Football. Australian-Lebanese have become involved in these and other sports as players, referees, administrators and supporters. As such, sport has assumed a number of roles in the Lebanese community: it has occupied an important place in the cultural lives of many immigrants; it has contributed to the preservation of ethnic networks; and it has provided an entrée to wider Australian culture; and society.[7]

Australian-Lebanese have been well represented as players in soccer, Australian Rules football and Rugby League. Each code has its own attraction for young Australian-Lebanese, most of whom were born in Australia or migrated to Australia as children. Soccer was known and played in Lebanon so its attraction was that of a familiar, world-wide sport. Australian Rules has always been the dominant football code in the southern states of Australia (Victoria, South Australia, Tasmania and Western Australia). The attraction has been attachment to a locality, especially in Victoria, where each team was originally identified with a suburb of Melbourne. Rugby League is perhaps the football code which has attracted the greatest number of prominent players and supporters from the Australian-Lebanese Community. This has been partly a function of locality as rugby league teams represented localities with large populations of Lebanese. It was also partly a function of the status of rugby league as a mainstream sport and an avenue of assimilation into Australian culture.

In addition to these elite sports, sports associated with leisure activities of ethnic groups and churches provided some young Australian-Lebanese with social, educational and support networks so necessary for newcomers in a strange land. Four case studies outlined below pick up some of these issues: St Nicholas Cricket Team, Melbourne; the story of Ray Garby, an early Australian Rules footballer; the champion Rugby League players Hazem El Masri and Robbie Farah; and Bachar Houli, member of Richmond's premiership football team in 2017. It is worth noting that each of these sports people were not only champion players and role models but also took initiatives to share their skills and encourage the young of their respective communities.

St Nicholas Church Cricket Team

The major sporting activity of St Nicholas Church over the years has been the game of cricket. St Nicholas Cricket team was established in 1934 and played in Melbourne's Northern Suburban Cricket Association for the first time during the 1934-35 season. The team met with only limited success during its first season, winning only two matches out of a total of ten and finishing ninth out of 13 teams. The following season, 1935-36, was more successful with the team winning six matches and coming fifth in a competition of 12 teams. Victor Batrouney won the batting average in both seasons and the bowling average in the first season while Don Bosaid won the bowling average in the second season.

St Nicholas Cricket Team played only three seasons before the Second World War. A number of the young men at St Nicholas were soon to join the armed forces or become employed in industries of national priority under manpower regulations. The joyful days of playing cricket against other local churches, factories and community bodies had to give way to conflict of a more serious kind.

Not long after the end of the Second World War and even before the arrival of Father Haydar, the second priest of St Nicholas, the cricket team was revived and played in the same competition in the 1947-48 season. With a number of younger players St Nicholas achieved immediate success, becoming runners-up in 1948-49 and third in the next season. However a premiership continued to elude them until the season of 1951-52.

In a detailed account of the premiership match against Prestige Knitting Mills we learn that in the first innings St Nicholas made a creditable 181 runs which included a score of 94 runs by Victor Batrouney. However, in reply Prestige was 4 wickets for 164 runs:

> Then a cricket miracle happened, during tea the Reverend Haydar, who was one of St Nicholas's strong supporters, had to leave and before he left, he blessed St Nicholas with the sign of the cross and after tea had been taken and play resumed Prestige lost their remaining six wickets for the cost of six runs, giving them a total of 171 and St Nicholas had a first innings lead of 10 runs.[8]

St Nicholas went on to win the match by 132 runs and to gain its one and only premiership. That night the team and its supporters celebrated at the home of the captain Leo and his wife, Martha Batrouney. The Presentation Night was a joyous evening of dancing, speeches, presentation of trophies, premiership caps and photographs, followed by a fine supper. Then to the tune of 'God Save the Queen' a very successful evening and a very successful season was brought to a close'.

1961-2 was the last season played by St Nicholas. Despite a break for the war years, the cricket team played an important role in the life of St Nicholas Church for some 30 years. During that time, it made for family and community interaction and cohesion as brothers, uncles and nephews played together and older members of the community attended matches and supported the team. Playing cricket under the banner of the Church meant that they could be Orthodox of Lebanese descent and, at the same time, young Australians. Although the St Nicholas Cricket Team was never revived in later years, the young people of St Nicholas played other sports and in doing so shared something of the spirit of the St Nicholas Cricket Team.

Ray Garby (1923–2009)

Ray Garby, one of the last surviving members of Carlton's 1947 premiership team, died in Rosebud at the age of 86. In a number of respects Garby's life was typical of some of the children of first wave Australian-Lebanese settlers. However, his family chose to remain in a country town rather than join the exodus to Sydney. He worked in his family business both before and after his wartime service and he excelled in football, which was to provide his entrée to Australian society. The occasional racist comments that he endured ensured that he was never allowed to forget that he was not an Anglo-Australian.

Garby, a dashing half-forward in 85 senior appearances for the old dark Navy Blues, was the son of a Lebanese migrant and raised in the northern Victorian town of Cohuna. He later attended school at the famed football factory Assumption College in Kilmore. After his schooling he returned to Cohuna and before long the teenage Garby enlisted for wartime service. It was 1942, and Garby's commitment to king and country meant his senior League career would not begin until the opening round of 1946.

Wearing the No. 20 his play was noted for his excellent high-marking and accurate torpedo punt kicking. Garby was a potent force on a flank in the 1947 Grand Final when he barrelled a glorious long goal late in the game as his team overran the red and blacks (Essendon) to win by one point.

In a final interview, recorded in October last year, Garby fondly remembered Carlton as a 'rough old place' in the post-war period. Perc [Carlton coach Perc Bentley] used to say to us that he got nine pounds a week which he used to put to on 18-gallon drum of beer for us blokes.

Doug Williams, now 86, described Garby as 'a lovely chap' and 'a real gentleman' who maintained his composure in the most difficult of circumstances. 'There's one thing that sticks in my mind... and I won't mention clubs or names ... but Ray was on a half-forward flank and I was on my wing, and Ray was on a chap who was noted to be a pretty rough diamond on the ground. Anyway, he was calling Ray the filthiest of names, he went on and on and on right through the game, and I just couldn't understand how Ray put up with it, still don't. I think it was just his lovely nature that helped him to play the game.'

Ray had a gift of taking a mark, then going back to take his kick, feigning the kick and spinning around the chap on the mark to kick the goal. He was noted for that and he often did it.

At the conclusion of the 1950 season, Garby returned to Cohuna to assist with the family business, and lend support to the local football team as both player and coach. He managed the Cohuna Hotel for nigh on 20 years (and, later, the local supermarket) before relocating to a retirement home in Rosebud.

Garby died peacefully on Saturday. He is survived by his wife, Jean, whom he married in that memorable year of '47, sons Greg and Trevor, nine grandchildren and seven great-grandchildren.[9]

Hazem El Masri

Hazem El Masri was born in Tripoli, north Lebanon on 1 April 1976 to parents, Khaled and Amal. He emigrated to Australia with his family in 1988 when he was 12 years old.

El Masri's first game was soccer, which he began playing at an early age. However, during his senior years in high school he switched to rugby league, eventually joining the Canterbury-Bankstown Bulldogs.

El Masri played his entire club football career with the Canterbury-Bankstown Bulldogs with whom he won the 2004 National Rugby League (NRL) Premiership. In 2009, El Masri took the record as the highest-ever point scorer in premiership history and for a record sixth time was the NRL's top point scorer for the season. Hazem El Masri became an international representative for Australia and a New South

Wales State of Origin representative playing on the wing.

El Masri also contributed his time and skill to developing rugby in his country of origin. He captained the Lebanon national side which qualified for their first ever World Cup in 2000 and played in all three of Lebanon's World Cup games.

El Masri is widely respected for his community work with young people, winning the NRL's Ken Stephen Award in 2002. The award recognises players who contribute to the betterment of their community away from rugby league. He was one of the first Australian-Lebanese to step forward in the name of friendship and understanding in the wake of the racially motivated 2005 Cronulla Riots.[10]

Robbie Farah

Robbie Farah was born in 1985 in Sydney of Lebanese parents. He attended a local primary school and De La Salle College in Ashfield.

As a promising junior, he first played and toured with the Lebanese Rugby League team at the age of eighteen in 2002. He played with them in France and Tripoli as part of the Mediterranean Cup.

By 2003, Farah made his debut with West Tigers in the NRL competition, playing four matches in his debut year. By 2005, Farah had slotted into the regular team as hooker and enjoyed success with West Tigers winning the NRL Premiership. In 2007, he was runner up in the Dally M Player of the Year and was also named Hooker of the Year. Having enjoyed success in his role in the team, by 2009, Farah was appointed captain.

Robbie Farah was named as hooker in the NSW State of Origin side in 2009. By 2010, Farah was runner up by one point in the Dally M Award for the best NRL player and again named Hooker of the Year. He also played in many representative teams. By 2012, he was voted as the player's player in the NSW versus Queensland

State of Origin match.

In July 2019, Farah played his 300th rugby league game. He has endured the highs and lows of a professional sportsman and has been a regular and well-regarded player in rugby league world in Australia.

Farah, alongside Hasam El-Masri, has set a path for several other Australian-Lebanese rugby league players to follow. He has also shown his support for Lebanon from an early age by playing with the Lebanon Rugby League team in World Cup competitions alongside many other Australian-Lebanese rugby players playing in the ARL competition.

Farah has also worked on mental health campaigns dealing with how men relate to each other. His Mates on a Mission charity has raised considerable funds for the Westmead Children's Hospital and Youth off the Street program.[11]

Bachar Houli

Bachar Houli, from the Melbourne suburb of Spotswood, has effectively blended his adherence to his Islamic faith and playing AFL football at the highest level. He has worked to build bridges that establish links between Islamic youth and football through an academy that he established. As a professional sportsman at the Richmond Football Club and an Australia Post AFL Multicultural Player and Ambassador, he believed that it was important to provide a pathway for young people of Muslim backgrounds to play with others of a similar background and develop their football skills in a national competition.

Participants from the Bachar Houli Cup may be selected into the Bachar Houli Academy – which has a focus on high performance football talent for emerging junior players aged between 15-18 years from an Islamic background.[12]

At a time of heighted awareness of radicalisation of disengaged Islamic youth, the Bachar Houli Academy works to create a positive pathway between young boys and girls, their Islamic faith and a sport that is uniquely Australian. In his own words:

> … at the end of the day I am a role model whether I like it or not, it's just if I choose to be a positive or a negative role model. That's my choice and I work extremely hard on being that positive role model to give young Muslim boys and girls someone to look up to that is proud of who he is, a proud Australian-Muslim.[13]

The Bachar Houli Academy grew out of an initiative in 2012 of the Bachar Houli Cup. The Bachar Houli programs engage around 10,000 students across 30 Islamic colleges nationally. The Academy is an opportunity for young Muslim men to be exposed to pathways to pursue AFL, while learning important leadership skills to take back to their respective communities.

The Bachar Houli Cup was initiated in 2012 in Victoria and, after a hugely successful event, it has become an annual tournament with the 2013 version played nationally. The Bachar Houli Islamic Schools' Cup is an opportunity for Islamic Schools to play Australian Football against other schools in a friendly, fun and safe environment. The aims of the Bachar Houli Cup are:

- To provide a football competition for Islamic Schools in Victoria as well as other states
- To encourage students in Islamic Schools to make the transition from school football into community clubs
- To provide an opportunity for participants to be selected into the Bachar Houli Academy.[14]

CONCLUSIONS

The Settlement of Lebanese in Australia

A degree of continuity may be found in the distribution of Lebanese throughout Australia. By the 1940s most of the pioneer immigrants had settled in New South Wales. This pattern continued after subsequent migrations, with New South Wales accounting for 75 per cent and Victoria around 20 per cent of Lebanese-born, with much smaller proportions in the other states. After the hawking period, there was movement from rural areas, to settlement in the capital cities where the majority live in the 2010s. In the 2016 Census, Lebanese immigrants and their children and grandchildren totalled some 228,347 people around Australia.

First-wave settlers initially congregated in inner-city areas which housed their dwellings and businesses. This concentration of Lebanese-born and their descendants was brought about by a number of interrelated factors: the demise of hawking in rural areas; the desire of Lebanese families to provide educational opportunities for their children; the first occupations of second-wave immigrants in manufacturing industries; the opening of small businesses in urban areas; chain migration and the reunion of families; and, finally, the concentration of Lebanese communities and organisations, especially in the cities of Sydney and Melbourne. While there was an initial concentration among second- and third-wave immigrants, there has been a clear tendency over time for dispersal throughout metropolitan areas in pursuit of jobs, businesses and better homes. However, more recent waves of Lebanese immigrants in the 2010s could still be found living in close proximity to others of the same religion or village.

Family

A major continuity in Lebanese settlement in Australia has been the central role played by the family in migration and settlement. The family has always been the primary group to which Lebanese belonged, followed perhaps by their religion and village. The decision to emigrate was often a family, rather than an individual, decision. This might involve borrowing money for fares from family members and collective decisions as to which family members should emigrate first and which should follow. The earliest arrivals from a family or village often sponsored and assisted other members to migrate to Australia.

Relative parity of the sexes, which has extended across the total period of Lebanese migration and settlement, testifies to the importance accorded by Lebanese to their families and to an early commitment to settle in Australia. Over time, a transition can be detected from the traditional extended family to a modified extended family, which might involve married children working with their parents and living in close proximity to them. The final stage in family transition is that of a nuclear family, largely indistinguishable from other Australian families. The notion of the extended family has been powerfully present among Lebanese and has been an important part of their business success over the years. Following migration, the family typically constituted an economic unit for collective involvement in hawking, shop-keeping, factory employment, clothing businesses and a range of other entrepreneurial activities. Not only did family members work together in business but they also offered each other emotional support and conviviality.

On the other hand, the influence of an extended family can be limited by migration and modernisation. For example, over the total period, extended families would sometimes be separated across various continents. This meant that, following migration, some first-wave immigrants might never or rarely see members of their extended family again. Even where a family lived in the one city, the demands of education, occupations, and diverse interests could have the effect of attenuating the bonds between members of an extended family. Nevertheless, family has remained for most Lebanese-born and their descendants the most resilient of bodies to which they belong and the one that is often the sole remaining bearer of Lebanese culture.

In some cases, Lebanese families have proved remarkably resilient. Some families maintain their connections over many generations. For example, a family reunion of the descendents of George and Annie Batrouney was held in Melbourne in March 2019. This celebration of 130 years in Australia was attended by over 200 members of the third, fourth and fifth family generations.

The family has been responsible for the preservation, at least in the short term, of ethnic elements such as language and religion. Especially through members of the first generation, the family has typically been the bearer of a cluster of traditional Lebanese values such as honour, shame, thrift, hard work, abstemiousness and support for family members. However, these values are being challenged by the more individualistic values of later generation family members, both in Australia and Lebanon.

Occupations and Businesses

Lebanese settlers have made a significant contribution to the Australian economy. Through hard work, entrepreneurial drive and the help of their families, many have established successful businesses across a range of industries, most notably in the clothing and food industries. There is a sense of continuity about this contribution. Some clothing businesses established by Lebanese spanned three generations. Likewise, a Lebanese grocery store or delicatessen, whether established in 1894 or 2014, provides an example of entrepreneurial activity, family involvement and sometimes a social centre for Lebanese settlers.

Joseph Saad, shop steward at Ford Motor Company
Broadmeadows, 1988. Many Lebanese immigrants between
the 1950s and 1980s worked in the manufacturing industry.
(Source: Latrobe Collection. State Library of Victoria)

Significant differences may be perceived in the occupational pathways
of each of the waves of settlers. The occupational pathway of the
first group and their descendants moved, over a long period, through
the stages of hawking, shop-keeping, working in manufacturing
industries through to professional and managerial positions. The
pathway of second-wave immigrants was marked by a movement from
working in manufacturing industries to ownership of their own small
businesses and then to larger businesses in the service sector. The
occupational pathway of second-wave immigrants has been shorter
than that of the first-wave settlers and typically extended to just
two or three generations, with some members of these generations
gaining access to professional and managerial positions. Third-wave
immigrants, who arrived in Australia after the trauma of the civil war,
encountered initial difficulties in gaining employment and accessing
education. However, over time, these difficulties have been partly
overcome with many achieving success in employment and business

while their children benefited from educational opportunities.

These common occupational pathways do not tell the whole story. Each of the immigration waves illustrated diversity in the Lebanese population in terms of education, family support and a range of other resources. In particular, Lebanese women made major contributions to the settlement of Lebanese during each of the settlement periods. Not only did these contributions include family support, but also employment in businesses and self-employment. With this support some of the second- and third-wave immigrants could open a range of businesses soon after arrival while others were able to continue with their education and enter the professions and other high-level occupations. Small numbers of Lebanese immigrants and their families achieved success in building as well as land and property development.

Lebanese Women

Over the period of their migration Lebanese women have played indispensable and diverse roles in their families and beyond. Not only did they have major responsibility in caring for their families and undertaking domestic duties but they also contributed to the family income by engaging in work in the wider community. For the earliest Lebanese immigrants this included some women's involvement in hawking in Australia's capital cities and country areas, with members of their family or sometimes alone. During this period other women remained at home, caring for their family and perhaps sewing garments for their husbands to sell on their journeys. Later, many women would work in the family business, whether in clothing, milk bars, coffee lounges or delicatessens. They were also involved with decisions about the development of businesses and enterprises. While these represent traditional Lebanese businesses, some women would also work as employees in a range of manufacturing industries. The fact that some Lebanese women worked as taxi-drivers and on baker delivery vans suggests that no occupation was out of bounds for these women.

With the advantage of education in Australia, second- and third-generation Lebanese women entered a wide range of occupations.

Education

Education, both of immigrants and their descendants, was an important element in Lebanese settlement. Throughout the total period the financial and social capital of Australian-Lebanese families were crucial in providing education for the younger generations. Across the immigration waves a number of patterns emerged in relation to migration and education.

Typically, most immigrants over the total period regarded earning a living as a higher priority than continuing with their formal education. Many acquired knowledge and skills informally from family members or other Lebanese, which enabled them to make a living in a variety of occupations and businesses. In addition, despite their lack of formal education in Australia, some engaged in self-education in their own time.

In cases where education was valued and family resources were available, children were provided with opportunities at school and in tertiary education. In fact, concern for the education of their children provided part of the motivation for emigration from Lebanon and relocating from country areas to cities within Australia. In some families there is evidence of Lebanese students gaining considerable success at school and in higher education. Another common pattern was for children to remain in education but also work part-time and thus contribute to the family income.

Nonetheless, in families where finances and valuing of education were lacking, young Lebanese students, perhaps particularly male students, perceived Australian schools as alien places which were not understood or valued by their families and peer groups. For some students school, with its emphasis on secular education, was at odds with the religious and family value system. In many cases these families required their children to leave school and enter the workforce as soon as possible. In other cases, the young people themselves chose to leave school to search for work. This is one element of a larger issue: the perennial conflict between work and education in the lives of immigrant Lebanese families.

Lebanese community organisations

In terms of their primary functions Lebanese community organisations fall into three categories. The first may be termed cultural maintenance organisations whose primary focus is to preserve and maintain valued aspects of their former culture such as family values, religion, language, music, dance, among others. The establishment of their own churches and mosques, in particular, has assisted in this by providing familiar institutions in a foreign land.

A second type includes those organisations which are primarily oriented towards Lebanon. They may support particular political parties or provide financial and other assistance to villages and charitable bodies in Lebanon. Many of these organisations arose during times of internal conflict in Lebanon when those in the diaspora felt impelled to support the groups with which they identified.

A third category consists of community organisations which engage directly on behalf of their members with the wider society. These include welfare organisations, that seek to meet the settlement and welfare needs of Australian-Lebanese, and socio-political organisations, which ensure that the needs and interests of Lebanese and other Arab-Australians are brought to the attention of both the public and authorities.

The divisions and civil strife in Lebanon have not been conducive to the establishment of united communities of Lebanese and their descendants in Australia. In this context, it has been difficult for umbrella organisations, such as the Australian-Lebanese

Associations, to provide a united voice, representing the needs and interests of all the Lebanese in Australia. Not only are divisions evident across religious and political groupings but the post-civil war immigrants, in particular, have not always received the degree of understanding and support that they might have expected from the established Lebanese communities. On the other hand, community organisations, despite their largely sectional clientele, reveal a willingness to provide services across the board.

Sectarian differences and conflicts

The Lebanese state was born amid sectarian differences and conflicts. This was recognised in the Lebanese Constitution which allocated political positions and power in accordance with the numbers of adherents of each of the major religious groups. Members of particular religious groupings looked to their leaders to protect and advance their interests. This led, at times, to an unstable political system, especially where dominant groups sought to consolidate their power at the expense of smaller and weaker groups. In these situations the major actors in the Lebanese drama were leading families from the dominant religious and political groupings, rather than the state and its agencies.

This instability had a major impact on migration and settlement during this period. The different historical periods, with their different 'push' factors, affected the religious composition of the three waves of immigrants. We have seen that the first two waves were predominantly Christian, while the third wave was predominantly Muslim. Muslims now constitute about one-third of the Lebanese-born persons in Australia.

The Lebanese communities in Australia reflect the religious divisions of their homeland, as indicated by the establishment of churches and mosques as well as by the variety of other community groups. Clergy and community leaders often adopted a proprietorial attitude to the particular groups they represented. On the other hand, religious leaders have typically gone beyond their own communities to offer assistance to any Lebanese immigrants in need.

In general, sectarian differences and conflicts have been more muted in Australia than in the homeland. Perhaps an explanation lies in the complex demands of settling into a new society and the many opportunities it offered Lebanese and their families.

Racial discrimination

In almost every country where they settled and worked Lebanese suffered from varying degrees of racial discrimination, especially in the early years of their settlement. In the late 19th century the occupation of hawking was heavily criticised in Australia as non-productive and parasitical. This merged with racial criticism of the 'Syrian' (as the Lebanese were then known) among politicians and in the popular press. In 1901 Australia enacted legislation to prohibit or severely limit the entry of this group, among others. A second form of discrimination was the denial of citizenship to Lebanese immigrants. Over time, both forms of official discrimination gave way in the face of efforts by the Lebanese to gain equal treatment with other groups. However, this has not prevented the periodic upsurge of racism and assertion of a crude form of nationalism against some immigrants, including the Lebanese.

A more recent manifestation of racial problems was illustrated by the Cronulla Riots in Sydney where Australian-Lebanese youth were challenged by some young people from the wider community over access to Cronulla Beach. Sections of the Sydney media fanned the flames of confrontation which clearly revealed latent hostility to an entity which they conflated into Lebanese/Muslim/Arab youth.

Class and mobility

As indicated by their earliest occupations, most Lebanese immigrants at first occupied a lowly socio-economic status in their countries of adoption. This was especially the case during the White Australia Policy period when many were denied citizenship and experienced a degree of racial discrimination. However, throughout their history in Australia many Lebanese families provided examples of substantial economic and social mobility. In most cases, this was based on their entrepreneurial business activities aided, in later generations, by their entry to the prestigious professions. The types of industries in which the Lebanese became successful varied but they were typically the product of the powerful Lebanese entrepreneurial spirit.

Lebanese Identity

Migration inevitably raises the question of national identity. Over the last 130 or more years identity has been a major issue for Lebanese immigrants to Australia. The earliest pioneers came from the province of Syria under Ottoman control. Although they identified themselves as Syrians, some were incorrectly described by Australian authorities and media as 'Assyrians', a term familiar to those in the west through Biblical stories.

A second confusion arose from the application of the White Australia Policy, which denied entry to Australia by immigrants from areas east of the Bosporus as well as rejecting applications for citizenship by immigrants from that region. This led some Lebanese to claim a birthplace within Europe, such as a town in Greece, and thus present themselves as eligible for Australian citizenship.

The application of the White Australia Policy led to a number of defensive responses on the part of Lebanese and their descendants. These included Anglicising and even changing surnames to more acceptable western ones; for example, Facoory became Carey, Dabes became Davis and Barakee became Mack. The same process applied to first names (see page 44)

Another defensive response, on the part of established earlier arrivals, may be described as 'othering.' This has taken many forms in Australia. During the hawking period some Syrian/Lebanese migrants were defined as a group who were clearly 'other than,' and inferior to, native-born Australians. Their 'otherness' was based variously on their appearance, their colour, their language and their hawking activities. In more recent times the notion of 'otherness' highlights the cultural foreign-ness of a group as a justification for it not being viewed as part of society. For example, whenever an unfavourable focus fell on the Lebanese they were viewed as a group to be distanced from mainstream society and blamed for any failings of group members. The 'othering' that took place during the Cronulla Riot in 2005 by some politicians and sections of the media provided a stark example of marginalising a total ethnicity.

'Othering' was not confined to relationships between dominant and subordinate groups in society. It also occurred within the Lebanese communities as a defensive response, on the part of established earlier arrivals. Some earlier immigrants, who had assimilated into Australian society, sought to disassociate themselves from later arrivals or 'other' Lebanese. This 'otherness' may be based on religion, cultural behaviours, education, economic and social class, or length of time in Australia. Given the complexity of the Lebanese community this may be seen as an inevitable development. On the other hand, where it is not accompanied by a widely recognised and accepted 'roof' body, the process of 'othering' in some cases, reduced the unity of the community.

The process of 'othering' also conveys the notion that some earlier immigrants sought to disassociate themselves from later arrivals or 'other' Lebanese. This 'othering' may be based on religion, education, economic and social class, or length of time in Australia. Given the complexity of the Lebanese community this may be seen as an inevitable development. On the other hand, the process of 'othering' can have the effect of reducing the unity of the community.

Religions such as Maronite, Melkite and Orthodox were often replaced by Catholic or Anglican faiths in the lives of Lebanese migrants. Part of the explanation for this lay in the fact that Lebanese churches were not established in most locations until many years after the arrival of Lebanese migrants. However, the desire to identify themselves as Australians and deny their immigrant backgrounds also played a part in abandoning their original faiths.

Migration has had a significant impact on the religious identity of some Lebanese immigrants. In some cases, it caused immigrants to move from their 'taken for granted' adherence to a church or mosque in their homeland, to discover a new-found interest and

involvement in their religious institution in Australia. In these instances, the church or mosque provided a familiar institution and community in a new land.

In societies of mass migration, such as Australia, most Lebanese embarked on the pathway of becoming full citizens and members of the host society. We have seen above how these people were confronted with choice in terms of how they identified themselves. Some defined themselves as 'Australians of Lebanese background' referring to their family's past rather than to their current status. In other cases, people chose to adopt a hybrid identity: 'Lebanese-Australian' or 'Australian-Lebanese.' Then there were a few who, given Lebanon's historical link with France, sought to identify themselves as 'French' or 'Mediterranean.'

In a more recent variant of identity some young people have chosen to proudly assert their Lebanese identity, even to the extent of ostentatiously proclaiming it on their tee-shirts. This they do in direct repudiation of racist slogans vilifying young Lebanese-Australians. And so, in terms of identity, the wheel has come full circle from defensiveness during the White Australia Policy period to assertiveness in the present.

As indicated, family, village, and religion are important as identifiers for Lebanese. In some countries and even internationally, there are conventions of Lebanese villages and towns, families and religions. In this way Lebanese can see themselves as members of transnational bodies linked by the latest in communications technology. This suggests that globalisation is making an impact on the social relations of Lebanese and their identities.

'Othering' was not confined to relationships between dominant and subordinate groups in society. It also occurred within the Lebanese communities as a defensive response, on the part of established earlier arrivals. Some earlier immigrants, who had assimilated into Australian society, sought to disassociate themselves from later arrivals or 'other' Lebanese. This 'otherness' may be based on religion, cultural behaviours, education, economic and social class, or length of time in Australia. Given the complexity of the Lebanese community this may be seen as an inevitable development. On the other hand, where it is not accompanied by a widely recognised and accepted 'roof' body, the process of 'othering' in some cases, reduced the unity of the community.

Migration has had a significant impact on the religious identity of some Lebanese immigrants. In some cases, it caused immigrants to move from their 'taken for granted' adherence to a church or mosque in their homeland, to discovering a new-found interest and involvement in their religious institution in Australia. In these instances, the church or mosque provided a familiar institution and community in a new land.

In societies of mass migration, such as Australia, most Lebanese embarked on the pathway of becoming full citizens and members of the host society. We have seen above how these people were confronted with choice in terms of how they identified themselves. Some defined themselves as 'Australians of Lebanese background' referring to their family's past rather than to their current status. In other cases, people chose to adopt a hybrid identity: 'Lebanese-Australian' or 'Australian-Lebanese.' Then there were a few who, given Lebanon's historical link with France, sought to identify themselves as 'French' or 'Mediterranean.'

In a more recent variant of identity some young people have chosen to proudly assert their Lebanese identity, even to the extent of ostentatiously proclaiming it on their tee-shirts. This was done in direct repudiation of racist slogans vilifying young Lebanese-Australians and their 'otherness'. And so, in terms of identity, the wheel has come full circle from defensiveness during the White Australia Policy period to assertiveness in the present.

As indicated, family, village, and religion are important as identifiers for Lebanese. In some countries and even internationally, there are conventions of villages and towns, families and religions. In this way Lebanese can see themselves as members of transnational bodies linked by the latest in communications technology. This suggests that globalisation is making an impact on the social relations of Lebanese and their identities.

Assimilation or integration?

The process of assimilation, whereby immigrants and their families come to adopt the language and culture of the wider society, may be seen as an almost inevitable outcome of migration and permanent settlement in the country of adoption. However, assimilation may be affected by many variables such as length of time in the new country; the amount and type of contact with the wider community and within the ethnic community; as well as the education levels and occupations of migrants. Other key factors are whether the wider society seeks to deliberately and formally encourage and support the process of assimilation and the extent to which the immigrant group is tenacious in retaining its language and culture.

While each of these applies to the Lebanese in Australia, the story of Lebanese assimilation in Australia exhibits some key characteristics. The occupations of first-wave settlers in hawking and shop-keeping, as well as their early settlement in small numbers in country towns, provided opportunities for them to acquire the rudiments of language and cultural elements of the wider community. On the other hand, the adoption of the White Australia Policy by governments and sections of the public and media delayed, for a number of years, their recognition as Australian citizens.

Although the occupational history of the second-wave settlers varied from that of the early settlers, they generally followed in their footsteps on the journey to assimilation and citizenship. With a shorter history in Australia and their background of civil war and divisions in Lebanon, some third-wave immigrants faced greater hurdles in achieving assimilation.

Over their 130 and more years in Australia the great majority of Lebanese immigrants have evinced a strong desire to be identified with Australia. This has taken many forms over time and has been dependent on the social and political context of Australian society, from the early settlers seeking citizenship in the face of the official policy of exclusionism, in their seeking the vote, and in their enlisting in the Australian armed forces in both World Wars. Yet another measure is the high proportion of Lebanese-born who became Australian citizens.

Over the total period of their settlement in Australia Lebanese have sought to become Australian and, at the same time, to retain valued elements of their home culture. This suggests that many Lebanese in the different waves of Lebanese migration have avoided full assimilation and instead have sought to integrate certain of their Lebanese values and practices with those of the wider Australian culture. We have seen this played put in the biographies of particular Australians of Lebanese descent.

Contacts between Australia and Lebanon

The means by which Lebanese migrants maintained contacts with family in Lebanon and other countries in the diaspora has changed over time. First-wave settlers used letters and photographs to maintain family contacts, send remittances back home and find suitable Lebanese marriage partners. Limited communication with their former homeland meant that these Australian-Lebanese communities developed in comparative isolation within Anglo-Celtic Australia.

The second wave was a transitional group who, early in their settlement, employed similar means of communication with their homeland to those of first-wave settlers. However, by the 1970s, Arabic media began to appear, and more return visits took place, so that contact with family and information about Lebanon were now more readily available.

Third-wave immigrants, with their urgent need to keep in touch with family and developments in Lebanon, have employed an extensive range of media with which to communicate with groups in Lebanon. The difference between the communication experiences of first- and third-wave migrants lies in the speed, immediacy, versatility and cost of communications.

'A changing mosaic'

The Lebanese presence in Australia may be likened to 'a changing mosaic'. The term 'mosaic' suggests the many disparate religious, village and political groups that constitute the Lebanese community in Australia. We have identified the many changes that have taken place over the major migration waves and their settlement patterns. These changes include religion, social background, occupations and educational levels. They also refer to the varied patterns of settlement of the Lebanese including location, family life, ethnic and wider community involvement, and changing attitudes to their former homeland.

Throughout the total period Lebanese settlers and their descendants have made significant contributions to Australia in the political, business, religious, military, sporting and educational fields. Although a small and divided group, the Lebanese and their descendants have helped make Australia a richer and more diverse society.

NOTES

1   SBS Cultural Atlas: Lebanese Culture
2   Interview Broheim and Hoda Aoun July 2014
3   redwatch.org.au/media/090303sshf
4   Khachan, G 2018, *Lebanese Identity and the Australian Armed Forces: Summary of PhD thesis*, Unpublished Paper, Australian National University.
5   Australian Lebanese Historical Society Inc., *Lebanese Diggers—Australian Lebanese in the Armed Services*
6   *Ibid.* p. 43
7   Mosely, PA, Cashman, R, O'Hara, J & Weatherburn, H (eds.) 1998, *Sporting Immigrants: Sport and Ethnicity in Australia*, Walla Walla Press. p. 11
8   St Nicholas Cricket Team Premiership Booklet, 1952
9   de Bolfo, T 2009, *Premiership player Ray Garby dies*, Carlton Football Club, <http://www.carltonfc.com.au/news/2009-03-17/premiership-player-ray-garby-dies>.
10 Woods, B 2007, *El Magic: The Life of Hazem El Masri*, Harper Collins Publishers.
11 Lane, D 2015 *Sydney Morning Herald* May 'Tragedy drove NSW State of Origin skipper Robbie Farah's mental health mission.'
12 richmondfc.com.au/news/2016-09-26/bachar-houli-academy-kicks-off
13 *Ibid.*
14 aflvic.com.au/multicultural/bachar-houli-cup

GLOSSARY OF TERMS

Cedar Revolution – a series of peaceful demonstrations in Beirut and elsewhere in Lebanon in response to the assassination of Prime Minister Rafic Hariri in 2005; its goals included the withdrawal of Syrian troops from Lebanon and a more independent leadership of the nation

Galbally Report 1978 – recommended major principles including equality of access to services for all members of society; the settlement needs of migrants to be targeted; and the right of ethnic groups to maintain their cultural distinctiveness

Hezbollah – a Shi'ite Islamic political party and militant group based in Lebanon

NUSRA – Islamic State

Koora – locality in the cities of Sydney and Melbourne where many early Lebanese immigrants had their first homes and businesses

Mishwaar – traditional afternoon promenade

Mutasarrifate – a ruling body established by European powers in 1861 which guaranteed the autonomy of the Mount Lebanon District of the Ottoman Empire; it included representatives of the main religious sects and lasted until the end of the First World War

Mudabbir families – ruling or leading families in Lebanon

Mukhabarat – Syrian Intelligence Organisation

Règlement Organique – a series of international conventions between 1860 and 1864 between the Ottoman Empire and the European powers which led to the creation of the Mount Lebanon Mutasarrifate

Syrian Ba'ath Party – The Baath Arab Socialist Party was founded in Damascus in 1947 as the only legal political power in Syria; it promotes secular Arab nationalism, Arab socialism, pan-Arabism and militarism

Taouli – backgammon

Ta'if Accord – an agreement by members of Lebanon's 1972 Parliament to provide the basis for ending the civil war in Lebanon; it adopted the general principle that Lebanon is a free independent country and a final homeland for all its citizens, one country in terms of the land, the people and the institutions...

Versailles Peace Treaty – the defeat of Germany and the Ottoman Empire was marked by the Versailles Peace Treaty in 1919 which realigned the states in the Middle East; the status of Lebanon changed from being part of the province of Syria within the Ottoman Empire to that of a French Mandate, which gained semi-autonomy in 1920

Wajah – communal reputation

Wasta – favouritism based on kinship or a close relationship, especially in business circles

Wejbet – network of mutual obligations that can extend to cultural, economic and familial spheres

Za'im – community leader or chief

BIBLIOGRAPHY

Abi Farah, A 2000, 'Estimations of the number of Lebanese emigrants in 1999', in As-Safir, December 2001

Abu-Laban, B 1992, 'The Lebanese in Montreal', *The Lebanese in the World*, Centre for Lebanese Studies in association with I.B. Tauris & Co.

Ahmad, Michael Mohammed, 2018, *The Lebs*, Hachette.

Al-Doumani, K, Dados, N, Maddox, M & Wise, A 2010, *Political Participation of Muslims in Australia: Final Report 2010*, Centre for Research on Social Inclusion.

Al-Shayk, H 1992, *Beirut Blues*, Allen & Unwin.

Ansell, K 2001, *The Business of Life*, Merlvic Schrank Pty Ltd.

Australian Bureau of Statistics, <http://www.abs.gov.au>.

——1988a, *Census '86: Australia in Profile – A summary of Major Findings*, Catalogue No. 2502.0, Commonwealth Government of Australia.

——1988b, *Historical Census Data*, Catalogue No. 2101.0 – 2109.0, Censuses 1947–1991, Commonwealth Government of Australia.

Australian Government Refugee Review Tribunal, archives.

Australian Lebanese Historical Society, <http://alhs.org.au>.

Asal, H 2012, *Community Sector Dynamics and the Lebanese Diaspora*, Fondation maison des sciences de l'homme e Diaspora.

Batrouney, A 1978, *The Lebanese Community in Carlton, Melbourne 1880–1920*, History Honours Thesis, Monash University.

——1981, *The Genesis of St George's Orthodox Church*, Unpublished Essay

——1991, *Ethnic Community Issues in Local Government*. Ethnic Affairs Commission of Victoria

——1996, *Care Options for Arabic Muslim Elderly*, Northern Migrant Resource Centre

Batrouney, A & Batrouney, T 1985, *The Lebanese in Australia*, A.E. Press.

Batrouney, T & Blatt, P 1982. 'Settlement Problems of Lebanese in Melbourne', Report for Migrant Settlement Council for Victoria.

Batrouney, T 1995, 'Lebanese-Australian Families', in R Hartley (ed.), *Family Values in a Culturally Diverse Australia*, Allen & Unwin.

——2002, 'Arab-Australians: From White Australia to Multiculturalism', in G Hage (ed.), *Arab-Australians Today: Citizenship and Belonging*, Melbourne University Press.

——2005, 'Australian-Lebanese: Return Visits to Lebanon and Issues of Identity', in P Tabar (ed.), *Lebanese Diaspora: History, Racism and Belonging*, Lebanese American University.

——2007, *Cherishing the Faith: The Antiochian Orthodox Church in Victoria 1989–2006*, St Georges Antiochian Orthodox Church.

——2008, *Living our Heritage: The Maronite Catholic Church in Victoria*, The Victorian Maronite Community.

——2015, *Memoir: Trevor Batrouney*, Unpublished Memoir.

Batrouney T & Goldlust J 2005, *Unravelling Identity: Immigrants, Identity and Citizenship in Australia*. Common Ground

Betts, K & Healy, E 2006, 'Lebanese Muslims in Australia and Social Disadvantage', *People & Place*, vol. 14, no. 1, Centre for Urban Research and Action.

Brotherhood of St Laurence 2016, *Opening Doors*, Brotherhood of St Laurence.

Burke, E 1988, 'Rural Collective Action and the emergence of modern Lebanon: A comparative historical perspective.' In Shehadi, N & Haffar Mills, D (eds) 1988, *Lebanon: A history of conflict and consensus* Centre for Lebanese Studies, London.

Burnley, I 1982, 'Lebanese Migration and Settlement in Sydney, Australia', *International Migration Review*, vol. 16, Spring, John Wiley & Sons.

Calligeros, M 2015, 'The faces of Melbourne: which migrants went to which suburbs', *The Age*, <http://www.theage.com.au/victoria/the-faces-of-melbourne-which-mighrants-went-to-which-suburbs-20150507-ggw90s.html>.

Callil, C 2001, *Memoir*, Unpublished Memoir.

Callil, J 2001, *Frederick Alfred Louis Callil*, Unpublished Monograph.

Castles, S & Miller, M 1993, *The Age of Migration: International Population Movements in the Modern World*, Guilford.

Castles, S, Vasta, E & Ozkul, D 2012, *The Internal Dynamics of Migration Processes and their Consequences for Australian Government Migration Policies*, University of Sydney.

Chittleborough, J 2000, 'Hassan Ali (Harry) Monsour (1884 –1959)' in *Australian Dictionary of Biography* Vol 15, Melbourne University Press

Collins, J (ed.) 2005, 'From Beirut to Bankstown: The Lebanese Diaspora in Multicultural Australia', in P Tabar (ed.), *Lebanese Diaspora: History, Racism and Belonging*, Lebanese American University.

Community of the Holy Name 1922, *Day Book*, Community of the Holy Name.

Convey, P & Monsour, A 2008 'Lebanese Settlement in New South Wales: A

Thematic History' for The Migration Heritage Centre, Powerhouse Museum. www.migrationheriage.nsw.gov.au

Copeland, S. 1995 *Julia's Diary*. Unpublished monograph.

Cruickshank, K 2006, *Teenagers, Literacy and School: Researching in Multicultural Contexts*, Routledge Taylor Francis Group.

Dan, E & Mansour, N (eds) 2004, *St George Cathedral and its people, past present and future*. Longueville Media.

de Bolfo, T 2009, *Premiership player Ray Garby dies*, Carlton Football Club, <http://www.carltonfc.com.au/news/2009-03-17/premiership-player-ray-garby-dies>.

de Lacey, P & Poole, M 1979, *Mosaic or Melting Pot: Cultural Evolution in Australia*, Harcourt Brace Jovanovich Group.

Department of Education and Early Childhood Development 2011, *Lessons learned: A history of migrant education in Victorian government schools – 1960–2006*, Department of Education and Early Childhood Development Victoria.

Elali, N 2014, *A Century of Immigration: The Lebanese Diaspora in the USA*, Now, <https://now.mmedia.me/lb/en/reportsfeatures/564540-a-century-of-immigration>.

El Khazen, F 1976, *The Breakdown of the State of Lebanon 1967-76*

El Khazen, F 1997, 'Permanent Settlement of Palestinians in Lebanon: A Recipe for Conflict' in *Journal of Refugee Studies* Vol. 10, No 3. American University of Beirut.

Engebretson, K & Ghosn, M 2010, 'National Identity of a Group of Young Australian Maronite Adults', *Crucible: Theology & Ministry*, vol. 3, no. 1, Australian Evangelical Alliance.

Fairbrother, K 2012 'Australia's Immigration Policy Following the Second World War' in E International Relations – Students. www.e-ir.info

Fersen, E 2010, 'Lebanese Migration (1880–Present): "Push" and "Pull" Factors', *Viewpoints (Special Edition) Migration and the Mashreq*, The Middle East Institute.

Foster, L & Stockley, D 1984, *Multiculturalism: The changing Australian paradigm*. Clevedon: Multilingual Matters.

—— et al 1994 *Gender Equity and Australian Immigration Policy*, AGPS.

Friedman, T 2015, 'Contain and Amplify', *The Sunday Age* reprint from *New York Times*.

Gates, C 1989 'The Historical Rome of Political Economy in the Development of Modern Lebanon' Papers on Lebanon Series, Centre for Lebanese Studies.

Hashimoto, K 1992, 'Lebanese Population Movement 1920–1939: Towards a

Study', *The Lebanese in the World: A Century of Emigration*, Centre for Lebanese Studies in association with I.B. Tauris & Co.

Hage, G 1998, *White Nation*, Pluto Press.

——2002, *Arab-Australians Today: Citizenship and Belonging*, Melbourne University Press.

Henderson, G 2015, '1970s Lebanese Commission led to an Immigration Debacle, *The Australian*.

Hooglund, E 1987, *Crossing the Waters*, Smithsonian Institution Press.

Hugo, G 1995, *Understanding Where Immigrants Live*, Australian Government Printing Service.

Humphrey, M 1984, *Family, Work and Unemployment: A Study of Lebanese Settlement in Sydney*, Australian Government Printing Service.

——1987, 'Community, Mosques and Ethnic Politics', *ANZ Journal of Sociology*, PUBLISHER.

——1998, *Islam, Multiculturalism and Transnationalism*, Centre for Lebanese Studies in association with I.B. Tauris & Co.

——& Kisirwani, M 2001, 'Impunity, Nationalism and Transnationalism: The Recovery of the

'Disappeared' of Lebanon', *Conference on Transnationalism*, Royal Institute of Inter-Faith Studies.

——2004, 'Lebanese identities: between cities, nations and trans-nations', *Arab Studies Quarterly*, Arab Studies Institute.

Hyndman-Rizik, N 2009, 'Balad Niswen – Hukum Niswen: The Perception of Gender Inversions

Between Lebanon and Australia', *Palma Journal: A Multidisciplinary Research Publication*, vol. 11, no. 1, Notre Dame University.

——2010, 'Migration, Wasta and Big Business Success: The Paradox of Capital Accumulation in Sydney's Hadchiti Lebanese Community', *Labour Management & Development Journal*, vol. 14,

——& Monsour, A 2014, 'Immigrant Business: Choice or Necessity?', *Labour and management in Development*, vol. 15, Special Issue, <http://pandora.nla.gov.au/pan/133884/2014097-0001/www.nla.gov.au/openpublish/index.php/lmd/article/viewFile/3330/3890.pdf>.

International Centre for Transactional Justice (ICTJ), 2014 (Jan) Failing to deal with the past: What cost to Lebanon'. https://www.ictj.org/publication/failing-to-deal-past-what-cost-Lebanon

Islamic Museum of Australia 2015, *History of Australia's Muslims*, Islamic Museum of Australia.

International Centre for Transitional Justice 2014, *Failing to Deal with the Past: What Cost to Lebanon?*, <https://www.ictj.org/publication/failing-deal-past-what-cost-lebanon>.

Issawi, C 1992 'The historical background of Lebanese emigration - 1800-1914', in Hourani, AH & Shehadi, N 1992, *The Lebanese in the World: A century of emigration*. Centre for Lebanese Studies, University of Oxford.

Jayasuriya, L 1991, 'Citizenship, Democratic Pluralism and Ethnic Minorities in Australia', in R Nile (ed.), *Immigration, Multiculturalism and the Politics of Ethnicity and Race in Australia*, University of London Centre for Australian Studies.

Jidejian, N 1992, *The Story of Lebanon in Pictures*. Librairie Orientale

Johanssen, K & Kyriazopoulos, H 2011, *Emerging Needs Scoping Study: Middle East & North Africa*, Office of the Aging.

Jordens, A 1994, *Promoting Australian Citizenship 1949–1971*, Australian National University.

——1995, *Redefining Australians: Immigration, Citizenship and National Identity*, Hale and Iremonger Pty Ltd.

Jupp, J 1991, *Australian retrospectives - Immigration:*, Sydney University Press

—— 1996, *Understanding Australian Multiculturalism*, Australian Government Printing Service.

Kasparian, C 2003 'L'entrée des jeunes libanais dans la vie active et l'émigration, St-Joseph University, Beirut.

Khalaf, S 1987, *Lebanon's Predicament*, Columbia University Press.

Khachan, G 2018, *Lebanese Identity and the Australian Armed Forces: Summary of PhD thesis*, Unpublished Paper, Australian National University.

Khoo, S, McDonald, P, Giorgas, D & Birrell, B 2002, *Second Generation Australians*, Department of Immigration and Multicultural and Indigenous Affairs.

Khoo, S & McDonald, P (ed.) 2003, *The Transformation of Australia's Population: 1970–2030*, University of New South Wales Press.

Labaki, B 1992, 'Lebanese Emigration during the War (1975 – 1989)'in Hourani, A & Shehadi, N (eds) 1992, *The Lebanese in the World: A Century of Emigration*. Centre for Lebanese Studies & IB Tauris & Co.

Lebanese Development Network: Newsletter, June 2016.

Lo Bianco, J 2009, 'Second Languages in Australian Schooling', *Australian Education Review*, ACER Press.

Maalouf, A 2008, *Origins: A Memoir*, Macmillan – Farrar, Straus & Giroux.

Mackie, F 1983, *Structure, Culture and Religion in the Welfare of Muslim Families*, Australian Government Printing Service.

Markose, S 2007, *Home literacy practices of immigrant families and Cultural Discontinuity: Two case studies*, Australian Association for Research in Education.

Mellick, R 2016, 'Tears for my Jiddee', May 2016 Newsletter, Australian Lebanese Historical Society Inc.

Martin, J 1976, *The Migrant Presence*, Allen & Unwin.

McIntyre, J 2014, *Making the Mid-North Coast: A Migration Report*, Port Macquarie-Hastings Council.

McKay, J 1986, *Phoenician Farewell: Three Generations of Lebanese Christians in Australia*, Ashwood House.

McRae-McMahon, D 2009, 'Sydney's first Lebanese restaurant Wilsons of Pitt Street Redfern', *South Sydney Herald*.

Migration Policy Institute – Lebanon Remittances Profile – Data Hub.

Monsour, A 2004, *Syrian/Lebanese Traders and the Customs Prosecutions of 1897*, Professional Historian's Association (Queensland) Conference.

——2009, 'Already Here: Writing Lebanese into Queensland History', *Journeys through Queensland history: landscape, place and society*, Professional Historians' Association (Queensland) Conference.

——2009, *Raw Kibbeh: Generations of Lebanese Australian Enterprise*, Lebanese Australian Historical Society.

——2010. *Not quite white: Lebanese and the White Australia Policy 1880 to 1947*, Post Pressed.

——2014.

Monsour,A and Convey, P.Once *Upon a Time in Punchbowl-* a T V Program 2010

Mosely, PA, Cashman, R, O'Hara, J & Weatherburn, H (eds.) 1998, *Sporting Immigrants: Sport and Ethnicity in Australia*, Walla Walla Press.

Mukherjee, S 1999, *Ethnicity and Crime: An Australian Research Study*, Australian Institute of Criminology.

Multicultural Task Force 1978, *Report of the Review of Post-arrival Programs and Services for Migrants* (aka the Galbally Report), Government Printer.

Nabti, P 1992, 'Emigration from a Lebanese Village: A Case Study of Bishmizzine', *The Lebanese in the World*, Centre for Lebanese Studies in association with I.B. Tauris & Co.

Naff, A 1992, 'Lebanese Immigration to the United States: 1880 to the Present',

The Lebanese in the World, Centre for Lebanese Studies in association with I.B. Tauris & Co.

Nasser, R 2001, *From Kousba to Clemount: The Nasser and Solomon Australian Story*, J.R. Durington & Sons.

Omar, W & Allen, K 1996, *The Muslims in Australia*, Australian Government Publishing Service.

Parker, B, Lancely, K, Owens, B & Fitzpatrick, R 2009, *Geography for Australian Citizens, Teacher Resource Book*, Macmillan.

Owen R *1992*, 'Lebanese in the world: a century of emigration' in Hourani AH & Shehadi N 1992, *The Lebanese in the World: A century of emigration*. Centre for Lebanese Studies, University of Oxford.

Parker, B, Lancely, K, Owens, B & Fitzpatrick, R 2009 *Geography for Australian Citizens, Teacher Resource Book*. Macmillan.

Pascoe, R 1990, 'Raymond Betros: Hawker', *Open for business: immigrant and Aboriginal entrepreneurs tell their story*, Office for Multicultural Affairs.

Pearlman, W 2012, 'Emigration and Power: A Study of Sects in Lebanon, 1860–2010', *Politics and Society*, vol. 41, no. 1, SAGE Publications.

——2013, 'Emigration and the resilience of politics in Lebanon', *Arab Studies Journal*, vol. 21, no. 1, Arab Studies Institute.

Pollard, R 2015, 'For families of Lebanon's missing, the war goes on', *The Age*.

Salibi K 1988 *A House of Many Mansions: The History of Lebanon Reconsidered*. University of California Press

Sbaiti, N 2003, 'Peasant Modernities: In Lebanon and in Immigration', *H-Net Reviews in Human & Social Sciences*, review of Khater, A 2001, *Inventing Home: Emigration, Gender and the Middle Class in Lebanon 1870–1920*, University of California Press.

Suliman, R & McInerney, DM 2006, 'Motivational goals and school achievement: Lebanese-background students in south-western Sydney', *Australian Journal of Education*, vol. 50, no. 3, Australian Council for Educational Research.

St Nicholas Antiochian Orthodox Church 1932, *Church Archives*, St Nicholas Antiochian Orthodox Church.

——1952, *St Nicholas Cricket Team Premiership Booklet*, St Nicholas Antiochian Orthodox Church.

Stamm, S 2006, 'Social networks among return migrants to post-war Lebanon' Working Paper, Centre for Comparative and International Studies ETH Zurich Research Collection

The Syrian World Vol.2, No. 6 1927-1930 Salloum Mokarzel (ed)

Tabar, P 2009, *Immigration and Human Development: Evidence from Lebanon*, Human

Development Research Paper, United Nations Development Program.

——2010, *Lebanon: A Country of Emigration and Immigration*, Lebanese American University,   <https://www.researchgate.net/publication/265411236_Lebanon_A_Country_of_Emigration_and_Immigration>.

——2014, 'The Maronite Church in Lebanon: From Nation-building to a Diasporan/Transnational Institution', *Presses de l'Ifpo Publication de l'Institut Français du Proche-Orient*, <books.openedition.org/ifpo/4788?lang=en>.

——, Noble, G & Poynting, S 2010, *On Being Lebanese in Australia*, Lebanese American University.

Tannous, A. 1949, 'The Village in the National Life of Lebanon', *Middle East Journal*, vol. 3, no. 4, Middle East Institute.

Traboulsi F. 2012, *A History of Modern Lebanon*. Pluto Press. 2nd Edition.

Thompson, E. 2000, 'The Climax and Crisis of the Colonial Welfare State', in S Heydermann (ed.), *War, Institutions and Social Change in the Middle East*, University of California Press.

Underabi, H. 2014, *Mosques of Sydney and New South Wales: Research Report 2014*. Islamic Sciences and Research Academy Australia, University of Western Sydney & Charles Sturt University.

Wilton, J 1987, *Hawking to Haberdashery: Immigrants in the Bush*, University of New South Wales.

Woods, B 2007, *El Magic: The Life of Hazem El Masri*, Harper Collins Publishers.

TABLES

Table 1 **Number of Lebanese settlers by State (1911–1933)**

Census Year		VIC	NSW	QLD	SA	WA	TAS	National
1911	Female	137	307	80	58	26	24	632
	Male	186	448	71	127	29	33	895
	Total	232	755	151	185	55	57	1,527
1921	Female	176	373	79	50	84	14	776
	Male	225	477	90	101	106	28	1,027
	Total	401	850	169	151	190	42	1,803
1933	Female	131	500	105	117	7	7	868
	Male	157	644	137	186	12	14	1,152
	Total	288	1,114	242	303	19	21	2,020

Source: Australian Bureau of Statistics

Table 2 **Number of emigrants from Lebanon (1923–1933)**

Year	Female	Male	Total
1923	n/a	n/a	16,500*
1924	n/a	n/a	13,500*
1925	n/a	n/a	11,000*
1926	n/a	n/a	16,000*
1927	1,775	1,950	3,725
1928	2,268	3,730	5,998
1929	2,208	2,839	5,047
1930	2.097	1,786	3,883
1931	714	673	1,387
1932	625	546	1,171
1933	772	744	1,516

Source: 1932 Lebanese Census
*Includes migration figures from other parts of the French Mandate

Table 3 **Lebanese migrants by religion and municipality 1921**

Municipality	Maronite	Sunni	Shi'ite	Greek Orthodox	Druze	Greek Catholic	Protestant	Misc.	Total	Emigrants not paying taxes
Akkar	1,422	280	-	1,538	-	55	-	9	**3,304**	6,935
Al-Biqa'	448	402	98	506	1	1,041	19	-	**2,515**	8,661
Ba'albak	134	4	79	42	-	200	2	-	**461**	2,583
Beirut	190	38	1	250	8	31	9	1	**528**	2,406
Dayr al-Qamar	305	-	-	1	-	19	1	-	**326**	254
Hasbayyah	56	133	-	341	68	78	16	-	**692**	2,048
Hermil	-	-	47	-	-	-	-	-	**47**	16
Jazzin	1,802	14	238	6	6	741	11	-	**2,818**	2,622
Kisrwan	4,441	24	61	160	-	16	3	1	**4,816**	9,474
Kura-Batroun	3,654	103	47	3,518	-	-	-	-	**7,322**	12,597
Maj'jayyun	111	1	82	465	-	124	91	-	**874**	2,241
Matn	5,115	12	61	1,674	832	496	25	98	**8,313**	4,922
Rachayyah	26	251	-	863	259	58	19	9	**1,485**	1,481
Shuf	2,700	168	32	710	2,618	787	228	2	**7,245**	8,227
Sidon	287	34	518	-	-	111	1	5	**956**	1,848
Tripoli	409	1,356	-	2,764	-	15	37	60	**4,641**	421
Tyre	147	-	615	1	-	121	23	-	**907**	5,347
Zgharta	2,233	4	-	54	-	-	-	-	**2,291**	9,160
Total	**23,480**	**2,824**	**1,879**	**12,993**	**3,792**	**3,903**	**1,819**	**336**	**49,541**	**81,243**

Source: 1921 Lebanese Census

Table 4 Emigrants from Lebanon and return migrants (1926–1933)

Year	Emigration	Return Migration
1926	16,000	5,000
1927	9,391	5,320
1928	14,288	4,407
1929	7,941	3,515
1930	7,346	3,978
1931	2,426	3,196
1932	1,640	2,744
1933	2,324	1,999

Source:1932 Lebanese Census

Table 5 Pt 1 **Population of Australia by State/Territory (1947–2016)**

		VIC	NSW	QLD	SA	WA	TAS	NT	ACT	National
1947	F	1,040,834	1,492,627	538,944	326,042	244,404	127,834	3,490	7,813	3,454,847
	M	1,013,867	1,492,211	567,471	320,031	258,076	129,244	2,193	9,092	3,380,324
1954	F	1,221,242	1,702,669	642,007	393,191	309,413	151,623	6,181	14,086	4,440,412
	M	1,231,099	1,720,860	676,252	403,903	330,358	157,129	10,228	16,229	4,546,118
1961	F	1,455,718	1,944,104	744,249	479,115	361,177	172,712	10,889	1,757	5,268,350
	M	1,474,395	1,972,909	774,579	490,225	375,452	177,628	16,206	30,858	5,374,304
1966	F	1,605,622	2,109,360	819,778	543,345	409,982	184,045	15,925	46,036	5,814,201
	M	1,613,904	2,124,462	843,897	548,530	426,691	187,390	21,508	49,977	5,890,642
1971	F	1,752,290	2,293,970	905,400	587,656	501,403	193,971	48,627	70,474	6,565,542
	M	1,750,061	2,307,210	921,665	586,051	529,066	196,442	56,504	73,589	6,632,838
1976	F	1,832,192	2,396,949	1,012,584	624,594	563,667	201,354	44,643	97,519	7,044,328
	M	1,814,783	2,360,146	1,024,609	620,160	581,188	201,512	52,447	100,104	7,065,779
1981	F	1,931,032	2,577,233	1,141,719	649,337	630,516	210,316	57,907	111,194	7,539,778
	M	1,901,411	2,548,984	1,153,404	635,696	643,108	208,641	65,417	110,415	7,514,339
1986	F	2,028,009	2,717,311	1,291,685	979,985	699,360	219,873	73,347	124,273	8,081,449
	M	1,991,469	2,684,570	1,295,630	665,960	707,569	216,480	81,501	125,134	8,057,326
1991	F	2,147,741	2,887,468	1,495,414	709,751	793,173	229,026	84,289	140,963	8,723,444
	M	2,096,641	2,844,438	1,482,399	690,879	793,877	223,825	91,587	139,169	8,663,579
1996	F	2,307,506	3,123,684	1,665,650	745,104	877,679	240,141	86,175	155,298	9,262,870
	M	2,252,649	3,081,044	1,673,040	729,149	887,577	234,302	95,668	152,953	9,157,444
2001	F	2,438,431	3,311,014	1,822,506	764,466	949,603	239,325	94,293	161,742	9,837,328
	M	2,366,295	3,264,203	1,806,440	747,262	951,556	232,470	103,475	157,575	9,691,946
2006	F	2,512,006	3,320,729	1,969,150	769,130	982,963	243,100	93,529	159,656	10,056,04
	M	2,420,416	3,228,449	1,935,383	745,208	976,123	233,380	99,368	192,897	9,799,244
2011	F	2,721,425	3,508,781	2,184,517	809,353	1,112,992	252,677	102,425	180,475	10,873,70
	M	2,632,615	3,408,877	2,148,220	787,218	1,126,179	242,674	109,518	176,744	10,634,01
2016	F	3,018,549	3,794,217	2,381,308	850,652	1,235,994	260,482	1,10,266	2,01,425	11,855,24
	M	2,908,077	3,686,014	2,321,889	825,997	1,238,419	249,478	1,18,570	1,95,432	11,546,03

Source: Australian Bureau of Statistics

Table 5 Pt 2 **Lebanese-born Population of Australia by State/Territory (1947–2016)**

Census Year		VIC	NSW	QLD	SA	WA	TAS	NT	ACT	National
1947	F	104	509	119	105	9	5	-	-	851
	M	113	609	141	148	12	9	-	3	1,035
1954	F	195	964	102	137	13	-	-	1	1,412
	M	283	1,802	139	197	20	6	-	2	2,449
1961	F	413	2,282	120	395	32	10	-	4	3,008
	M	558	3,289	150	334	33	6	-	3	4,245
1966	F	583	3,284	49	179	19	-	-	7	4,121
	M	897	4,772	178	237	55	2	-	11	6,152
1971	F	1,576	7,619	138	259	61	3	2	14	9,672
	M	2,369	11,424	183	328	128	10	78	20	14,546
1976	F	2,709	11,620	221	385	126	10	1	31	15,103
	M	3,240	14,036	314	452	208	20	18	43	18,331
1981	F	4,759	17,118	294	562	180	25	6	57	23,001
	M	5,384	19,832	395	630	242	44	14	81	26,622
1986	F	5,317	19,769	344	645	236	28	4	97	26,440
	M	5,970	22,272	446	775	310	42	15	121	29,901
1991	F	6,576	24,406	461	706	370	42	16	196	32,773
	M	7,110	26,987	636	760	445	58	16	210	36,222
1996	F	6,791	25,051	494	735	393	31	9	181	33,685
	M	7,170	27,270	620	764	441	43	16	215	36,539
2001	F	6,874	25,540	501	720	405	18	7	175	34,240
	M	7,294	27,745	621	757	450	31	10	201	37,109
2006	F	7,263	26,842	568	746	404	20	4	169	36,015
	M	7,686	28,935	687	785	485	38	21	165	38,833
2011	F	7,641	27,278	579	708	478	27	12	189	36,912
	M	8,228	29,015	715	749	554	43	38	196	39,538
2016	F	8,036	27,743	632	748	496	33	11	188	37,879
	M	8,643	29,632	795	791	610	40	37	214	40,772

Source: Australian Bureau of Statistics

Table 6 **2016 Census: Age of Lebanese-born residents by gender**

Age	Female	Male
0 – 4	168	178
5 – 14	641	647
15 – 24	1,576	1,633
25 – 44	10,595	12,064
45 – 54	9,422	9,495
55 – 64	8,126	7,751
65 – 74	4,419	6,041
75 – 84	2,105	2,377
85 +	808	595

Source: 2016 Australian Census

ABOUT THE AUTHORS

Dr Trevor Batrouney OAM is a fourth generation descendant of Lebanese migrants who arrived in 1889. He is an historian and sociologist who has written extensively on migration, settlement, citizenship and religious issues in Australia. He has authored several books and articles on the Lebanese and other immigrant groups.

Andrew Batrouney, is an historian and sociologist who has written and researched extensively on the history and settlement of the Lebanese community in Melbourne and Australia at large. He has authored a number of government and community publications.

Publications by the same authors
The Lebanese in Australia 1985
Legacy of the Hawker 1989 (with David Mansour)
Care Options for the Lebanese Muslim Elderly 1996

Selected publications by Dr Trevor Batrouney
Australian Lebanese Welfare: Serving all Arabic-Speaking Communities 1984-2004
Cherishing the Faith: The Antiochian Orthodox Church in Victoria, 1989-2006
Cradle of Orthodoxy: St Nicholas Antiochian Orthodox Church, Melbourne 1932-2007
Living our Heritage:the Maronite Catholic Church in Victoria 2008

Selected publications by Andrew Batrouney
Managing Community Diversity in the City of Whittlesea 1991
Making the Links: Ethnic Issues in Local Government 1992

INDEX

www.ingramcontent.com/pod-product-compliance
Lightning Source LLC
Chambersburg PA
CBHW070909100426

42814CB00003B/106